A LIFE IN SMOKE

A Memoir

Julia Hansen

FREE PRESS
New York London Toronto Sydney

FREE PRESS
A Division of Simon & Schuster, Inc.
1230 Avenue of the Americas
New York, NY 10020

FREE PRESS and colophon are trademarks of
Simon & Schuster, Inc.

For information about special discounts for bulk purchases,
please contact Simon & Schuster Special Sales:
1-800-456-6798 or business@simonandschuster.com

Designed by Kyoko Watanabe

Manufactured in the United States of America

1   3   5   7   9   10   8   6   4   2

Library of Congress Cataloging-in-Publication Data
Hansen, Julia.
A life in smoke: a memoir / Julia Hansen
p. cm.
1. Hansen, Julia. 2. Cigarette smokers—United States—Biography.
3. Nicotine addiction—United States. I. Title.
HV5731.5.H36 A3   2006
616.86'50092[B]—dc22   2006043744

ISBN-13: 978-0-7432-8959-7
ISBN-10: 0-7432-8959-5

To my son
and
to my family, John, and Matt

A NOTE TO THE READER

The names and identifying characteristics of some individuals portrayed have been changed.

I fell into a burning ring of fire
I went down, down, down
And the flames went higher
And it burns, burns, burns
The ring of fire
The ring of fire.

"Ring of Fire," Johnny Cash

CONTENTS

A LIFE IN
SMOKE

PROLOGUE

6:26 a.m.

I lean over John's broad back to peer at the clock. Flopping back on my pillow, I pull the heavy quilt up to my chin and stare at the ceiling.

I am not ready for this. Who quits smoking on four hours of sleep?

Last night I'd wandered the house until 2:30 a.m., smoking cigarette after cigarette, trying to commit the act to memory. A taste: hot, a drought in the mouth. A smell: stale, like poverty. The way cigarette smoke ribbons, turns to cloud and drifts sullenly to the ceiling. I grieved the satisfying snap! of a lighter. The first stinging lungful of smoke over morning coffee or after a good meal. Scraping the ash from a lit cigarette to lay bare its hot glowing heart.

Having smoked almost a pack in the three hours before I went to bed, I was wired; nicotine triggers a rush of adrenaline into the blood. Adrenaline is the hormone of cokeheads, skydivers, women who lift cars off their children. So minutes after I settled between the sheets, my heart began to hurl itself against my chest like a guard dog against a chain-link fence. The palpitations had plagued me almost every night for two years, and each night I was sure my heart would explode as my husband snored peacefully beside me. In the past year, I'd developed sleep apnea, too, so all in all, I dreaded going to bed. I knew I would drift off, over and over, only to start awake, gasping for air like a fish on the end of a hook.

There's no way I'm getting back to sleep. I shrug into my bathrobe and head downstairs. My pack of Basic Menthol Lights waits on the kitchen table. It holds one last cigarette, forlorn, bent. Any other morning, a fresh pack would have awaited me, neat and glossy in its cellophane wrapper. To me, a new pack of cigarettes is as pretty as a party invitation, to be opened with the same small thrill of pleasure.

I brew coffee, and then it's time. The clock reads 6:32. The Last Cigarette is a momentous event. It deserves respect, even if it's commemorated every other day. So I smoke with the solemnity of a pallbearer, paying my last respects to a beloved friend. I throw my mini-Bic into the trash, a gesture I've made more times than I care to admit, and a wave of sadness breaks over my head. When I think of living without cigarettes for the rest of my life, the world goes gray.

An executioner's drum roll sounds in my head, crescendos, and I put my cigarette to death.

I smoked my first cigarette at age nineteen, in my freshman year of college. Why so late? I have no good answer. Though no weed fiend, my mother enjoyed the occasional

Camel Light, and I'd spent high school eyeing the popular kids, fantasizing that, with the flick of a Bic, I could join their ranks of smoky cool. Perhaps, as a girl, I even sneaked a puff with friends, and turned green—I don't recall. But that first retch-producing, eye-flooding Benson & Hedges Menthol Light 100 was worth waiting for. Smoking was perfect, one more billboard on the self-destructive road I traveled. I was drinking then, and cutting, and in comparison, smoking felt benign and even fun, another facet of my life to withhold from my parents.

During the summer of 1982, home on summer break, I hid my packs of Newport Lights and books of matches in the glove compartment of my VW Bug. I hadn't yet started to use lighters. I became a true smoker when I stopped using matches—which feel flimsy and temporary and, in smokers, provoke a certain anxiety—and started to buy lighters, smooth and solid and dependable. To a smoker, hell is a cigarette and no fire.

Every Friday night that summer, I made the forty-five-minute drive from my parents' home in Burlington, Connecticut—then a hick town, not the upper-class enclave it is now—to the Lit Club in Hartford, which booked punk bands on the weekends; it was the oasis in my suburban desert. I had discovered punk music in Washington, D.C., where I attended college, and its bellowing rage eased my surly self-consciousness.

I was interning for the rinky-dink local newspaper. All week, as I filed my stories and photographed scenes of summer revelry around the city, I thought about the drive to Hartford. On some level, it wasn't the music that drew me. It was the trip itself. With every mile I put between me and my parents, the bigger and brighter and more *me* I became. The pack of Newports was a totem that conjured the embryonic self I'd so painfully cobbled together.

And yet, as the week wore on, the thought of that drive made my stomach clench. A nervous driver, I drove a matronly fifty miles an hour and could not bring myself to venture into the passing lane.

I was afraid behind the wheel—of what, I didn't know. Fear was just a part of me, always had been, like the birthmark on my back, and the rage with which I covered it was a bandage too small for its wound. But my will to outrun my life—a life that was already too complicated—was stronger than my fear of rolling down the dark highway, alone, pursued by the silver stream of headlights in my rearview mirror.

Smoking helped me make that trip and the many others that mark the map of my life—alcoholism and recovery, failed relationships, marriage and divorce, the birth of my son. Cigarettes were my constant and unwavering companion on those dark, twisting roads. I'm still not sure whether I found them or they found me.

I've been locked up most of my life. First, I was shackled to my mother's love, chains of sadness and anger and guilt. As I grew, the chains lengthened, rattling like Marley's ghost, each new link forged in depression and vodka and razor blades and obscured by a haze of cigarette smoke. It took me years to discover that it was only my emptiness that I dragged behind me, so heavy it made me stagger.

Maybe that's why in November 2003, when I chained myself in my Allentown, Pennsylvania, home for a week in a last, desperate attempt to quit smoking, the act felt strangely familiar, like a perfume you've smelled before or a person whose face you've forgotten but whom you once swore to love forever.

I was forty, with a beautiful seven-year-old son, a new husband I adored, and a successful career as a health editor at a large publishing house. A health editor. Who smoked. A decade ago, I'd found the irony amusing. As the years passed, however, I began to develop this sick feeling in my gut, an irrational certainty that I would die if I didn't stop. But I couldn't. Something inside me compelled me to keep lighting up, even when my eyes swelled and my lungs burned and my heart seemed ready to burst the muscle and bone that separated it from the outside world.

I wanted to quit, but I didn't want to stop smoking.

Ambivalence is the addict's root affliction. For five years before I finally quit, I bought nicotine patches but mostly didn't use them. I'd open the box, toss the cassette tape and booklet into the trash, and put the patches on the kitchen counter, next to my ashtray. They languished there, like birthday cards that you mean to mail, but never do.

I'd tried to quit countless times, and succeeded twice. The first time was in February of 1996, when, newly married to my first husband, Matt, I discovered that I was pregnant. I lasted until Daniel was about a year old. I quit again, for eight months, in January of 2002, a few months after meeting John, my second husband.

After that were the countless miniquits, when I'd slap on

a patch for two or three days until I crumbled. My failures first shamed and then hardened me; I accepted the certainty of my untimely death with gallows humor and a calculator. I'd read somewhere that each cigarette you smoke knocks seven minutes off your time on the planet. To amuse myself, I multiplied the estimated number of cigarettes I'd smoked—a pack a day for twenty-one years, that's 153,300—and did the math.

$$153,300 \times 7 \ minutes = 1,073,100 \ minutes$$
$$= 17,885 \ hours$$
$$= 745.2 \ days$$
$$= 2.0416 \ years$$

Two years of my life, up in smoke.

I continued to forfeit my days, seven minutes at a time. I smoked in the house and in the car, snuck out of Daniel's third birthday party at Chuck E. Cheese's, closing my eyes as the nicotine entered my bloodstream and lit up my brain like a Fourth of July sparkler. I puffed apologetically at his soccer games under other mothers' accusing eyes.

I won't say that I loved cigarettes more than my son, but I did love them more than I loved myself. From 1998 to 2001, the years that encompassed an affair, my divorce, and another doomed relationship, I smoked up to two packs a day. I wanted to care that I could die and leave Daniel motherless, but I didn't. At least, not enough. When you're consumed by self-hatred, there's no room for anyone else. Not in any way that counts.

The Lockdown, as I call my voluntary house arrest, was a variation of an idea I'd given my mother in the summer of 2003, during one of our countless discussions about her weight. "You should chain yourself to your computer, set up a webcam, have Dad bring you water and cottage cheese, and share your weight-loss journey in streaming video," I'd said. "It's a metaphor for your addiction to food. You'd get a million hits a day. Oprah would flip."

"You're nuts," my mother said, and that was that, or so I thought. But the idea stuck in my head with the stubbornness of an advertising jingle. Months later, on a balmy Friday night in October, John and I and his parents sped up Route 476 from Philly on our way back to Allentown after a night out. I sat in the back next to my mother-in-law, and the smoke from John's father's cigarette filled my throat like a gag. So what. His smoke or mine, in twenty years I'd be breathing through plastic tubing anyway. I tried to imagine one of my lung cells at the very moment of its cancerous mutation. Would I feel its first murderous division, the way some women feel the moment they conceive?

Then, from nowhere, a thought illuminated the inside of my skull, blazing with the kind of light reserved for celestial visitations. I blinked.

"Yes," I said.

"What," John said, eyes on the road.

"I'm going to chain myself in the house for a week to quit smoking."

John Senior laughed. My husband said, "You're demented." Fair enough. But I was also desperate. The plan seemed like my last hope, and possessed a peculiar logic: If

I couldn't control my impulse to smoke on my own, I'd impose that control.

On Monday, I put in for a week's vacation. Lockdown, a month away, began on Monday, November 17. The next Saturday, John and I went to Home Depot and bought a 72-foot length of chain—brushed-nickel finish, heavy steel, purchased off the roll at 69 cents per foot—and two small combination locks. We'd worked it all out. We'd use one lock to fasten the chain around my left ankle and snap the other to the radiator in the dining room. John would shackle me each morning before he left for work. I'd have the run of the first floor, my computer, and my cell phone. John would release me when he got home. (We decided against shackling me to the bed at night. I am a restless sleeper, and John said that the chain would rattle as I tossed and turned, keeping him awake.)

The chain was as unwieldy as a corpse. At Home Depot, when John gathered it up and heaved it on the scale, I noted its weight: forty pounds. But it was lighter than the weight of the habit I'd dragged behind me for twenty years.

My chain, to which I would be attached for up to eleven hours a day, was my addiction to nicotine. I could see it, hear it, hold it; it had heft and weight. Each link was a story, a story about cigarettes and me. Rasping across my wooden floors, its weight disabling my stride, the chain would narrate my life in smoke.

DAY 1

6:33 a.m.

The end is quick—one defiant hiss as I pass the lit end under the tap. It dies like any other I've held under faucets, dropped into toilets, and inserted into half-empty cans of flat Diet Pepsi. After the murder there is the ritual disposal of the ashtray—this one the orphan saucer to a cracked teacup—and the sigh of relief and regret. The deed done, I head into the living room to watch CNN. The last cigarette has soured my stomach, but sweetened my mood. When John comes downstairs, showered and shaved, I can smile. Pausing at the couch for a kiss, he ambles into the kitchen, with me at his heels.

I take a seat and watch him work. Opening the refrigerator, he roots for a moment, then shuts the door with his elbow, cradling the carton of eggs, the butter and bacon, a wedge of Cheddar. John cooks breakfast every morning; he is Pennsylvania Dutch and needs his eggs and bacon. He's a big man—5 feet 10, 240 pounds—and before we started dating he'd lost one hundred pounds, twice. He still strug-

9

gles with his weight, and loves his bread and potatoes as much as I love my smokes.

As he cracks eggs into a bowl, I say, "Don't make me any. I'm not hungry. I had coffee and a cigarette." (Not a cigarette. The cigarette. The last one.)

He ignores me, keeps cracking. "Hon. You have to eat." He whisks the eggs into froth, pours them, hissing, into our cast-iron frying pan, then drops bread into the toaster. "You want bacon?"

"Sure." I sigh. He will nurture me into a size fourteen.

We eat in the living room in front of the TV news, as we do every morning. I wolf my food, as usual, but John eats the way his people do everything: slowly.

Finally, he lays down his fork and looks at me. "Ready?"

The chain lies in the corner in glinting disarray, one end already locked around the dining-room radiator. Gathering an armful, John drags it to the couch and searches for the free end, letting each heavy coil drop upon the last. Spooked by its clatter, my eleven-year-old cat, Frankie, crawls out from under the coffee table and skitters into the kitchen. I'm inclined to follow him.

John pats the coffee table. I sit and extend my left leg, a maid of honor accepting a garter. He kneels at my feet and, with the other lock, attaches the chain to my ankle with a firm quiet click. Suddenly, I am a chain gang of one. Where are my prison stripes? John is right: I am demented. But this is the only way.

John tugs gently on the chain, then sets me free again. "You better wear socks. This"—he rattles the chain—"will hurt in a few hours." I head upstairs, returning in socks but *still wearing my bathrobe. I see no reason to get dressed.*

*John reshackles me, then checks the time on the VCR:
7:24. "I've got to go." John maintains and repairs machinery in a plant that makes car seats and high chairs, and has
an hour's drive ahead of him. Stepping over the puddle of
chain, he gathers his gym bag and keys and picks up the bag
of trash I've placed at the door.*

*I lower my head, blinking back tears. It's my first day of
kindergarten and my mother has just walked out the door.
How will I survive this day, my life, without cigarettes?
Without my trusty pack I don't exist, like that falling tree in
the forest that no one hears.*

*I clank to the front door with him. We murmur the usual
endearments, kiss, and then he's down the front steps. At
the Jetta, he turns.*

"You're okay with this? You're sure?"

*"Yes, yes, I'll be fine. Go." What else can I say? My hus-
band has chained me inside my house, because I've asked
him to, and now he's got to go.*

*"I'll call you later." He gets in, pulls away from the curb,
and is gone.*

*I shut the door gently, rattle back to the couch, and wait
to go crazy.*

For the first three years of my life, it was my mother and
grandmother and me. We lived in my grandmother's little
brick house on New Pear Street in Vineland, a small city in
southern New Jersey populated by the working-class Ital-

ians and blacks who worked in its many factories. On the outskirts of the city was farm country. In August, tomatoes and corn burst from the fertile earth; peaches, swollen with juice, dropped from the trees.

My grandmother's woodsy backyard abuts a house with stables. The horses press against her split-rail fence; she lifts me high, my legs dangling, my dress riding up, so I can pat their velvety muzzles. It is late spring; I love the heavy clusters of lilacs, with their dew-silvered leaves and distinctive scent of honey and rain. I close my eyes and inhale.

There was Elisa, my mother; Julia, my grandmother, the woman for whom I was named; and me. My father, Nicholas, was just gone. Both eighteen, they'd met waiting tables at a Chinese restaurant in Atlantic City, and he had gotten her pregnant under the boardwalk. Weeping, my mother confessed to my grandmother, who promptly flew at her daughter, slapping and screaming: Her *putana* of a daughter carried a bastard in her belly. Her brother—my uncle Art, four years older than my mother—cornered Nick, held both fists under his nose, and suggested that he marry her. Art had been my mother's protector since kindergarten; small, pencil-wristed boys in his elementary school had paid him to act as their bodyguard. He fought anyone, anytime, for a buck or for free. And so, in November 1962, a justice of the peace in Harrisburg, Pennsylvania, performed a quick, quiet ceremony attended only by Art.

My mother didn't want to be married any more than Nick did, however, and they divorced several months before I was born. No real harm done; everyone eventually got what they wanted. My grandmother's pride was restored:

I had a last name. Nick got his freedom back. My mother got me, a shining bowl into which she could pour all her inchoate yearnings.

I got something, too: a ghost. Nick's ghost—short, wiry, with black hair and olive skin, like mine, and small, delicate hands. It shadowed me everywhere. As a child, I could not understand the pain his desertion caused me; as an adolescent, I denied it. In time, it would consume me like a slow-growing cancer.

But that came later. When I was two, my mother enrolled in community college as an English major. During the day, she attended classes while my grandmother, a talented seamstress and a supervisor in a factory that made coats and uniforms for the army, terrorized the women who worked under her. Her next-door neighbor, Irma, watched me while they were gone. In 1965, this was day care. Each day, fat, kind Irma, in her faded housedresses and sturdy shoes, took me for walks and sang to me in lilting Italian. In the late afternoon, I played on her kitchen floor while she prepared dinner for her equally gentle husband, Jules. When my mother returned from her classes, we'd head outside to the swing set in our backyard, or I'd color in the kitchen as she cooked. Dinner, bath, my mother's crooning in the dark, eventually, her warm body next to mine in our shared bed. We lived in a world without men, and were content.

All that changed when my mother met my stepfather.

He was tall, this Kurt Hansen, with a high forehead and

pale blue eyes. Looking at photos of him during their courtship, I see what she must have seen: strength. Wide shoulders, the shoulders of a man who would make everything all right. He courted me along with my mother, but there was no way I would let him be my father, as my mother sometimes hinted. Perhaps, at three, I was dimly aware that I already had a father, and believed he would return to me one day. What would he think if he knocked on my door, bearing love and gifts, only to find me living with another man?

But my mother married Kurt anyway. Their union was a huge wave that deposited me, gasping, on an unfamiliar shore. My mother and I moved out of my grandmother's house and into the furnished trailer he had purchased to accommodate his new family.

I was enraged as only a three-year-old can be. This man had taken me from my grandmother, the horses, my lilac tree, my beloved Irma. He had stolen my mother. As angry as I was with him, however, I reserved my fury for her. One morning soon after their marriage, she kissed him good-bye at the door of our trailer before he left for work. Suddenly, she screeched and clutched her lower leg, kicked blindly against the pain. There I was on the floor, scuttling away like a scorpion. I'd bitten her calf.

My brother was born a year later and named after his father. I can't say I welcomed his arrival. Perceiving the three of them as a family, myself as an intruder, I was too proud to step inside their shimmering ring of love. I was also confused. On the one hand, I resented my stepfather for displacing me in my mother's heart, or so I thought. On the other, he was my father, the only one I knew, and I had begun to crave his love and approval. I feared I would never win it and scratched at this anxiety constantly, as if at an infected mosquito bite. Nick's ghost whispered in my ear: *Who could ever love you?*

I had to admit, he had a point. My stepfather had to love my brother; my brother was his. But I was my mother's, so she had to love me. Didn't she? Or would she decide she didn't need me after all?

Looking at family pictures from around that time, I have the sense I was caught in the act of disappearing. In a photo taken just after he was born, my brother and I sit in our trailer on our couch. My mother has put him in my lap, but I refuse to hold him. My arms are under his swaddled body, stiff like a doll's, and he lies sideways across my lap, his eyes puffed, his face stamped with that wizened expression newborns have. I stare into the camera, my eyes blank as pennies. In another picture, I sit in the backseat of my step-father's old red VW Bug, wearing a pink dress. My brother is strapped into his car seat next to me. This time, there's murder in my eyes. I can only imagine what I was feeling—betrayal, perhaps, an aching furious betrayal.

That's why I refused them all. Why I would not smile and take my stepfather's hand if he offered it. Why I pinched my baby brother. Why I lagged behind on family walks, kicking rocks and humming as if I didn't have a care in the world. We picnicked on the beach in Ocean City, fed peanuts to the elephants at the Philadelphia Zoo, but I was like the wobbly leg of a kitchen table, always the cause of upsets. My sullenness frustrated my mother and irritated my stepfather—he was trying, wasn't he? My mother assured me of his love, threw us together, forced him to kiss me good night. The harder she tried to draw me into the family circle, however, the more I withdrew.

I wanted to hurt my mother and drive a wedge between her and her new husband. If I could not share in their love, then I would sabotage it. But there was another motive for my self-exile: survival, pure and simple.

My mother's love for me knew no bounds. She believed we shared the same heart and that she could see her every thought and feeling reflected in my eyes. If she was blue or anxious, then so was I. If she believed that it was the two of us against my father—as she did more fervently with each passing year—who was I to dissuade her? I don't know when I made my first primitive attempt at deductive reasoning: My mother is life; I am alive; therefore I am my mother. All I knew is that when I looked inside myself, I saw my mother's face. More confusion. Who was I? Who was she? Was she a part of me, and if she ceased to exist, would I? I couldn't be sure. I yearned to merge with her; I felt engulfed by her. Her oppressiveness terrified me; so did my fear of her abandonment.

My mother was beautiful—an Italian Marilyn Monroe, all light and perfume and curves. She claimed the drawers in our bathroom for her zippered bags of cosmetics, and her dresser held stacks of neatly folded clingy sweaters in the bright colors she favored, orange and turquoise and pink.

(My mother also wore tube tops. Oh, the shame of meeting a classmate and her mother in the aisles of the local department store.) Men beamed when they saw her; their wives tightened their mouths. She was like Mardi Gras: loud and colorful, all jingling bracelets and clicking stiletto heels, and disconcerting to certain temperaments. She laughed too loud in front of strangers. Profanities tumbled from her soft mouth like dice from a Yahtzee cup. And every morning after her shower, she smoked one cigarette—a Camel Light—as she applied her makeup. The bathroom was right next to my bedroom. Each day I woke to the fragrance of one of her overpowering perfumes, all with the same top note: smoke. When this suffocating yet comforting scent settled in my throat, I knew it was my turn in the bathroom.

If my mother's fingers smelled of nicotine, her heart was as soft as the marshmallow chicks she tucked into our Easter baskets. For most of my childhood, she worked with abused and neglected kids. When she couldn't place children with a foster family for the night, she brought them home, and they slept in our spare bedroom. This was against the rules, but she couldn't stand the thought of them spending a long, lonely night in a detention center. She read to my brother and me, made up her own fantastic stories about shy violets that talked, smothered our stomachs with lipsticky raspberries. She painted our faces, and her own, with chocolate pudding. And she threw the best birthday parties. Every year, beginning in first grade, she invited my whole class into our small backyard, popular kids and nose pickers alike, no one ever left out. There were games and lovely chaos and her beautiful smiling face above a thickly frosted birthday cake.

I learned kindness and compassion from her. When I was around seven, our next-door neighbors allowed my brother and me on their children's swing set, but not the kids who lived on the other side of them. I was outraged; I knew those kids had nothing. They were scented with that musky smell of poverty, and their father was often in jail. I told my mother.

"Those goddamned sons of bitches," she said. "Get in the car."

My brother and I clambered into the backseat of our banged-up Bug, now pocked with rust on the driver's-side panel. The car often stalled when we sped down the highway, which always froze my heart, but we made it to a local department store without incident. My mother raced through the electronic doors, my brother and I hurrying behind her, excited, a little scared—what was she going to do?

She bought a swing set on credit. My father assembled it when he got home from work. Something about the way he dug the holes for the swing set's legs, and the way my mother shook the frame to make sure it was securely rooted in the ground, made me feel, for once, like a part of them.

The next day, my mother invited the neighbor kids to swing. She pushed them first, and then my brother and me. I swung high, higher. Her palms against the small of my back afforded me a rare moment of peace. Happy, I showed my heels to the sky.

But for all my mother's zany energy and fierce maternal love, she was often engulfed by her own demons. At those times, I sensed something struggling inside her, like a sack of kittens destined for the river.

My mother grew up invisible, neglected by her parents, who worked long hours. My grandfather, a carpenter, loved his little girl, but it was his sons—one a high-school football hero, the other in medical school—who would bring honor to his name. My grandmother—primitive, simple as bread or a cup of water—didn't need or give love. All she needed was food on the table and shoes on her feet.

Need ran through my mother like a fault line. Fat, bullied by the other kids, she talked compulsively in class; her teachers sat her in the hall outside her classrooms. Each day after being savaged at school, my nine-year-old mother trudged home to an empty house, packed the hole inside her with food, and cleaned. Cleaned and cleaned and cleaned. She mopped the gray linoleum of my grandmother's kitchen floor, scrubbed the toilet and the tub, ironed her father's and brothers' shirts, cooked the family meal. At fourteen she turned exquisite, but the fat, lonely girl she had been was locked in her heart forever.

By the age of eight, I believed it my job to protect her and ensure her happiness. My father certainly wasn't doing it. She and my father raged in the night. I listened to their fights with a fistful of blanket in my mouth, my eyes wide and dry, silently chanting *stopitstopitstopitstopit*. He would thunder back for a while, then storm from the house.

When he's gone, the house is quiet. I can hear her wandering from room to room, keening. After a while, the hall light flicks on; a slice of it slides under my door. Seconds later, she opens my door gently, switching on the lamp with the purple flower inside the glass—she is always buying pretty things for my room, frilly curtains, fluffy bed-spreads—and sits on the edge of my bed.

"Sweetie," she whispers. "Are you awake?"

I peer up at her from under the bedcovers. In the light of the hall, I can see the tear tracks on her cheeks.

"I came in to see if you were okay. I'm sorry if your father and I scared you. Are you okay?"

I nod, because she needs me to.

"Are you sure?"

Another nod. She cups her palm to my cheek and drops down, down, down into me, like a miner into a tunnel. "Come here," she says, gathering me in her arms. I smell cigarette smoke.

When she and my father fought, she smoked in the house—in the family room, *his* room—to spite him. Some-times I stayed up with her while she waited for him to come home. She'd switch off the lamps and lower the volume on the TV to an almost inaudible level; the murmuring voices and muffled laugh track could have been the drone of bees. The room seemed to grow smaller then, as cozy as a cave, but scary, too, as if we'd never find our way out, never see daylight again. In the flickering glow of the television, her smoke appeared blue. I stayed very still, my mind drifting like her smoke, my eyes open against her chest.

"Your father and I . . . honey, we just don't get along. He's a rotten sonofabitch—he doesn't care about this family. And I know he treats you differently from Kurt—he's so much harder on you. He's just a selfish, selfish man. I should leave him—take you and Kurt and just leave. We could go live with Mom-Mom again and everything would be like it was before your dad. Do you remember when we used to go to the beach, just you and me? I don't want you to worry, honey, but we might have to get a divorce. What would you think if we did? Tell me the truth, sweetie. I really want to know. You can tell me. You can tell me anything."

I'm not sure what she wants me to say. Does she really want to know if I am okay? Or should I stay still and quiet, as I am? And what is this about my father treating me differently? I'd always suspected it, but having it confirmed so directly deflates me. My awkward position on her lap is making my back ache, and my stomach clenches at the possibility of divorce, every child's worst nightmare. I feel small and utterly overwhelmed.

Eventually, she gently pulls away and examines me, holding me at arm's length. In the light of the hall, her eyes glow soft and bright. "I love you more than anything in the world, honey. I love Kurtie, too, but I can't talk to him the way I can to you. He's too little. I don't know what I'd do without you. Are you okay? Are you sure? Because you can tell me if you're not."

No, I can't. It is my job to eat her pain, piece by piece, as dutifully as I eat my broccoli at dinner. So I nod solemnly against her chest: Yes, I am okay.

"Okay then, sweetie-pie—back to sleep. You have school in the morning. Sweet dreams."

She tucks me back in bed, lingers in the doorway for a second, her silhouette shimmering against the hall light, and shuts the door. After she leaves, her scent lingers—faded perfume and cigarette smoke, the smell of comfort and of need.

10 a.m.

I huddle in the fake-fur tiger-striped blanket my mother made me for Christmas three years ago, the chain curled at my feet like a faithful dog. Half of me watches a talk show—a guilty pleasure, the only kind I allow myself. The other half wonders why I'm not craving a smoke. I've never quit cold turkey, and imagined sweats, shakes, agony— Frankie Machine's withdrawal scene in The Man with the Golden Arm, *only with cigarettes. I didn't expect to feel so spacey, so profoundly alone. The couch is an unmapped island, and I am marooned.*

During commercials for technical schools and slip-and-fall attorneys, I look around my living room, my universe for the week ahead. Dust blankets every surface. A pile of books, Daniel's school papers, and unpaid bills spill from the desk in the computer room, off the living room. Acceptable under normal circumstances, the disarray disturbs me today; my defenses are down. If my mother were here, she'd offer to clean. Insist on it, in fact. She'd scrub my bathrooms and the kitchen, strip the sheets from our beds, and declutter closets, occasionally crying out over such wanton filthiness. I finally had to tell her to stop bringing her rubber gloves, bucket, and scrub brushes when she came to visit. She honored my request—reluctantly—but still offers advice. "Don't waste your money on those expensive cleaners. There's nothing better than bleach. It kills everything."

Pushing past coats and shoes and rolls of Christmas

wrapping paper, I drag out my vacuum cleaner. Redemption smells like bleach and lemon oil. If I can't smoke, I will clean—purge my house of cobwebs and dirt as I purge my cells of nicotine.

I vacuum the living room—ignoring behind the couch and under the coffee table—and picture my mother shaking her head, her mouth puckered in disapproval. When I'm through, I stand there for a moment—this small effort has drained me—then clank back to the couch, abandoning the vacuum in the middle of the room.

But still I see through my mother's eyes. The living room walls are painted a cheery yellow, but cobwebs lace the ceiling. Though expensive, the wool rug in soft greens and browns, patterned in flowering vines, is too small to cover the scratched wood floor. The knotty-pine entertainment center, from a naked-furniture outlet, is still naked. (We'd planned to stain it cranberry, but never did.) This very couch is my mother's castoff, as is the love seat across from it. I've covered both with pseudo-suede slipcovers in a shade of red she calls cayenne. Her hope is that, someday, I will buy a new dining-room set. Or a couch—at least a couch. When we talk on the phone, she pleads, "Break down and buy yourself some new furniture, Julia, will you? And don't be cheap. Spend a few bucks and get something nice. You'll have it forever."

Usually, I roll my eyes. Not today. Nothing matches: there's no color scheme, no theme. My house is wrong, pathetic, ugly. My mother has a flair for the decorative arts; she loves bright colors, wills beauty into her life. I grew up in rooms painted pumpkin and periwinkle, filled with lush potted plants, thick carpets of wine and teal, furniture and dishes that matched. A stranger would be seduced by the comfort she'd created, believing that nothing could go wrong in her house. Plenty has gone wrong in mine.

I have lugged around my mother's castoffs for twenty years—chairs, couches, lamps, end tables, sheets, curtains. But the photographs on the painted wooden mantel above the fireplace are mine, scenes from my own life: John blows out his candles on his thirty-ninth birthday. Daniel perches on John's shoulders outside our house. The three of us, a new family, pose bashfully in front of our crooked tree last Christmas morning.

I rattle over to the mantel and take down a photo. Through a film of dust, my son sits on John's broad shoulders, his button-brown eyes and mouth wide in mock panic. I see a gap, and smile; I keep his baby teeth with my jewelry.

He is why I am here, locked up like a chimp in the zoo. Both our lives are at stake and I won't let him down, even though I hear my Last Cigarette, giggling like Satan. Like dogs hear high frequency humans cannot, smokers hear cigarettes. They can sound like distant music, white noise, the crooning of a mother to her infant. Sometimes all you hear is the whisper of burning paper or the pop of tobacco. But you hear them. You hear them and you heed their call.

Like the moon circles the Earth, my father orbited the vast unknown planet of his family, trapped by its powerful pull.

My father was the director of a not-for-profit workshop that employed the physically and mentally handicapped. His job was to land business and government contracts that put them to work. His employees—of all ages and levels of disability—did things like sort ball bearings and assemble Val-U-Paks, small boxes of samples that companies mailed to people to entice them to buy the full-size products. For filling and sealing the boxes they were paid a small wage. When my father landed the Val-U-Pak contract, we had these little boxes of mouthwash, moisturizers, and shampoos all over the house, in every closet.

The gods visited a terrible fate upon my father. They made him an artist with a day job and a family to support. He defied them, however, escaping his life—us—through his art. He spent most of his weekends in the basement, transforming logs or slabs of wood into the visions in his head: twenty-foot-long plaques of wild, waving sunflowers, naked women with pendulous breasts and bulging eyes, gargoylesque figures with bared teeth and wings. He always carried a dog-eared sketchbook, and drew his figures in pencil before he put chisel to wood. When I snuck into his workshop and looked through it, touched his chisels and rasps, I saw the inside of my father's intelligent, twisted mind.

Back then, my father was a cold man, as distant from us as the stars. "Oh," he would say on Christmas mornings, holding up our gifts—the Old Spice from me, the sweater from my mother and brother. But he always drew out that stingy syllable and tipped it down at the end, so it sounded more like "Aw." He gave us brief, awkward thank-you hugs, explaining that he didn't want to catch our colds. We always seemed to have colds on Christmas Day—all winter, in fact—and for months he'd keep his distance, as if we were contaminated.

Our table manners were a constant source of irritation to him. If my brother or I put our elbows on the table, he'd jab his fork into the tender flesh of our forearms. One night—perhaps my brother was eating too fast, or I was smacking my lips—he snapped. "Jesus Christ," he snarled. "You kids are pigs. Look—this is you." He picked up a gob of whatever was on his plate—spaghetti?—and ground it against his mouth. I must have been ten or eleven. My brother stopped laughing in a hurry; he saw that my father wasn't joking. Ashamed, I lowered my eyes to my plate.

More than once, it occurred to me that my father came home every night not because he loved us, but because we belonged to him, and it was a man's duty to care for his property. Maybe his coldness stemmed from the fact that he was dyslexic. Could it have been that reading people's feelings and motives was as difficult for him as reading words on a page? But he read anyway, because the world captivated him. His nightstand was piled with books about ancient Greece and prehistoric art and how to make beer.

I was shy around him. We would sit in the living room, watching some sitcom, him in his avocado-colored vinyl recliner and me on the couch, and he was as out of my reach as a diamond ring down the drain. Convinced that I disappointed him in some profound way, I vowed to develop some singular talent to prove to him that I was worthy of his love.

It couldn't be art. I loved to draw, but my efforts looked

pitiful next to his. So I took up the guitar and judo, only to quit them both because I could not bear to perform in front of him and risk his ridicule. Why in the world would he want to listen to me plink out "Red River Valley," stupidly tapping my foot to keep the beat, as my teacher insisted I do? And the thought of him watching me in judo class made me sweat. He often picked up my brother and me from our Saturday morning classes, and each week I prayed he would arrive late enough to miss my clumsy kicks and rolls.

I thought I had to earn love from him as I earned my allowance, and was furious that my brother did not understand this. Kurt didn't seem to care what our father thought of him. He didn't seem to care about anything, or at least the things that bothered me—our mother's unhappiness, our father's indifference, their constant fighting. He accepted the way things were in our house with the composure of a cow in the rain. My brother was a charmer, with red-brown eyes and freckles and hair the color of an old penny. I hated him for the way he came and went, with easy confidence and a ready smile, collecting friends as I collected resentments.

11:17 a.m.

The coffee is almost five hours old, as bitter as a department-store Santa. Yet here I am at the pot, pouring my fourth cup. This is pure stubbornness. A cup of coffee without a cigarette is like Vegas without Wayne Newton, pizza without cheese: just not right. But caffeine is the only drug

I have left. I will not give it up. In fact, I drink even more coffee than usual when I quit, and take it black hoping that its bitterness will drive the lust for nicotine from my brain.

It never does. Coffee and cigarettes—a more life-affirming duo does not exist. The Turks knew it, even coining a proverb in homage: Coffee and tobacco are complete repose. On summer Saturdays, when lawn mowers droned to life at seven a.m., or January snowstorms tucked me into my house for the day, I'd sit at my kitchen table with a pack of cigarettes and a fresh pot of coffee and live one perfect hour.

Having collected vices like men's phone numbers in my youth, I now cling to one: caffeine. How humiliating. Obviously, I am a pussy, as afraid to live as to die. Smokers are risk-takers, rebels, iconoclasts, artists. They foment revolution and walk on the grass. I am an old woman who frets about her bowels. My only consolation is my sure knowledge that I will never quit red meat. I may be able to survive as a nonsmoker, but would never make it as a vegetarian.

On the first day of seventh grade, I sit in Honors English, my last class of the day, trying to decide where to sit on the bus. We've moved to a new town and I am the new girl, even more the outsider than usual, and my decision may well chart the course of my life. When the bell rings at 2:15, my class stampedes toward the door. I merge into the sea of feathered haircuts and jean jackets already in the hall, and we all stream into the warm golden air.

Six buses snake around the school's circular driveway, motors running, drivers at the wheel. As I try to find mine, I bump up against a few kids who have stopped in the middle of the moving crowd. Girls and boys. Their Levi'd legs are planted against the surge of the crowd, their eyes narrowed in cool indifference. I look closer. Surprise snatches my heart and squeezes, hard. They are *smoking.* I watch them pull on their weeds and spew out thin blades of smoke. They look like rock stars. They've thrown an impromptu party, right here in the parking lot, and haven't invited me.

Kids weren't allowed to smoke. Were they? Astounding as it seems, they were. The junior high was connected to the high school, and every kid from the lowliest seventh-grader to the most anointed senior ate lunch in the same large cafeteria. One wall of the lunchroom, made entirely of glass, had a door that opened out into a courtyard. This narrow, sunless strip of lawn was where the kids smoked, with the sanction of both schools. Called the smoking lounge, it was hallowed ground, the domain of the stoners who brazenly displayed their packs of Marlboros and lighters in their front pockets. They congregated there before school and during lunch and study hall, the boys in their army jackets and work boots, the girls in their gauzy Indian shirts and clogs.

I'd felt like an outsider all my life, but the smoking-lounge kids *were* outsiders, literally. They could be seen from the cafeteria, and I watched them as I ate with my group. I was a Brain, according to the unwritten junior-high and high-school social hierarchy, but only because I didn't fit into any other category. I didn't play sports (my one anxious season of soccer didn't count), so I couldn't be a Jock. I didn't bring a hash pipe to school, so I wasn't a Burnout, either. I took Honors classes but loathed math and chess and didn't make the National Honor Society. The Brains were polite, but distant; they sensed my internal chaos, and it made them skittish. The smokers seemed more like me: sullen, suspicious, frayed around the edges. Their seeming inviolability intrigued me. I liked to think that if I opened that cafeteria door one day, stepped outside, and lit up, they would embrace me as one of their own.

Clearly I sensed the appeal of smoking early, and not just because of the parking-lot rock stars. Everyone in my mother's family smoked. My uncle Art chain-smoked. So did JoAnn, his intelligent, sharp-tongued wife. My grandmother's brothers and sisters—Uncles Johnny, Mingo, and Pep, Aunt Mary, and many of their wives and husbands— all smokers. Fun, handsome, vital people, they brought a party wherever they went. When we visited my grandmother in Vineland, the *famiglia* would bang at the screen door off the kitchen, take a seat at my grandmother's battered Formica-topped kitchen table, sip musty-smelling red wine, and chain-smoke, my mother included. (A social smoker, she got caught up in the conviviality of these reunions.) They filled one heavy glass ashtray with crushed butts within an hour; a toxic plume hovered above the table like a benevolent spirit. To me, they looked every bit as cool as my smoking peers.

It seems impossible that I never experimented with smoking: I don't recall taking so much as a puff on a cigarette before my freshman year in college. Probably, before that point, smoking was too open an admission of rebellion. My insurrections were performed in my head, away from the family I'd come to loathe in typical adolescent fashion. In photos of me from age twelve through my teens, I look at the camera with disdain, as if into the eyes of a firing squad.

By now, we were a family of strangers. I threw pots and pans at my brother. My mother continued to complain bitterly to me about my father. My father and brother talked neither to us nor to each other. Dinnertime was an agonizing though necessary event, like a trip to the Department of Motor Vehicles.

"Stop picking the salad out of the bowl with your fingers," my father snaps. At twelve, my need for his love and approval coexists with my simmering resentment of him. All that anxiety and anger has fermented into a mighty strong brew. "If you want more, put it on your plate."

"Jesus, Kurt—what's the big deal? We're finished," my mother says. I hunch over my plate, humiliated and angry. I am sick of her always coming to my rescue, elbowing me out of my own life.

"Shut up. Am I talking to you? I'm talking to her."

"No, I want to know, God damn it! Why are you so much harder on her than on Kurt?"

"I think Kurt's stoned," I offer, to distract them. He sits there quietly eating his dinner, but his eyes have this jack-o'-lantern glow, as if lit from within.

After dinner, we scattered. My brother blasted KISS or Ted Nugent in his room and leafed through the dirty magazines he kept under his mattress. I read or wrote bad poetry in mine. My father retired to the living room to watch the news. My mother cleaned the kitchen or did laundry. At eight o'clock, my parents and brother reconvened in the family room to watch TV.

Almost every night, my mother tapped at my door and stuck in a crescent of face. I'd look up from my bed, my finger holding my place in *Steppenwolf* or *The Bell Jar*.

"Please come downstairs, Julia," she would say, softly. She was still begging me to join the family, and I was still trailing three feet behind them, scuffing my shoes.

"I'll be right down, Mom. Just let me finish this chapter."

But I rarely joined them. I felt calmer in my room, more sure of my boundaries. Here, the air had not passed through my mother's lungs first. This was *my* room, *my* bed, *my* desk, *my* shoes there in my messy closet, a Great Wall of footwear hiding glass jars of booze. I'd begun to steal my father's liquor and squirrel it away in old condiment bottles. I drank ketchup-flavored vodka, and gin with the faintest taste of Italian dressing.

3:14 p.m.

Is this what life without cigarettes sounds like? This aimless hum inside my head that I cannot bear for one more second?

Despite the coffee, lethargy has closed over me, as murky as lake water. Actually, this whole day has the feel of a drowning: After a brief struggle, I let it happen. I sleep, stare at the television, sleep, rattle to the bathroom, sleep.

I know this torpor. When it finally burns off, my depression will float to the surface like a body. My sadness is as much a part of me as my eyes or my hands. I've carried it always, this isolation, this nagging suspicion that I am incomplete and unlovable and unworthy. Despite twenty years of therapy, my sadness persists, coming and going as it pleases, sitting on my chest like a fat housecat. A cigarette always shooed it away. Not anymore, not ever.

My urge to sleep is as unrelenting as a pillow over my face, but hunger finally drives me into the kitchen, where I slap peanut butter between two slices of whole-grain bread. As John predicted, the chain hurts, I slip my index finger beneath the links to ease its weight, but when I remove it, the steel resettles on bone. I lick my knife, add it to the pile of dirty dishes in the sink, and carry my sandwich to the couch without a plate. As I cross the dining room, a craving cleaves through me.

Screw this. I'll dig through the trash for my Last Cigarette and dry it in the oven on a piece of aluminum foil. Then I'll turn on my electric stove, bend to the heated front coil with the butt in my mouth, and puff until it catches. In the process, I will singe a lock of my hair, the odors of burnt hair and tobacco smoke sharp in my nose. It's happened before. Many times. Fuck it. In seven seconds, the time it takes nicotine to travel from the blood to the brain, life will be Technicolor again, clearer, sharper, brighter.

Then I remember: John took out the garbage this morn-

ing. The bag is sitting in front of the house. Even I am not desperate enough to rattle out the door in my robe like an escaped sex slave. Yet.

That I can even entertain this thought depresses me. How many times have I acknowledged to family and friends that I know smoking is a filthy habit and I'm paying Big Tobacco to kill me and it's dumb to stand in the rain/snow/cold to smoke and I'm pathetic to worry about gaining weight if I quit and I can't give up my self-destructive, death-dealing habit even though I'm forcing my son to suck down my secondhand smoke. I know that I am an idiot. Don't I know it. Yet I persist. Why does no amount of knowledge, guilt, shame, or scary statistics dissuade me?

Lectures don't work, either. My mother should know; she's phoned in her nagging for over five years. I wonder if she feels responsible. Parents who smoke tend to raise children who smoke, and children are marked by their parents' tobacco use shockingly early. But did my mother's smoking really influence my own? She rarely smoked more than one cigarette a day, for God's sake—ours was a one-ashtray household—and so beautifully. There's a photo of her, in her twenties, that I pull from her collection every time I visit. Wearing a sleeveless black pullover and white slacks, breathtakingly beautiful, my mother stares unsmiling into the camera. A cigarette nests in the V between her index and middle fingers. Even as a child, I admired that picture, was caught in her gaze like a wrist in a strong man's grip. This was not my mother. This was Cleopatra, right down to her black-rimmed eyes.

Day 1

If that cigarette intensified her beauty—if I saw the slim white cylinder between her fingers as a magician's wand, conjuring poise and a regal distance—it's possible that her morning Camel Light made a lasting impression. Just as her childhood runs to the corner store for her father's packs of unfiltered Camels influenced her. Her father died at fifty-one of pancreatic cancer, one of several cancers thought to be smoking related, nineteen days before I was born.

The Last Cigarette stays buried in the trash. The peanut butter sticks in my throat. Sadness hums on the edge of my consciousness, as the rumbling of a distant truck causes a thrum in a pane of glass. I need a cigarette. I must have a cigarette. If I don't, my sadness will gather, crest, and smash into my consciousness like a tsunami wave. The sound of sadness is the groan and splintering of wood, the screech of bending steel. The sound of collapse.

Seventh grade went on and on, like a bad dream that sucks you to your pillow. One Friday afternoon, I board the bus for home, grateful for the weekend. A group of backseat girls get on a few minutes after me, wrapped in the sharp corrupt scent of smoke. They are in my grade but seem much older in their long denim coats and Candies slip-ons and dangly peacock-feather earrings—very Stevie Nicks. When they walk down the hall together, I study the bulletin boards or duck into the nearest classroom.

Now, I keep my eyes on the rip in the green seat in front

of me and will them to walk on by. The leader, nicknamed Kermit because her eyes bulge alarmingly behind her huge plastic frames, stops at my seat, third row from the driver, where I sit alone. Kids bunch up behind her and her mean-girl clique, waiting to pass.

"We're going to kick your ass on Monday," says Kermit. Terror surges through me, that deep shocking thrill in the chest, like when you've been startled. I say nothing, just keep studying that rip, imagine crawling through it as they all high-five each other and saunter to the back of the bus.

It isn't the threat of a beating that freezes my heart. It is the certainty of their hatred of me, which confirms my own. What about me invites an ass-kicking? My Levis, are they wrong? Wrong cut, wrong color? My shoes? No. It is me, just me. They smell my weakness like blood and, like sharks, are hard-wired to rip me apart. I can understand that. I want to kill my weakness too. Carve it right out of me, like a tumor. To get a head start, I dig my fingernails into my forearm, leaving angry, pink half-moons.

The bus drops me off in front of my house. My father has stuck one of his carvings in our front yard. That house on the corner of Punch Brook Road with the totem pole? That would be mine. There is no hiding my pathology; I am a door left ajar, and anyone can walk right in whenever they feel like it. I am the girl with the totem pole, the girl who walks the halls alone with her head down, the girl who stinks like a loser.

I was sick to my stomach all weekend, anticipating my beating, but those girls never did kick my ass. Life, that ball-breaking bitch, went on.

3:27 p.m.

I am dying. At least, some part of me is dying. It takes seventy-two hours for all traces of nicotine to leave the body. I imagine the nicotine fading from my brain, molecule by molecule. Each molecule is a piece of the puzzle of me, and the puzzle is coming undone.

With my index finger, I trace a small stain on the pseudo-suede slipcover over and over again. The movement soothes me. Keeps me from thinking too hard about the unwashed dishes in the sink, the vacuum cleaner left out, the dust that floats serenely in the wan winter light. There are most certainly dust balls behind the couch, or worse—on the rare occasions I've looked, I've found crusts from Daniel's breakfast toast. At his age, I pressed my Flintstones vitamins between the cushions of the couch, which annoyed my mother—they were expensive. She could have bought the generic kind.

But what she really hated was dirt. By the time I was in high school, I hated Saturday mornings, which were not for family breakfasts or team sports or music lessons but for vacuuming and Pledge and tears—sometimes my mother's, sometimes my own.

"God damn it!" she roars from downstairs; it is maybe eight o'clock, my brother isn't even watching cartoons yet. "This house is filthy! Julie! Kurt! Get the fuck up and help me clean this pigsty! I am not your maid!"

As her footsteps pound across the kitchen and up the stairs, I don my mental armor. While my mother's internal disorder still scares me, her rage now fuels mine. I want to douse her, shout her down, shut her up. I am sick of her tantrums, her constant scrubbing and polishing. Sometimes when she cleans, her face gets white and sick, like right after you throw up.

Then she is at my door, snorting like a bull. "Get the hell out of bed, get downstairs, and start vacuuming! And get behind the couch—pull it away from the wall! I'll check, and I swear to God if I see filth, I'll make you do it again!"

One morning, I fight back. "Jesus Christ!" I roar, throwing my legs over the edge of the bed. "You don't have to fucking scream! I can hear you!"

"Don't you raise your voice to me! I'm your mother!"

"Get out of my face. Go scrub a toilet."

"Bitch," she breathes, and lunges at me. Her hands, roughened by years of bleach and hot water, clamp down on my shoulders and she drags me from my bed. Tangled in my flannel nightgown, I grab her forearms so I won't fall, recover my footing, and shove her toward my door. Cat fight! I start to laugh; the situation is absurd. My mother thinks I am laughing at her, of course.

"You're a monster. A monster." She surges against me one more time, and then pushes me away, her face collapsing in defeat. "Get dressed and help me."

I would forgive her, and she me. We loved each other, were bound together forever. Still, I lived for our fights. For the few seconds this battle had lasted, I felt perfectly myself, comfortable in my own skin. But I did not forget, not for a second, that it was her or me. I remember our ragged breathing, our locked eyes, and my certainty that if I lost this fight, I'd lose them all.

My cell phone rings, interrupting this warm and fuzzy memory. I check the number: it's John. "Hey," I say, tracing the stain.

"How you feeling, Hon? You holding up all right?"

"Yeah." No. My numbness lifts like a curtain, pain pirouettes across the stage, the curtain falls again. I squeeze my eyes shut, hiding them with my hand, and sob silently, mortified that less than nine hours into Lockdown, I am falling to pieces.

"Well . . ." John knows I need comfort, knows he has none to give. "I'll let you go, then. I'll be home at five thirty, six. Need anything?"

"Cigarettes," I say dully, wiping my eyes. "Just kidding. Love you." I push End on my cell and toss it back onto the coffee table.

I don't know what I was thinking. I can't do this. I must do this. Failure is not an option. I've told too many people about Lockdown—my family, John's family. Made a huge stink that this was it, I was quitting for good this time. Why did I use the word "quit"? How foolish. In the past, I didn't "quit." I "cut down." I hedged my bets, the only sensible strategy. Now, trapped in the web of my bluster, I'll have to white-knuckle it for a month, at least, even if it kills me.

For some reason, I recall the boil that erupted in my right armpit when I was eight. Frightened by the hot swollen cyst, imagining a long, slow demise, I'd kept quiet about it until I couldn't lift my arm. My father took me to the doctor to have it lanced. It had been an evening appoint-

ment; I remember the porch light shining as we made our way to the car. Dead girl walking. I don't know where my mother was.

My father holds me down on the examination table while the doctor cuts into the boil and presses out the poison inside. The pain is hallucinatory. I writhe on the table, the crisp paper crackling beneath my bare skin. "It's almost over," my father says, in a rare display of tenderness. "It's all right, you're going to be all right."

But I wasn't all right, would never be. Pain and smoking, smoking and pain, inseparable as the links in this chain. I recall screaming on that table, but my father says I never made a sound.

I was graduated from high school in June. Class of 1981—rah. I skipped the prom and the senior dinner. In September, I started my freshman year at George Washington University. In February, I bought my first pack of cigarettes.

On that gray Saturday afternoon, I stood in the liquor store around the corner from my dorm, buying a fifth of vodka. Hung over from the night before, I felt the acid in my stomach churn with free-floating dread. I was fucking up big time—drinking every night, cutting classes, waking up every Saturday morning in a different boy's bed. No structure; no parental restraint. Staying sober on a Tuesday night was as unfathomable to me as riding a unicycle.

The summer before, I'd wanted desperately to be free of my parents, counted the days before we packed the car and drove the eight hours to D.C. When my parents lingered in my dorm room, reluctant to leave, understanding the hugeness of this moment, my mother with proud and happy tears in her eyes, I thought I would explode. But now, hundreds of miles from home, I felt like a balloon released by a child, sailing toward its certain demise by tree branch or telephone wire.

As I paid for my vodka, I noticed the cigarettes on the wall behind the old man at the cash register. They looked pretty—small, neat, multicolored packs, stacked like oversized LEGOs. A thought leaped into my brain like a flying fish: *I should try those.* So as the old man behind the counter slid my fifth into a paper bag, I said, "And a pack of Benson & Hedges Menthol Lights 100s, please," as if I'd been buying them for years. The box was a pale luminous green, like copper patina.

He gave me a hard pack. Once outside, I tore off the cellophane, flipped up the neat little lid, and pinched out one of the tightly packed cigarettes between my thumb and index finger. I placed it in the center of my lips, the way I'd seen my mother do. An errant piece of tobacco stuck to my tongue; I picked it off, then ripped one match from the book. The phosphorus on the tip ignited with a satisfying sizzle. I touched the match to the cigarette, inhaled, and Jesus Christ—my eyes went wide, flooded with water; I swore I felt my pupils dilate. I coughed, then retched. The six glasses of watered-down apple juice I'd had for breakfast, my hangover remedy, sloshed sourly in the back of my throat. An icyhot burning gripped my chest. It didn't occur to me to stop.

Gingerly, I smoked the cigarette down to the filter, then

tossed the butt into the street. I leaned against the store and closed my eyes. My head buzzed; my mouth crooked into a big wobbly grin.

A month later, my roommate—a hearty, preternaturally cheerful girl from Cape Cod—found me drunk on my bed, slicing my arms with a razor blade I'd pounded out of my Lady Schick. My bleary eyes met her shocked ones. She raised her hand to her mouth.

"Oh Jesus, oh Jesus." She inched toward me cautiously, as if attempting to befriend a snarling dog, and held out her hand. "Come on. You need to go to the emergency room."

"Just let me get my cigarettes."

When the resident on duty saw the gaping cuts on my arms, he wouldn't let me leave. I spent three weeks on the locked ward.

I don't remember much about that time. It is sealed somewhere inside me like a pickled tumor in a jar. I know I didn't eat for more than a week. Or talk. Or sleep. Every night until dawn, I sat on the vinyl couch across from the nurses' station and smoked while the nurses drank coffee and gossiped. Patients weren't allowed matches or lighters. The nurses were the keepers of the flame. When I needed a light, I shuffled sullenly to the station, held out my cigarette, and waited. The gesture was my one admission of need.

When my parents arrived, I lay facedown on my bed and refused to look at or speak to them. I don't remember what I felt. Rage, probably, like a balled-up rag in my mouth. Fear right behind it, surging in my throat. My parents drove to my dorm and packed my things. We made the eight-hour drive to Connecticut in silence.

My parents enrolled me in an outpatient therapy program at a local hospital—day care for the mentally unhinged.
My mother drove me there at eight in the morning and
picked me up at four. At home, I felt her red-rimmed eyes on
my back, through the closed door of my bedroom, willing me
to live. We attended family therapy once a week, but didn't
talk about what had happened to me because eventually we
had to walk through the dark parking lot to our car, knowing that what we'd said couldn't be taken back.

Slowly, though, I came back from the dead and fell in
love with my therapist, Joe, an acerbic balding Italian with
eyes like searchlights. I fantasized that he would fix me and
we'd marry and I'd raise his black-eyed children, even after
he told me what the psychiatrist at the hospital hadn't: I was
an alcoholic. I told him he was full of shit. He merely raised
his eyebrows.

After three months, Joe pronounced me sane and released
me into the world. I enrolled at a local college but dropped
out after the first week, depressed by the tiny campus and its
embarrassment of business majors. A few months later, I
applied for a reporting job at the paper for which I'd interned
the summer before, wearing a long-sleeved blouse to the
interview—which was in June—to hide my shredded arms.
To my surprise I was hired, fresh from a psych ward and
without a college diploma.

I forgot about Joe and fell in love with Eric, the paper's
copy editor. Pale and thin-lipped and dreamy-eyed, slightly
tubercular-looking, Eric looked like the pen-and-ink illus-
trations of princes in my favorite book growing up, *The
Blue Fairy Book*. He was my first adult relationship, the first

of my blue-eyed men, and he smoked too: Marlboros. Six months after we met, we were engaged. I wore the ring for a month before locking it away in a safe-deposit box. I told Eric I was afraid I'd lose it.

In the fall of 1984, I left the paper to give college another shot. Eric talked about quitting too. He wanted to return home to New York City to be a photographer. "You'll love the city," he said. "You can get a part-time job, finish school. When I'm making decent money, we'll get married."

"Okay," I said, and dropped out of school for the third time in two years. One morning in the summer of 1985, we packed the back of my father's old black pickup with domestic detritus from my parents' basement. My mother stood next to my father, her fist to her mouth, as I rolled down their dirt driveway toward my future.

9:22 p.m.

Wrapped in my blanket, John by my side, I stare through a rerun, the TV, the wall, until my gaze reaches the end of the world.

"Tell me about your day," he'd said when he got home and unshackled me, a conquering hero liberating a prisoner of war. I shrugged. I didn't want to. I didn't want anything. Not dinner, not a shower, not even a cigarette. I'm spent. Hollow as a chocolate Easter bunny. Somehow I'd forgotten that, at least for me, the first month without cigarettes is like running a marathon. Every day.

John draws my foot into his lap; his fingers feather gently over the sole, across the arch. "You holdin' up all right?"

"Uh-huh."

"You're awful quiet."

"Yeah."

Shh, I want to tell him. Danger, Will Robinson. I feel it. Animals sense imminent disaster—earthquake, tidal wave, volcanic eruption—in subtle shifts in barometric pressure and infinitesimal vibrations under their feet. They flee on foot. I flee into an electronic device that converts light and sound into electromagnetic waves and displays them on a screen. The less I talk, the less I hurt. The less I move, the safer I am. Without cigarettes, I am not safe.

Then again, I don't recall ever feeling safe. As I stare into the TV, a fragment of memory breaks loose like a clot. More sensation than memory: sun, wind. My mother at the wheel of a car; I sit beside her on a wide bench seat. I can't be more than two, which means my mother has not yet met the man who will steal her from me forever. For now, there is just me and her, two halves that make a whole.

There's just one thing: I can't see.

Wind lashes my eyes. I squeeze them shut. Gray squiggles float across an orange field. Wind whistles around my ears and drowns out the world. I am scared, so scared. Flattening against the scratchy front seat, I press against her hip, searching for a spot that feels safe.

We don't wear seat belts. When protection is warranted, she throws her arm across my chest. Her will is all that stands between me and disaster, but I trust her. What choice do I have? She loves me. Her love is all around me, heavy like her perfume. And I love her. She is inside my head at all times, fills me up, squeezes me, enormous with her love, her bright lipsticked mouth, her eyes as luminous as the moon. Every so often, she gropes for the wrinkled pack of Camels that lies on the seat between us, fishes out a cigarette with her painted lips, and pushes in the car's lighter.

"Hon."

My mind goes white like the projection screen after a home movie. My husband stands next to the couch, about to go into the kitchen. "You want anything?"

"I'm good."

"A peanut-butter sandwich?"

"No thanks."

John plods into the kitchen. He walks slowly. Talks slowly. A glacier could melt in the time it takes him to season, prepare, and eat a slice of meat and a baked potato. I can't stand it.

Fast scares me, but so does slow. Slow affords you time and space to think, unearths pain you plowed under years ago. I don't want time and space. I want tight deadlines and crowds and urgency. I discovered this in my first yoga class, which was also my last. A colleague had dragged me to a class at the company gym, and the mindfulness of it all—the nostril breathing, the Gumby poses, the stink of sweat and serenity—made me want to howl and bark and bust up the place.

John returns with a lager and a small box of pretzel sticks, the skinny kind mothers pack for their children's lunch. Carefully, he extracts one pretzel and takes a tiny bite.

Day 1

My apathy burns off like mist. Finally I feel something: irritation. I know from experience that John can make a box of pretzel sticks last an hour.

He takes a sip of his lager.

One minute passes. He bites, sips.

Another minute. He's still on his first stick.

Dreamily, he bites the nub.

"Eat the fucking pretzel already," I snarl, the hard poisonous bubble in my gut bursting like an infected eardrum. I reach for his hand, contrite, but John's eyes let me know that it's too late for apologies.

"Screw you," says my husband, and trudges upstairs with his pretzels and beer.

I deserved that. Good night, John-Boy.

DAY 2

6:20 a.m.

*The smell of pancakes, all vanilla and burnt butter and con-
tentment, drifts into the living room and penetrates its
chill—the furnace kicked on only a few minutes ago.
Frankie purrs beside me, eyes closed, paws tucked under.
Wrapped in my blanket, I sip black coffee, muttering snide
commentary on the morning's top stories. I've been flipping
channels for almost two hours. At 4:28 a.m. my eyes
snapped open like switchblades—nicotine withdrawal tends
to disturb sleep—and I am agitated. A wasp in a jar, trapped
by the day ahead. When John came downstairs, pink and
wet-headed from his shower, he took one look at my sneer-
ing, rumpled self and fired up his griddle. My husband
believes in the restorative power of sugar and fat. But I
chew the inside of my cheek, hungry only for smoke.*

Headline News *cuts to a commercial. A patrician-looking
man behind a podium addresses a packed auditorium of
employees. He tells them that he has an announcement that
will brighten their day: He has ordered them new printers*

48

and copiers from a certain company. "Tell them why, Andy,"
he says. A man in the audience rises, grinning like a chimp,
and burbles, "They're people-friendly!"

This ad runs every day on CNN. To John, it's about
printers and copiers. To me, it's about the subjugation of
the common man to Big Business. Why should Andy, who
probably hasn't received a raise or a word of praise from his
boss in years, have to fake enthusiasm about new copiers?
I'll bet the elitist bastard at the podium didn't even buy
American. As I'm swept along on a swift current of rage, I
know my reaction is way out of proportion, even factoring
in nicotine withdrawal and my antipathy for corporate
America. Then it hits me.

John enters the darkened living room with plates of pancakes and bacon. Taking mine, I say, "I think I need to start
my Wellbutrin again." Oh, shit. I haven't taken my anti-
crazy pills for several months, but John didn't know that.
I'd let my prescription lapse, telling myself I was too busy
to meet with my psychiatrist to renew it.

At least, that was my excuse. The truth is, I've stopped
and started my antidepressants dozens of times over the
years, repeating a painful and predictable cycle: bridle at my
dependency on the pill du jour (I've tried them all), convince
myself that I don't need them, slip back into depression,
crawl back to the pills for relief. Stupid, self-defeating
behavior. Why do I do it to myself? I should have called my
shrink weeks ago, when I conceived Lockdown. Not to take
my antidepressant while I was smoking was bad enough.
Not to take it while trying to quit is just stupid. Without
nicotine to stabilize it, my mood is spinning like a gyro-

scope, and I need the Wellbutrin to make it stop. Of course, I've realized this too late.

John scowls at me. "You stopped taking it? When?"

"It's November, so . . . July, I think. I told you before."

"You did not." He cannot stand me when I'm off my medication. "Well, that explains a lot."

It's true that I've become even more irritable than usual. The week before, I'd asked Daniel to undress and get into the tub. Twice. The third time, I'd roared at him, my eyes shooting twin laser death rays of rage. Regarding me in hurt surprise, my son squinched his eyes shut, turned his face to the ceiling, and howled. Nor has John escaped my wrath. Lately, I find myself watching him with clenched teeth: Must you have your soda in a glass with ice? Can't you drink it out of the fucking can like everyone else?

"Why do you do this?" John asks, flooding his pancakes with sugar-free syrup. "You know what happens to you."

"I felt fine. Also, I hate taking off work to drive across town to his office. The guy only makes me come in so he can fleece Blue Cross."

I know that my accusation is unfair. I like this guy more than my last psychiatrist, who tented his fingers as he regarded me with the flat, dead gaze of a lizard. I always imagined him rubber-gloved, expectant, at a dissection table.

John sighs and spears a forkful of pancakes. "When will you get back on it?"

"I'm calling him today. I'm hoping he'll call in a pre-scription." My mood bucks again. Fighting tears, I place my hand over his. "I'm sorry. I swear, I'll never go off again."

He lays down his fork and draws me to him.

"Isn't it ironic," I say, my cheek against his chest. "Of all the people you know, who gets the most stressed out? Who most needs to relax?"

"You," says John, who knows his line

"And here I am. Can't drink. Can't smoke."

I don't want him to chain me up and go away. I stay against his chest, my eyes closed. If I don't move, I will remain in this pocket of peace.

Gently, John pulls away and tips up my chin. "You okay?"

I nod.

"All right, come on. I've got to get to work."

Pulling myself together, I place my ankle on the coffee table. I remembered to wear socks. "How's your ankle?" John asks as he loops the chain around it.

"A little sore. Not too bad."

"Well, try to stay off your feet." He snaps on the lock. After rattling to the front door to see him off, I call my psychiatrist's office.

"He schedules his own appointments," says the receptionist, "but I'll take your name and number."

"Can you ask him to call in a prescription? For Wellbutrin—150 milligrams, twice a day. I know I haven't seen him in a while, but I'm not doing well. I think I should start it today."

"I'll give him the message," she says, unmoved.

When he calls three hours later, I describe my black mood, adding, "I quit smoking yesterday, too." I don't mention that I've chained myself in my house to do it.

"I'll call in the Wellbutrin, but I'd better see you in my office," he says. "December ninth."

"I'll be there." And I will. Quitting smoking could launch me into a major depression. My shrink knows it, too. That's why he's calling in the prescription without making me come in.

The metal around my ankle is a child's paper chain. How stupid to think it was a match for nicotine's invisible shackles. Nothing but a cigarette can fix what is broken.

Eric rented us an apartment in Queens, three subway stops from Shea Stadium. From the moment he double-parked in front of our building I knew that the city—all relentless sirens and sour Dumpster odor and militant ugliness that melted into sudden moments of beauty—was my Oz. Each morning on my way to the 7 train, I picked up a *New York Post* at the newsstand outside the Jackson Heights stop and savored the headlines. My favorite: HEADLESS BODY IN TOPLESS BAR. By day, I sold art supplies on Lexington Avenue while Eric photographed wannabe models and actors. By night, we smoked and drank. I'd long since graduated from Heinz-flavored gin. Vodka was my poison. It tasted like a slap.

Actually, I did most of my drinking with my colleague Celeste, a failed actress ten years older than I who trailed the scent of gin like a feather boa. Every night after work, we headed for the nearby Blarney Stone and sat there for hours, drinking and smoking, cursing when we lit the wrong end of a cigarette. There's nothing worse than the taste of scorched filter—Bhopal, right there in your throat.

Celeste was not pretty. Her teeth were pearl gray, from years of cigarettes and booze; her hair was thin. But when she smiled, her chin tipped down, her eyes bright like a puppy's, so flawed and so real—she had you. Her hand on your arm, her desire to please, the way she waved her Eve Menthol Lights like batons, her audience her music—I couldn't touch her. I slumped at the bar beside her and watched her bewitch diplomats and captains of industry, charm even women into buying her drinks.

A year passed. I experienced my first panic attack and filled my first Xanax prescription. The *Challenger* burned in the sky. Eric returned to Connecticut, where his old job awaited him. His dream of becoming the next Scavullo hadn't panned out. Neither had our relationship. That was my fault. I drank too much and wouldn't wear his ring or set a wedding date. I went off with other men, lured by their cocaine.

Eric left me on a Sunday afternoon in June. His eyes shone with tears. Mine shone with Xanax. He gathered me in his arms and sobbed into my neck, his shoulders heaving. I patted his back, *Shh, shh. It's all right. Everything will be all right.* And it was. Alcohol and cigarettes and Xanax shoved the pain of his departure into the deepest part of me.

Soon after Eric left, my godmother died and left me some money, enough to live on for a few years if I was careful. I gritted my teeth, quit my job, and enrolled at Hunter College.

On my last day at work, Celeste and I went for a drink.

"We'll never see each other," she said. She stared into her gin and tonic, stabbing her stirrer in and out of the cubes.

"Sure we will," I replied, but I was lying. A year ago, Celeste's drinking made me feel better about my own. Now it scared me. Her drinking had a relentless quality. As her charm settled to the bottom of her glass, trapped by melting ice and gnawed wedges of lime, her eyes glazed, like those of a pet put to sleep, and she developed an English accent, as if performing Evelyn Waugh. Her smile wobbled; her audiences drifted away. She bought her own gin and tonics now.

Occasionally, averting my eyes, I mentioned treatment centers and AA meetings—for her, of course, not for me. Celeste made excuses and continued to black out and wake in urine-soaked sheets. I gave up, smelling tragedy in her like dogs are said to smell cancer.

Celeste's tailspin into late-stage alcoholism didn't make me confront my own drinking, or even drink less. I just drank alone, after class. Somehow, I was graduated in 1988. I think. I didn't attend the ceremony, and Hunter didn't mail me my diploma. I didn't call to ask about it, either. I just let it slide.

Around that time, I lost my Connecticut driver's license. Literally lost it early one Sunday morning in a taxi, crossing over the Queensboro Bridge, on my way home after spending the night with a stranger. I remember my relief: *I'll never have to drive again.*

Like the chaos that defined my life, my smoking had assumed a consistent pattern, as familiar as a lover's imprint

DAY 2

in the mattress. Now there was an ashtray on the milk crate beside my bed and a lighter in every room. I smoked my first cigarette of the day still wrapped in my blankets. The second with my first cup of coffee, the sour blend of nicotine and milky caffeine spreading like a stain in my mouth. The third outside, on my way to the F train. The next as I emerged from the station and walked the few blocks to work. Ten to twelve more during the work day, finishing the pack—or tearing into a new one—at night.

I smoked faster than anyone I knew: short puffs, a little catch in my breath, like a sob. Then the hard discharge, as if blowing out the candles on a birthday cake. Two or three seconds between each inhalation. Constantly tapping, flicking, rolling the ash, often knocking it off so I'd have to light it again. I smoked when I was hungry, tired, bored, angry, lonely, after sex, in the bathtub, on the toilet. When I couldn't smoke, I bit my lips or chewed the insides of my cheeks.

Like all compulsions, my smoking was tinged with anxiety and nerves, but the act soothed me. Muted a need I couldn't meet on my own: to belong somewhere, be a part of something. My yearning for connection shamed me; it was weakness, a boot on my chest. Preferring loneliness to rejection, I kept the world at arm's length. From a distance, behind a cigarette, I appeared attractive, intelligent, in control. Up close, I looked like what I was: an unlovable defective stain.

Men didn't seem to think so, however, and like cigarettes, they calmed me. Fortunately, I'd discovered they

were as interchangeable as cigarette brands, merely varia-
tions of the same poison. I couldn't commit to any of them,
of course. I couldn't even commit to an apartment. After
Eric left, I moved every year. By 1989, I had left Queens and
settled in Brooklyn Heights, the affluent neighborhood just
across the East River at the lower tip of Manhattan, favored
by artists and hip young professionals.

My apartment was as small as my life. The door opened
into a kitchen the size of a large closet. In the bathroom, I
could barely raise my arm to lift my blow dryer. But my
bedroom was beautiful—light and airy, with a view of
Court Street and the grocery store across the way where
the cashiers ran up your bill if you didn't watch the register. My parents had given me a metal bed frame and head-
board, but I left them on the street the last time I moved
and bought a cheap futon bed. I spent a lot of time in it,
passed out or in the company of men I didn't know and
would never see again. Drunk or sober, I knew that love
and happiness were beyond my reach. But cigarettes would
always be there. Cigarettes, those small doors I closed
gratefully, again and again, against the sadness and tedium
of my days.

On a Sunday morning in July, I lie on my bed, staring at
the ceiling. My windows are open; the rich odor of softened roof tar fills the room. The white curtains, purchased
by my mother, billow in the breeze. The leaves of my ficus
tree tremble. Cars pass below my window, pouring throb-

bing hip-hop music into the street. Occasionally, a siren wails.

Summer always evokes anger and a peculiar longing in me. The hot bright weekends bring people into the streets, hungry for pleasure. Hispanic families descend on Prospect Park with their huge coolers, charcoal grills, boom boxes, and Frisbees, and party until dark. Yuppies read the *Times* under trees, glide by on inline skates, or wander through street fairs. I try to do these things, but they fall away from me, tumble down some endless dark chute inside. I cannot muster interest in anything, possess neither talents nor hobbies, and take care to hide my shameful dullness from musician boyfriends and colleagues who write their novels at night. My depression is exhausting, like a ragged cough, and cuts me off from the raw material of creative endeavor.

I've always been this way. I remember soft, damp summer nights, when I rode my bike or played tag with the neighbor kids to please my father. He hated when I moped around, as he called it. But I took no pleasure in flying down the street, my feet sure in the pedals, or in watching the red tassels on my handlebars stream straight back.

Now that I'm grown, I can spend the whole summer inside if I want to.

It is 11:00 a.m. I wander into the kitchen and pour another cup of coffee. Attempt the crossword puzzle in the *New York Times Magazine*. Listen to the digital alarm clock on my milk-crate nightstand flip each minute into the next. If I'm going to leave, it has to be now.

Last week, I'd promised myself I'd take the A train up to the northern tip of Manhattan to the Cloisters, the branch of the Metropolitan Museum of Art devoted to the art and architecture of medieval Europe. But now, torpor flows through my veins like Darvocet. I am twenty-four, living in one of the most vibrant cities in the world, and can't think of a single reason to leave my apartment on a sunny Sunday morning in July.

I wander back to my bed and light another cigarette. Its stream of smoke wafts to the ceiling like a soul freed from its carbon-based shell. By now, lighting up is like sitting down at the kitchen table for a short but intimate conversation with a trusted friend who will never reject or abandon me. Truly, cigarettes are my best friends; as long as I have them I'm not alone. I can spend whole weekends in my apartment, talking to no one, not picking up the phone if it rings, watching television or reading or painting my toenails or drinking until I pass out or doing anything, anything, but connecting with another human for any reason.

Today, however, I am restless. I can call one of the men in my life. But if I do, I must be prepared to sleep with him, and I'm not in the mood. I can take the F train into Manhattan to sit in some outdoor café and sip Bloody Marys, but I'm too hung over from last night. I think about Celeste. I'm used to going to bars by myself, but sometimes I miss her and the easy and unapologetic way we drank together. I wonder how she is and if she drinks alone too.

Calling her is out, though. Her life is fading like the tiny star that appeared in the center of an old TV when you switched it off, and I can't stand to watch. It's bad enough fielding her occasional 4:00 a.m. telephone calls, during which I bear witness to the unfolding catastrophe of her life. She'd started showing up drunk at work, lost her job at the art store and never found another. Her wealthy parents have written her off, but send a check each month. She rarely leaves her apartment, has her whole life delivered, her cigarettes and her gin and the cartons of Chinese food that rot uneaten in her refrigerator.

I could, however, have lunch with my landlords. I have a standing invitation.

Married fifty years, the De Ciccos have lived on the first floor of their brownstone for almost as long. Mrs. De Cicco is small and birdlike and speaks about five words of English; I've never seen her outside their apartment. Mr. De Cicco is the cock of Third Place. He is almost as small as his wife, but his effusiveness—and his abundant and unruly hair, the color and texture of steel wool—make him seem larger. He strolls the neighborhood in his wife-beater T-shirts and high-waisted polyester pants, gossiping with the neighbors and trailing a cloud of cologne, and like my mother, he worries about me.

Earlier that morning, returning from the corner bodega with the *Times*, I'd run into him at the gate. "Hey," he yelled cheerfully. "Come see my tomatoes."

Embarrassed to be caught with a cigarette—Mr. De Cicco was virulently house-proud, and I didn't want him to know I smoked in his apartment—I made a grand show of stubbing it out on the sidewalk. Then I let him lead me around the back of the brownstone.

"Look at this," he said, and waved grandly in the direction of his basil, peppers, and zucchini, which he'd coaxed from a patch of earth the size of a beach towel. What beauty. Leaning forward to smell the sun-warmed basil, I caught a whiff of the cigarette butt in my hand. My hangover had weakened my defenses, and its smell, close and dead, seemed to sum up my life. I blinked away tears.

"Come in for lunch and have some *pasta fazool,*" he said as we walked to the front of the house. "You know *pasta fazool*—pasta with beans? Very good, you'll like it. I make it every week, fresh."

I pictured him puttering at the stove, Grace slicing bread on the counter, their lives entwined like the vines in the tiny grape arbor beside their garden. My own life drought and dust. I liked this kind man who could make things grow, instead of making them die as I did. Of course I couldn't enter their Eden. I didn't belong there.

Arranging my face to convey regret, I said, "I wish I could, but I have plans." I lied all the time now—to my parents when they called, to men, to myself.

"Ahh," Mr. De Cicco said, touching his nose, giving me a wink. "A boyfriend, eh? Bring him too. Come anytime."

"Definitely," I said. "Next week for sure." My smile a coat of cheap paint, hiding a multitude of sins. I'd figure out how to get out of it later. But I felt bad that I would never sit on the plastic-covered plaid couch in his living room, which I saw when I brought him the rent. That I'd never asked about the photos of his children, long grown, on top of his television.

"Okay, *bella,* you have fun now," he said, and watched from the front walk as I pulled on the heavy front door and trudged up the wide staircase to my apartment.

I won't have to venture out again today, not even for cigarettes. Making my drunken way home from the city this morning, I'd wavered into a deli and bought two packs of Newport Lights, one for the day ahead and one just in case. Somehow, in the one tiny part of my brain unaddled by alcohol, I'd known I wouldn't make it to the Cloisters.

I always made it to work, though: I was an editor at *Play-girl.*

Housed in a Second Avenue high-rise, *Playgirl* was one of several porn magazines—including *High Society* and *Cheri,* for men—owned by a wealthy businessman. The men's magazines shared office space with *Playgirl.* Each morning, I rode the elevator to the thirty-second floor, passed through the mauve reception area, and opened the door to depravity.

My *Playgirl* colleagues were sweet young teetotalers with husbands and boyfriends. Of course, I befriended the editors of the men's magazines, who shared my fondness for alcohol. Somehow, when we drank together, one after-work cocktail took eight or more hours to finish. The next morning we crawled to our desks, pale and sick, to pore through manila folders bulging with transparencies of strippers—in my case, from Chippendales.

Most of my porn posse smoked, which made sense. Smoking and sex go together—the greedy rhythmic suck, the gush of creamy vapor over rouged lips. Now, Internet fetish sites show fully clothed women chain-smoking— "chaining," in the argot of devotees—French inhaling, or demonstrating "deep cone exhales," which look like tiny cyclones spinning out from between their thickly glossed lips. The popularity of these sites doesn't surprise me at all. In this culture of health hysteria, smoking is almost as depraved as porn—filthy, immoral, deviant.

If my colleagues and I deserved that characterization, it wasn't because we smoked. My friends plastered their offices with posters of nude women with the hard, slick, silicone-looking skin of dolls, images that commanded no more of my attention than their desk staplers. These same women— some of the sweetest girls you'd ever want to meet, all tanned skin and plunging cleavage—occasionally visited our floor, for reasons that I never understood. Each month, I sifted through snapshots of naked men, culling the best for publication in *Playgirl*'s back pages. (Alas, men one wouldn't want to see nude are those most eager to doff their clothing.) We hooted over our letters—pornographers get inordinate amounts of mail from people who believe that the CIA drugged them and implanted transistors in their molars. Once, a new editor at *High Society*—from the Midwest, I believe, and heartbreakingly innocent—was ambushed at his desk by his sobbing mother and tight-lipped father, who somehow had heard that their son worked in a den of iniquity. Hushed, embarrassed for the poor kid, we watched as they dragged him off, never to be seen again.

One morning soon after the fall of the Berlin Wall, I walked down the long carpeted hall to the art department. The publisher wanted *Playgirl* to run a special issue: Men of the Eastern Bloc. Normally, Freddie left it to me and my art director, Donna, to select the centerfold. But Men of the Eastern Bloc! Freddie smelled the sweet scent of publicity. He'd called me to his office the day before to review the aesthetic principles that should govern our choice.

The pickings were slim. While I don't remember specific flaws—an underbite, a lazy eye—their general unsightliness remains fixed in my memory. But Freddie didn't care about their faces. As I recall, he leaned back in his plush office chair, his shrewd eyes caged behind aviator frames, gnawing on an unlit cigar the size of a turkey leg. His exact words are lost to me, but the gist was: Let the largest popo win.

Studying the manila folders in my lap, I chose my words carefully. "The thing is, sir, all of these guys are unattractive. I mean, *really* unattractive." I didn't add that they weren't from the Eastern Bloc. This was a detail, and Freddie was a man of vision.

Pick one, he said. And if his . . . member isn't big enough, airbrush it.

I'd told Donna about my meeting with Freddie a few days before. This morning, I had to break the news. At her desk, I silently placed several transparencies of my first choice on her light box and switched it on. Picking up her loupe, Donna examined them. After thirty seconds, she looked up at me.

"Did you see his *teeth*?"

"Oh, yeah. And it gets better. We have to retouch his wiener. Freddie wants it big. Halfway-down-his-leg big."

"At least it will draw attention away from his face." Then, this unpleasantness dispensed with, she looked at me and cocked an eyebrow.

"Let's go," I said.

This was the late 1980s, and a growing number of companies in the city were giving smokers their walking papers. Our banishment created a kind of perverse camaraderie. Fellow exiles from the nonsmoking world, we stood in a haze of brume, sharing the pleasure and pain of our compulsion as well as rain, snow, and unpleasant extremes of temperature.

Donna was my smoking buddy. Every hour, when the nudging need forced us to the elevator, we descended the thirty-two floors to the lobby and shuffled through the heavy revolving doors, clutching our cigarettes and lighters. We'd become almost like friends on our cigarette runs. Not clubbing-on-Saturday-night friends, although I would have liked that. She smoked like me—short hard puffs.

And once a week, I visited my therapist, Hannah. My weekly trip to her office on the Upper West Side, around the corner from the Dakota, where John Lennon lived and was shot, gave my chaotic life some small but comforting measure of predictability. She, too, had banned cigarettes from her office. I nicotine-loaded before and after our sessions.

Hannah was tiny, with luminous skin, wavy brown hair that reached halfway down her back, and a quick, brilliant smile. I was compelled to tell her things.

"I called Nick last night," I said at the start of one session. I still hadn't met my biological father, but I'd talked to him. In fact, I'd called him every six months for the past several years—late at night, after hours of swigging Smirnoff's. My mother had given me his number. She couldn't explain why she had it or how she knew that Nick lived alone in a large midwestern city. He worked in a factory—doing what, she didn't know. I imagined him in a grim industrial setting, standing at a conveyor belt with black-hooded eyes, performing some repetitive, soul-numbing task.

"So what happened?" Hannah asked.

"The usual." Though sporadic, the conversations between Nick and me were as predictable as the pornography I wrote. They could last an hour or, like this one, minutes.

I sit on my bed, the only light from the neon-green buttons on the receiver. I punch in his number. *Ring-ring.*

"Hello."

"Nick," I say. "How's every little thing?"

"Who is this? It's almost midnight." His nasal midwestern twang a mosquito's whine in the dark.

"It's me, the amazing invisible daughter. How long has it been?" My attempt to shame him fails, as usual.

"Julie, this business has gotta stop. You been drinkin'? Am I gonna have to call your mother again?"

I ignore him. "If Muhammad won't come to the mountain, the mountain must come to Muhammad. Wait, wait, I screwed that up. But it doesn't matter. I'm your mountain, Nick. Hold on."

I shove the Newport in my mouth and light it with shaky fingers. A moment of peace. Then the kaleidoscope pattern in my head shifts into a sodden sadness. Why do I bother to call him? There is nothing to say. He hasn't forgotten about me. I have never existed to him at all. I am a lone shoe in the road: How did *that* get here?

I drop the phone on the bed and hunch over, holding my stomach as if I'd been shot. I hear his voice, tinny and faint as if he were in Africa: "Hello? Hello?"

I rock in the dark, my eyes closed. My blood father has erased me from his life as cleanly as chalk from a blackboard.

When I was in the sixth grade, I'd looked up "tundra" in the dictionary. Its definition—a vast treeless plain in the arctic regions—intrigued me less than its etymology. In the language of the Inuit, it means "nothing."

The word took root in my brain. Eventually, when I pictured myself, I didn't see a petite, slender young woman with wavy black hair and dark eyes. I saw a stretch of cold, white, barren land. I wasn't in this image. I *was* this image.

I rock. See white sky darken, feel cold need whistle right through me.

After a while, I pick up the receiver and hold it to my ear. He must have heard me breathing.

"You there? Talk to me if you're there."

"Mail me a picture of you," I whisper. What a whiner I am, begging for scraps.

"Why?" he asks.

That's when I hang up.

I was crying by the time I finished the story. I hated tears;

they advertised that you'd been caught wanting something. In every session, I played a game with myself: If I didn't reach for the box of Kleenex on the table beside my chair, my crying didn't count.

I kept my head low, but a tear fell on my wrist. I covered it with my other hand.

"Good girl," Hannah said, softly.

No, I wasn't. I'd cried. I hated her for her softness, myself for mine, and did not want to see the kindness in her eyes. Without looking up, I rose and walked out of her office, fumbling in the pocket of my leather jacket for my cigarettes.

8:43 a.m.

I took a short nap and now I feel better. Not great, I'm slightly on edge—okay, a lot, I want a cigarette, I can admit it—but I'm strong. I'm going to make it this time. I feel it.

I can't help but note, however, that more than twenty-four hours have elapsed since my last cigarette. If I lit up now, I'd experience that pleasant, about-to-black-out wooziness that results from a long gap between cigarettes. I miss that feeling, but that's okay. Today marks the start of a new and improved me. I'm going to lose ten pounds. Start running again. Save a ton of cash. Let's just rattle on over to our desk for our calculator and figure out exactly how much. Four bucks a pack times $28 a week equals $1,560 a year.

I have an idea. Dropping the calculator, I extract a ten-

dollar bill from my wallet and clank to the kitchen. The racket startles Frankie, who streaks in front of me. I trip over him—out of the way, shit for brains! In the pantry, I remove my can of Folgers and a box of plastic freezer bags. Dumping the coffee into the bag, I drop the ten into the empty can. Voilà—my new face-lift fund. This is great. Everything is great.

Except that my spices are poorly organized. I don't use a spice rack, preferring to jumble all the bottles on one crowded shelf. I see now that this is wrong, so wrong. Tiny plastic containers of ginger and cloves should not mingle with huge, bargain-store shakers of garlic powder and oregano. No one needs more than one box of cornstarch in her lifetime, and here I have two. Another may lurk behind the tiny army of McCormick and Spice Island bottles.

I will organize my spices. A project, that's what I need. Get things a little more organized around here. Inspired, I transfer what seems like one hundred bottles of spices from the pantry to the countertop.

Which was a bad idea. I realized this immediately. I own too many spices, way too many, and God knows how old some of them are. It's quite possible that I imported a few from Brooklyn. How do I know which to discard? Do spices have expiration dates? How should I organize them, anyway—by size? Small containers in front, large ones in back? By frequency of use? Should I segregate the baking spices—cinnamon, nutmeg, lemon rind—from the rest? Oh, God. I count three bottles of vanilla extract, one unopened, two tins of cinnamon, two bottles of cumin. Cumin? I can't recall ever using cumin. What a fucking mess.

Opening one tin of cinnamon, I transfer its contents into the other. Cinnamon spills all over the countertop. Shit. My bowels begin to churn. I want a cigarette, but I am a non-smoker now. I am strong. I am invincible. I am woman.

I am going mad.

I rattle back into the living room. I imagine flinging open the front door and running into the street screaming, my chain rattling like the sabers of the Mongolian hordes. I need a cigarette badly, but I have quit. Fuck this. Not smoking sucks ass. Not smoking is bullshit. Not smoking is the worst thing that has ever happened to me. Why must I quit? Everyone else gets to smoke, and they're fine. Why do you torture me, God, with thoughts of menthol? I should just call John and tell him to pick me up a pack of cigarettes on his way home. Then I'll grovel like the weak, pathetic loser I am.

I can't. Think of Daniel. Imagine him holding your hand as you lie in a hospital bed, begging you not to die. I can't do that to him. I have to make it, have to hold on.

At twenty-five, I still saw myself as the outsider in my family. My bond with my mother, though volatile, was at least defined: I loved and loathed her in equal measure. My relationship with my father, however, remained as stratified as Neapolitan ice cream: vanilla sadness, chocolate resentment, strawberry love. This story shows just how skewed was my perception of my place in his heart.

Early in 1989, my father called me in Brooklyn and said, "I want to adopt you." If he offered an explanation, I don't remember it. What I recall is humiliation; on the other end of the phone, I burned to my toes. *Mom put him up to this,* I thought. *She made him call.* This was a pity adoption.

I couldn't refuse his name, however, even to save my pride. I loved him. I didn't understand him, couldn't talk to him, but I loved him. When I was four, he'd hidden Chiclets in his navel for me, saying he made them from belly button lint. A year later, he made my mother take me to an ear doctor because I didn't answer him when he spoke to me. (The doctor found significant damage.) He stood by me during my brief foray into insanity. Unlike Nick, he'd *stayed.*

For that reason, I boarded a train to Connecticut ten days before my twenty-sixth birthday and, after a half hour in probate court, was reborn as Julia Hansen. The elderly judge assigned to our case thought it charming: adopted at twenty-five. He insisted that we commemorate the event with a picture. Great. Just what I needed, a memento of my humiliation. Not wishing to hurt my father's feelings, however, I sat on the judge's lap while my father stood by his side. "Smile," my mother sang, and we grinned like chimps for interminable seconds until she snapped the photo. Silently, I begged my new father's pardon.

More than a dozen years later, I summoned up the nerve to ask my mother about this day. Had she suggested the adoption?

No, she said. It was his idea. They had been preparing their wills, and he didn't want Nick's consonant-heavy Eastern European surname to prevent me from collecting my inheritance.

My father hadn't tried merely to be a father to me. As far

as he was concerned, he *was* my father. I was his daughter, and always had been. How sad that it took me so long to feel his love, or anyone's.

—

You didn't drink margaritas at the Blarney Stone on Third Avenue between Forty-fourth and Forty-fifth streets. It was beer, whiskey, or nothing. That night it was beer.

After a hard day in the porn mills, it was my night out with the posse. We went to the Blarney, one large, dim room with a jukebox stocked with Mel Tormé and Tony Bennett for the old-timers nursing their shots of whiskey. We'd planned to leave after one quick drink. But there we were at 11:30 on a Wednesday night, huddled around a rickety little table sticky with spilled beer, next to the bathroom with its rank, perpetually overflowing toilet.

It was my turn to buy. Pushing back my chair, I crossed the empty room to the bar to refill our pitcher and get change for the cigarette machine. I'd bought a pack of smokes that morning, had two left, and would smoke another half pack before I got home. Tomorrow morning my lungs would feel crumbly, like charred wood in a fire ring. Leaving the beer on the bar, I fed quarters into the cigarette machine by the door. When I returned, the pitcher was gone.

"Damn, couldn't you wait one minute?" I said, holding out my glass.

"Nope," said David, pouring all around. David, my best friend: a melancholy saxophone solo of a man, tall as a telephone pole, skin the color of oatmeal. An unlikely pornographer, David was no good with women, and his body was as smooth and downy as a seven-year-old boy's. I'd seen it the one time we had sex. I'd apologized the next morning—wormed my way out of being his girlfriend—while he, gloomy in plaid boxers, sat on the edge of my bed. His body hummed with discontent and lack of love, his shyness a bruise you wonder about but don't mention.

We left around 12:30, unwilling to go home to our loved ones or—in my case—to Frankie the cat, adopted after Eric left. We lurched up Third, crossed over to Park at Fifty-third, and headed for some bar, I don't remember which. With no late-night shops or bars to draw traffic, Park Avenue—primarily residential, filled with luxury apartment buildings—was deserted. The cold moon washed our faces and the trees in a pewter glow. It was early January, and the city had recently taken down the celebrated Christmas trees that, during the holiday season, stretch for two miles up and down Park in a glittering necklace of lights. Staggering up Park, we found their grave: the narrow strip of earth that divides the wide avenue. They were stacked eight or nine feet high, dead and silent, but the smell of pine was still strong. I stopped, mesmerized, and the guys sighed, knowing what was coming.

"Let's climb," I said—although inebriated, I retained my characteristic dubious judgment. I thought we could find a gap in the branches wide enough to crawl into, and make ourselves a little pine-scented womb.

The guys groaned and kept walking, except for David. He stood by silently, his fists jammed in the pockets of his thrift-store overcoat.

"Come on, help me." I grabbed some branches and pushed them apart, trying to create the womb I'd imagined, but they were too dense. David waited, shifting in his high-top sneakers. "Damn it," I muttered. Dropping my purse, I began to climb, hampered by my bulky coat.

Reaching the top, I settled on my back and stared at the moon, set in the sky like an opal on black velvet. My breath unfurled like glass wool, as if I were smoking, and I could have reached for the cigarettes in my coat pocket but didn't. My need had quit rattling its tin cup across the bars inside me, and I settled into something that felt like peace. I lay limp on my pine-scented bed, the moon like nicotine in my veins. My sadness parted for a second and I thought, *This is me. This is me.* I felt my smallness, understood that I could be crushed as easily as a butt under a boot and it was all right. I could bathe here in sky, forget myself a while. I didn't need to fight here, or to hide behind a scrim of smoke.

"All right, come on now," David said below me.

"Shit," I said, the spell broken. Shinnying down the stack of trees, the sweet-smelling branches rough against my cheeks, I hopped to the pavement and lit a cigarette. David turned toward our friends, already several blocks ahead, and regarded them glumly. For him, the martini ship had sailed.

"You should have come up," I said. "I could have stayed there all night. Forever."

"Yeah," he muttered and brushed my coat, now streaked with bark and pine tar. Sighing, he took my hand and led me back toward Third Avenue, where the cabs still trolled for drunks.

David raised his hand, and a gypsy cab swerved to a stop in front of us. He opened the door. "Don't tell him you're going to Brooklyn until you start moving," he said. (New York cabbies are infamous for turning down fares to Manhattan's sister boroughs, even though they risk being fined if caught.) I think he kissed my cheek. I don't remember getting home.

11:57 a.m.

If I can't smoke, I want an electrode permanently implanted in my nucleus accumbens, one of several brain regions known collectively as the reward pathway. This area does the Snoopy dance when jolted by so-called natural rewards like food, water, and sex. Artificial rewards turn it on, too— money, the face of a beautiful woman, addictive drugs like heroin, cocaine, and nicotine.

Forget nicotine patches and gum. Smokers need intracranial self-stimulation—do-it-yourself shock treatment. Why not? Rats love it. Psychologists James Olds and Peter Milner learned that in the 1950s, when they delivered a mild electric shock to a certain part of a rat's brain and the rodent came back for more. Intrigued, the researchers rigged up a system that allowed rats to buzz their own gray matter. Depending on where they implanted the electrodes, the rodents shocked themselves up to 5,000 times an hour, sometimes forgoing food, water, sleep, and mating.

Smoking is like those rodent shock treatments. All

addictive drugs—including nicotine—are thought to rev up the release of dopamine, a brain chemical central to the experience of pleasure. "That feels good," this rush of dopamine tells the brain. "Do it again." Essentially, nicotine creates a lasting impression of its pleasure, which ensures that smokers light up again and again. Just like Olds's rats pressed the lever.

Crave a cigarette, buzz your nucleus accumbens. I'd sign up for that. Of course, I'd buzz until I dropped to the ground, twitching. Anyone who grinds up Vivarin tablets and tries to snort the granules like cocaine, as I once did, has a reward pathway in need of serious stimulation.

That Vivarin burned my nasal passages horribly; I might as well have snorted Drano. I suppose I experienced pleasure when the pain stopped. The writer William S. Burroughs wrote, "Perhaps all pleasure is only relief." Burroughs would know. He was a heroin addict. And a smoker.

I left *Playgirl* in February 1990, after landing a job as managing editor for a *TV Guide*–type magazine. It wasn't the *Times,* but the job was a step up and came with a huge raise, and I felt as if I'd arrived. But four months after I'd started, the executive editor called me into his office. It wasn't my fault, he said. There simply was not enough for me to do. But to me, being fired was a confirmation of my unsuitability, of my loser nature.

After he let me go, I walked through the office in a daze, saying good-bye to my colleagues. They were gentle with me—over the months, they'd seen me sinking and tried to help, the way people extend a stick to a man in a swollen river, only to see him swept away. I took the elevator to the ground floor. The sidewalk shimmered in an angry haze. I walked to the Grand Hyatt, sat at the bar and drank three Bloody Marys, and then rode the F train back to Brooklyn. I got home at 11:00 a.m., and the summer yawned before me, a vacant lot of days.

That summer, I occasionally met my brother for lunch at a Greek diner near my old office at *Playgirl*. Now twenty-two, Kurt had graduated from the School of Visual Arts and lived in Williamsburg, an isolated and vaguely menacing part of Brooklyn. Although we were still not close, my earlier jealousy had softened. I enjoyed his company; we got each other's jokes; he was of my blood, my tribe, in this city of strangers. I helped get him his first job, as an art director at *High Society*. He still worked there, and was as he'd always been—hysterically funny, slippery as black ice.

We didn't see each other much. He had his own friends, his own life. If my hobby was drinking, his was painting. His art was as fantastical as my father's, but more attuned to technique. I'd visited him once at his studio and watched him paint. With a brush so fine that it looked like it held a single hair, he rendered one veined leaf for what seemed like hours. He seemed to live inside that leaf.

Once in a while, Kurt joined me and the porn-mill gang for cocktails, but he was a light drinker—one beer, maybe two, only occasionally staying long enough to watch me light the wrong end of a cigarette, pick a fight with a large man, or curse our friends and stagger off alone into the night. We'd laugh about my behavior the next time we met, but I was always vaguely ashamed. All my emotions were vague then, fogged by alcohol and smoke. I longed to escape the prison of me and live in my brother's body, to see the world through his eyes.

"So how are Mom and Dad?" I asked, dipping a French fry in ketchup. Ashamed of my life, fearing that I might let slip my distress and they'd ride in like cavalry to save me, I rarely called or visited my parents. Kurt, the Good Son, gave me periodic updates.

"They're fine," he said. "Can I bum a cigarette?" Like me, he started smoking in college, burned through a pack a day.

I pushed my pack across the table. "Sure, but they're menthols." I knew his brand—Camel Lights, like my mother.

"Shit—oh, all right. I'm going to quit anyway."

"Me too." I reached for the pack. "You going home for Labor Day?"

"I don't know yet." He scraped his ash against the side of the ashtray. "I might just hang here, chill with my friends, have a little barbecue on the roof." I waited for him to invite me, but he didn't, and I didn't ask. Couldn't ask.

"Well, if you're not going, neither am I," I said, faking relief. I had a choice: Go to Connecticut or spend Labor Day weekend alone. I didn't know which was worse.

Sitting across from my brother, I wanted desperately to ask him about our family. What did he remember of our childhood? When our parents fought, had he been as scared as I? What had it felt like to zip away on his minibike, leaving that strife behind? How had he managed to slide out of fights with our mother, when I just had to take her on? Did he ever feel as lost and empty inside as I did?

But I remained silent, picturing my words skittering across the table like pebbles. My brother smoked his cigarette, so normal, a bright young man with many friends, his freckled redhead's skin rosy. I'd never seen him drunk, never seen him cry.

I wondered what had built this wall of reserve between us. I knew that he didn't sense it—he was always affable, seemingly untroubled by anything in our relationship. Maybe he was put off by my self-destructive behavior. What normal, well-adjusted person wouldn't be? Perhaps he simply perceived me as someone with whom he had nothing in common.

Regardless, at that confused and painful period of my life, his indifference put me in mind of my father's. It never occurred to me that what separated him from me—what separated me from everyone—was me.

2:37 p.m.

I am daydreaming about Diet Pepsi and a cigarette. Caffeine and nicotine, the ultimate adrenaline cocktail, two great tastes that taste great together. The Diet Pepsi in a can, because I never finish those twenty-ounce bottles. The cig-

arettes, Basic Menthol Lights. *Menthol menthol menthol; minty peppermint-patty goodness. A mentholated cigarette is almost like dessert. Someone I knew in New York said she sometimes paired her Newports with YooHoo. The cooling smoke would dry the back of my throat, and then the crisp combination would tumble over it like a mountain stream. I feel like a volunteer in a sleep deprivation experiment who fantasizes about the softness of sheets, how cool a pillowcase would feel against his cheek.*

With misgivings, I call my mother's cell phone. Confiding in her is a double-edged sword. If she's having a good day, she will be able to comfort me. If not, she will ask about Daniel, then launch into her own problems—her weight issues, her boring job, my impossible father.

"Hey, it's me," I say when she answers.

"How you doin'?," she says, faking a Brooklyn accent. Just four words, but I hear that edge in her voice. Those kittens in the sack are clawing and yowling.

"Not great. I'm tired—I can't believe how tired I am. Depressed, too, I guess. I haven't gotten dressed in two days."

"How's my little boy?"

Here it comes. My heart touches bottom, like a sinker sending its hook to the floor of a river, her question the bait.

"Mom, he's fine. You know he's at Matt's for the week."

"All week? In that filthy apartment that smells like cat shit? Oh, Julie, go get him."

"Mom, I'm trying to do something important here. I sent him to Matt's so I'm not a screaming maniac around him. I'm doing this for him. Besides, he loves it there."

"*Of course he does. All those toys, everywhere. All those figures.*" *A talented artist, Matt sculpts movie- and comic-book characters for companies that turn them into model kits. His tiny apartment is filled with them.*

"*Oh, Julie, you have to go get him. You don't really need to be chained up for a whole week, do you? I mean, this whole thing is a little ridiculous, isn't it? Just don't smoke. That's all there is to it.*"

"*Mom, don't you think I've tried that?*"

"*Don't yell at me.*" *Her voice a sheet you could bounce a quarter on.* "*Why are you getting so upset?*"

"*Because this is fucking hard, and you're not making it any easier! Why can't you encourage me, tell me I'm doing the right thing? Why can't you just say I'll be all right?*"

"*A child should be with his mother—*"

I hang up on her.

I know she loves me. I know that when she thinks about her life, all she sees is regret after regret—the years of fighting with my father, which she believes scarred her children, the novel she'd deleted from her hard drive—strung out across the years like telephone poles on an endless shimmering road.

"*You and your brother are my greatest creations,*" *she once told me during one of my weekend visits. She'd spoken in a moment of détente, just me and her after midnight, me on one couch, her on the other, sipping tea in her tasteful living room. I believed her, but her voice held the faintest chill. By then I had decades of therapy under my belt and a child of my own, so I recognized the ambivalence that characterizes motherhood, that blend of love and resentment, as rich and bitter as coffee.*

Yet we could do one thing companionably: smoke. As drinkers do, smokers forge a bond; when we happen upon someone who shares our habit, we believe that we know this person in some deep way. So it was with us. On my infrequent visits, she'd pull her Camel Lights from her cavernous handbag and say, "Let's have a ciggie!" in the same tone one might say, "Let's do a road trip!" For a few minutes, the air would soften between us.

We loved each other, no question of that. We just didn't understand each other. Our mutual lack of empathy triggered pitched battles about everything: my lack of domestic skills and her lack of boundaries, my harshness and her emotionality, my readiness to attack and her readiness to meddle, all of which belied the real problem: We could not let go of each other. We were like Chang and Eng, the cranky Siamese twins who toured with P.T. Barnum's circus. The intensity of their bond led them into bitter, intractable struggle. Ultimately, I believed that my mother did not trust my ability to survive—a reasonable fear, given my history— but it enraged me. Harboring the same fear, I couldn't bear to hear it in her voice, see it in her eyes.

Did she think that without Daniel to ground me I'd sail off into nothingness like a kite snaps its flying line? If I were to disappear, where did that leave her? Or maybe I just reminded her of her mother, who caused her so much pain. As my mother and I hurt each other—often by accident, but at times intentionally.

There was a time when I thought, if love hurts this much, I don't want it. And then a softness, when I learned, finally, to bear it.

*It would be so good to smoke right now. I'd close my
eyes, inhale deep, exhale long. My deep cleansing breath.*

It was a week before Thanksgiving 1990, and I was on my
way home to Connecticut for turkey and conflicted love. I
was thankful for Newport Lights.

I exited the Amtrak station in Hartford and found our
Pacer in the parking lot, my father in the driver's seat. My
mother wasn't with him. My stomach tightened: forty minutes in the car with him, alone. Our relationship hadn't
changed much since he'd adopted me; we still circled each
other cautiously, like dogs that meet in the park. Part of our
continued distance stemmed from my sense of shame about
who I was and my understandable desire to keep my alco-
hol-fueled exploits under wraps. I was secretive; he must
have sensed that and respectfully kept his distance. I hungered for his love and approval as much as I had when I was
four, but when I tried to talk to him, my thoughts scattered
like mercury from a broken thermometer.

"Hey, Dad." I threw my bag into the back, slammed the
door, and stood by the passenger's side for a second to finish my cigarette. The drivers behind us leaned on their horns.

"Come on, come on," my dad said, his watery blue eyes
tight.

"This is my first one since New York," I replied, puffing
furiously.

The driver behind the Pacer tapped his horn. I stepped
on the butt, slid into the passenger's seat, and slammed the

door. The Pacer was warm and the radio tuned to NPR, my father's favorite station. The host was discussing the collapse of the Soviet Union. Unlike me, my father cared. As always, I envied his curiosity about the world, a quality that I'd long since abandoned. How did he do it? How did he continue to give a shit?

My father shifted in his seat. "How's it going?" he asked. I checked my watch: thirty-five minutes to go.

"Oh, you know," I replied. Then I stopped. A part of me had just collapsed, like a beam in a burning building.

The night before, I'd gotten drunk and attacked my boyfriend, Andy, because he didn't want to live with me. I'd met him in June, when I was still living on unemployment. A former colleague from the TV magazine, who lived a few streets from me in Brooklyn, had set us up. Andy pretended to write novels and cashed his wealthy father's checks. His most serious flaw, however, was that he made me go outside to smoke.

Our battle was one of those morning-after fights, the kind where your eyes snap open and the universe allots you a second of grace before the memory of what you've done wells up like a cut. Unfortunately, I remembered everything.

"We've only been together four months," he'd said. "I'm not saying no, but it's too soon. Let's wait and see how things go."

My heart ignited with rage, hurt beneath like tinder. I was determined to hide both.

"You're right," I said, amazing even myself with how easily I lied—it was a talent, a gift. "I put you in an awkward position, and I'm sorry."

The relief in his eyes only increased my fury. "So we're okay?"

"Uh-huh," I said, picking up my coat.

"Where are you going?"

"Just to smoke. Be right back." I clattered down the stairs and lit up by the side of his building, watching gift-laden shoppers fight their way down Spring Street.

Fuck you, I thought. *Fuck your commitment issues and for not letting me smoke inside where it's warm.*

When I went upstairs again, he was waiting for me. "Mike just called. He wants us to meet him and Cathy for dinner," he said. "Want to come?"

Why would I want to go? I'd never met them. We should be talking about our relationship—how to make it work, *where we were going.* Obviously, Mike and Cathy were more important to him than I. But I smiled, smiled, smiled.

"I'll meet you there. I want to do some Christmas shopping first."

The restaurant was just a few blocks from his apartment. After he left, I waited five minutes, then headed to the liquor store around the corner, bought a pint of vodka, and let myself back in, using the key he'd given me. I finished a third of the bottle, then lit a cigarette—fuck it. I smoked a second, third, and fourth, staring at the smoke haze in front of the television.

It was past eight by the time I got to the restaurant. I saw them immediately, talking and laughing, their plates pushed away, nursing glasses of wine. I walked unsteadily to their table. Their laughter stopped. I don't remember what I said, but suddenly Andy was walking me toward the exit, his fist wrapped around my elbow. He propelled me to the corner and into a cab.

When we reached his apartment, Andy pulled me from the taxi and pushed me up the stairs—the nice Jewish boy in him wouldn't allow him to leave me on the street. The next morning, as he slept, I crept out of his apartment and returned to Brooklyn. Another relationship, *finito*. I invented another game: If I didn't move, it wouldn't hurt.

I lay on my bed and chain-smoked until my cigarettes were gone, moving only my left arm to flick the lighter in front of my face or to bring the cigarette to my lips. In the early afternoon, I got up and showered, trembling under the warm spray. Then I packed a bag with enough clothing to last a week and boarded the train for Hartford.

My father's voice interrupted my thoughts. "You okay? You're so quiet."

"Just tired," I said. The NPR announcer droned on. I watched my father's hands on the wheel. I hadn't yet admitted to myself that I'd come home to get sober. It was November 19, 1990.

I spent my first week of sobriety in Connecticut. Those seven days, an intermission between my past and future, passed as quietly as clouds. During the day, after my parents went to work, I read or nosed around their bedroom. Frightened by the train wreck my life had become, equally petrified at the prospect of life without alcohol, I needed their comfort, to feel them near me. I fingered the coins on my father's nightstand that had come from his pocket. Studied my mother's closet, smiled at her shoes tucked sweetly, in pairs, inside their canvas holder. Smelled their pillows, inhaling their presence. At night I slid into thick dreamless sleep, wrapped in the 600-thread-count scented sheets on which my mother insisted.

I didn't tell my parents I'd stopped drinking—I wasn't sure I could do it. I'd called AA a few days before I left Connecticut and went to my first meeting, on Thirty-seventh Street between Lexington and Park, directly from the train. I sat in the back and left immediately afterward. I wasn't ready to talk.

I was, however, seized with a mad compulsion to create. A few days after I got home, I hungered for beads, tiny bottles of gold leaf, thick sheets of watercolor paper, oil pastels. I purchased enough supplies to stock a summer camp and began to make odd little crafts—mobiles, altars, paintings on three-inch-square canvases. My life revolved around AA meetings and art projects. Every morning, I rode the subway into Manhattan for a meeting, purchased the supplies I needed that day, returned to Brooklyn to craft, rode back to Manhattan for dinner and another meeting, then went home to work into the night. It's fair to say that AA and Pearl Paint on Canal Street saved my life.

That Christmas, I gifted these sad, strange items to my family. My brother and father received mobiles. His chestnut eyes kind yet puzzled, my brother praised his and pecked me on the cheek. My father lifted his out of its box. It was snarled, like our love. He untangled it. Examined it.

My heart stopped: He hated it. I thought of "Red River Valley" and judo class, and wanted to die.

My father turned to me. His eyes held neither ridicule nor pity but caution, borne of his desire to do and say the right thing.

He said, It's beautiful. Really nice. My heart reset itself. He leaned toward me, supporting his weight on one arm, and pulled me to his chest with the other, wedging my head under his chin. In that awkward embrace, I felt as proud as a five-year-old who'd just handed her dad a Popsicle-stick pencil holder.

My mother's gift was a picture frame to which I'd glued beads in every color of the rainbow. It looked like an item a mental patient might make in occupational therapy and in a way, it was. The beads began to drop off almost immediately, but she displayed the frame for years, until the last stubborn bauble released its hold.

5:47 p.m.

I have to pee, but I don't want to get up because I can't stand the scrape of the chain against wood and linoleum. I'd hoped to hold out until John got home, but can no longer ignore the increasingly desperate signals from my bladder. From the couch, I gird myself for the arduous journey across the living room, dining room, and kitchen to the bathroom, thirty feet away.

Picking up my cell phone—if it rings, I can't run back

into the computer room to retrieve it—I rise. The chain awakens, stirs. Click-click-click across the rug. Rasp and scrape across bare wood. Click-click-click as I reach carpet again. And then its hideous clatter on the kitchen linoleum.

I wonder what my mother would say if she could see me now—her daughter, sitting on the toilet in a purple bathrobe, a willing prisoner in her own, ill-furnished home. I'm sure that she'd suggest a new pair of curtains for the bathroom. Neither of us has called the other back, and I'm anxious, as I always am when we fight. We might make up tonight, tomorrow, in a week, there's no telling.

I flush and stagger back to the couch. I need Lifetime movies; they're like Valium to me. When John walks in, I sit slack-jawed in front of a drama about a teenage stripper. I poke my shackled ankle from under the blanket. "Thank God. Get this off."

John hands me a CVS bag. "Take it." I dry-swallow two Wellbutrin. I'm only supposed to take one, but I need to push my brain's serotonin levels as high as possible as quickly as possible.

"I feel better already. Unchain me and let's go out to dinner."

I throw on some sweatpants and we make the ten-minute drive to Applebee's. It's a raw, rainy Tuesday night, but the teenager who holds open the door for us reveals, as usual, a crush of eager diners ahead of us, waiting for tables. People around here love to go out to eat and cheerfully wait two hours for a table, which I cannot for the life of me understand.

Two days ago, I could have slipped outside for a cigarette. Now I must endure the perky waiters and ersatz Americana without nicotine. The restaurant hums like a hive. I watch an older couple wait for their table with the terrifying patience of age, and think, I cannot stand this.

John knows that the sight of overweight people waiting eagerly in line for mediocre food annoys me. "Let's eat at the bar." He nods toward the gleaming swath of wood. Only a few youngish businessmen sit nursing beers, their cell phones on the bar in front of them. He takes my hand and we thread our way through the crowd.

The bartender hands us menus. John orders a black and tan and I my usual Diet Pepsi. My spirits are inexplicably high, mostly because I've spent two days locked in my house and am grateful for any diversion.

My bright mood collapses, however, when I take a sip of the Diet Pepsi the bartender sets in front of me. It's flat. A line from an eighties pop tune wafts through my head: Don't drink, don't smoke, what do you do?

I covet.

A young couple comes in from the rain and settles at the bar across from us. The woman is in her mid-twenties, fresh and pretty, her face bare of makeup. Fishing in her bag, she removes a lighter and a pack of Newports. I watch her smoke with the focus of a businessman in a strip joint. The empty space at the back of my throat demands to be filled. I start to chew the inside of my cheek. Tomorrow morning, it will be sore, covered in little pits and gashes.

Noticing that my face is twisted up like a little girl's underpants, John tries to distract me. "Need anything from Target after we eat? More gum?"

"A pack of Basic Menthol Lights." I mean it as a joke, but my words sound bitter even to me. I'm ashamed of myself until the bartender takes our order.

My husband orders what he likes: wings, steak topped with blue cheese, mashed potatoes, and garlic bread. I order a cup of chicken soup and a grilled-chicken salad, dressing on the side.

My hands are empty. I have nothing to hold on to, nothing to hide behind.

DAY 3

4:17 a.m.

John nestles closer and drapes his thigh over mine. Our faces are inches apart; his breath brushes my eyes, drying them out, but I don't turn away. It's safer to stay still. To brace for the terror that jolts my brain every few minutes, twitching and sparking like a downed power line.

Supposedly, you can't die in your dreams—your unconscious won't let you. But a panic attack is a glimpse into your own final exit. Doom swoops down like a falcon and snatches you midbreath. Your heart crashes against your ribs, a sparrow caught suddenly, miserably, indoors. Light is too bright, sound too loud, the lightest touch a splinter under your fingernail.

For the past few years, my panic attacks have funneled up from my depths only when I try to quit smoking. I've come to expect these pointed dispatches from my subconscious: Smoke or die. My last attack hit last year, about three weeks after another failed attempt to quit. Watching News at Ten *with John, I forgot how to breathe. I thought I was having a heart attack. John thought I was ridiculous.*

"Hon, you're not even forty years old. Your heart is fine. You're nervous, is all."

"How do you know? People in their late thirties have heart attacks all the time. One minute they're fine, the next they keel over."

My heart fluttered. Lurched. Heaved again. This was it—the Big One, Fred Sanford style.

"Take me to the hospital," I said as calmly as I could. John shut his eyes in irritation. "Hon, I have to get up for work tomorrow. You know what this is—nerves. You'll be fine in the morning. Let's just go upstairs."

By 11:30, we'd reached an impasse. His patience worn as thin as a cat's ear, John stomped off to bed. Hyperventilating, furious, I drove myself to the emergency room, humming along with the radio so I wouldn't drive off the road. Physical exam, EKG, questions: How much coffee do you drink? How are things at home? The resident shrugged; he could find nothing. By then, of course, my heart had resumed its calm, steady throb. I drove home in humiliation, tiptoed up the stairs, and wound myself around John's warm, comforting bulk.

A hot bath always helps. If I must die, let it be in warm water. I crawl over John, trying not to wake him. When my feet hit the carpet, my knees almost buckle. Numb from the waist down, as if I've been slipped an epidural, I stumble down the hall, clutching the walls to stay vertical. Once in the bathroom, I kneel by the tub and turn the taps. You're supposed to keep calm during a panic attack, talk yourself down. My eyes open in the dark, my cheek pressed against the tub's cold porcelain, I chant silently. You're OK, you're OK, you're OK.

Smoke a goddamn cigarette already, sneers the demon in my head.

The bedroom door creaks open. A second later, John flips on the bathroom light. Pitching forward onto the edge of the tub, I shield my eyes in the crook of my forearms, the water's dumb, dull roar at my forehead.

"What are you doing?" His voice is furred with sleep.

"Shut the light. Panic attack." I lower myself into the steaming tub.

"Is it out?" I ask.

"Uh-huh. Can I turn on the hall light?"

"Yes." Eyes still closed, I crouch directly in front of the tap, my chin inches from my knees, and hold my palms under the hot water.

"I may need to go to the hospital."

"Hon, you know what this is. You're not dying."

"You don't know that."

John sighs and rests his big hand on my shoulder. "What can I do?"

"Please don't touch me. I'm sorry. I love you."

His hand retreats, but he stays close, his breath a small warm breeze. He squats by the tub, all 240 pounds of him, watching over me. I grope for his hand.

"I have a joke for you," I say, in a lame attempt to lighten the moment. "What's the difference between a corporate CEO and a hooker?"

"What?"

"A hooker screws only one person at a time." I peek up at him; he is smiling.

"Here's another one. How do you torture a smoker?"

"How," John sighs.

"Hide all the lighters."

"That was a joke?" He strokes my hair.

"Sorry. When I can't smoke, my brain shuts down. Nothing makes sense. Life feels like one big run-on sentence."

"Hon . . . can we go back to bed now?"

"Ten more minutes."

John by my side, I drain a few inches of tepid water and blast the hot until the tub steams like a lobster pot again. Finally, sleep calls, a mother on a dusk-shrouded porch. John helps me out of the tub. Under my waterlogged fingers, his skin doesn't feel like anything I've touched before.

I think of the chain downstairs, as patient as a sniper.

Back in Brooklyn after Thanksgiving, I floated for weeks on an incredible sense of well-being, as serene as a leaf on a pond. The Pink Cloud, as this phenomenon is called, is a cosmic gift the newly sober experience early in recovery. No more hangovers. No more guilt. I felt cleansed, renewed. God had touched his thumb to my forehead, dissolving my urge to drink. I still bar-hopped with the porn posse, but nursed Diet Pepsis, watching my friends drink the way a researcher observes monkeys.

I also attended AA meetings in churches and community centers all over the city. Invariably, I walked into a shabby, ill-lit room, helped myself to coffee from a gleaming industrial-size urn—standard issue in the rooms, as AA meetings are called—took a seat in a metal folding chair in the back, and listened to people talk about what it felt like not to drink. More often than not, they held a cigarette. So did I. Our smoke floated above our heads like a communal halo.

This was me in my first year of sobriety: ashamed of my past, searching for redemption, studying "normal" people to figure out who and how I should be. And smoking, smoking, smoking. I'd always been a pack-a-day girl, but early in sobriety, I started to burn through forty sticks a day. I smoked more because I felt more—mostly I felt frightened—and smoking made those emotions less intense. The world seemed enticing but treacherous, and I lurched through it like a teenager learning to drive a stick shift.

Weeks into sobriety, a hip young couple in my AA home group, both painters, invited me to their party. "You must come," they trilled, after I mentioned my *Playgirl* gig. In the early 1990s, government-funded art was under attack and New York City the epicenter of the culture wars. My friends considered pornography a form of artistic expression and me a freedom fighter. Okay.

Stephan and Christiane lived in Williamsburg, an hour away by subway, and I almost didn't go. I spent the whole afternoon before the party in a controlled panic, chain-smoking and planning my strategy. I settled on a time-honored tactic: Ask questions. To ask the guests about themselves would demonstrate my interest in others, a quality those "working their program"—tending to their sobriety—were supposed to develop.

I rehearsed on the subway on the way to the party. But then Christiane opened her door, releasing the revelry within like a swarm of wasps.

"Julia!" She drew me into a hug. "I'm so glad you could make it."

"Hi," I said, fixing my smile like a bayonet. Why had I come? I knew little about painting, didn't read *ArtForum*. I was a no-talent, bead-stringing alcoholic and I didn't belong here. The guests would smell my fraudulence, sneer, and abandon me in a corner with my shame and a paper plate of hors d'oeuvres.

It was too late for regrets. Christiane took my coat and led me through the hallway. We passed a floor-to-ceiling bookcase. I longed to sit out the party there, hiding behind a fat book of art theory.

The hall opened into a small dark kitchen, where a few people sat talking at the food-covered table. I knew one of them, a woman from my home group. The rest, dressed in thrift-store garb—a man in a bowling shirt, several women in dresses last worn, perhaps, by Tricia Nixon—were strangers. One or two held wineglasses.

"Soda's in the fridge," said Christiane, giving me a wink. "Help yourself." I reached past the slim green bottles of wine, drew out a can of Diet Pepsi, and popped the tab, feeling like a child at a grown-up's party.

"Guys? This is Julia," said Christiane. "She edits porn magazines."

"Well," I said, "I used to."

"Cool!" said a woman with Buddy Holly glasses and a buzz cut. She asked if I'd ever slept with a centerfold. No, not their type, I said, *wink wink*. "Does size matter?" asked the bowling-shirt man. "Sometimes," I said, and told them about Mr. Eastern Bloc's retouched manhood.

"I had to write an article to go with the centerfold," I said. "Guess what I called it."

"What?"

"'A Man Called Horst.'" They laughed, getting my allusion to the Richard Harris film.

Two hours and five thousand Diet Pepsis later, no one had sneered. I said my good-byes and headed home, giddy with relief and triumph, thinking, *I did it! I did it!* Meaning, I'd stayed sober at a party, acted like a normal person. I felt exhausted but virtuous, like I did after a good workout.

Most of the time, however, I felt like an alien. To an alcoholic, sobriety is a sudden move to a foreign country—you don't speak the language, you don't get the habits and customs of the natives, you're adrift. You cling to the things that carry over from your old life. Smoking represented continuity amid chaos, reassurance that not everything had changed. While I could envision my life without alcohol, I could not imagine it without cigarettes. I needed them like air or water, and especially now that I wasn't drinking, smoking helped me feel normal, if not better.

Nicotine was my meager comfort. I passed the Korean delis and Hispanic bodegas on my way to meetings, cheered by the knowledge that while I could no longer dash in for a six-pack of Corona, there was still something in there for me: Newport Lights, as many packs as I wanted. And coffee, served by their surly proprietors in those blue-and-white take-out cups with the Greek key trim, the phrase "We are happy to serve you"—what a lie—printed in gold above three steaming cups. Coffee is the alcoholic's lifeblood. I sat in coffee shops for hours with my AA buddies, slugging it down, cup after cup after cup, and stinking up the place with smoke. Our waitresses had to empty the ashtray every hour. I left very good tips.

With neither job nor relationship to distract me—I hadn't worked in five months, since my ignominious firing—I could devote all my time to the serious business of sobriety. Gathering my courage, I asked a young woman to sponsor me, and we met for coffee each week. I attended at least one AA meeting a day, sometimes two. I volunteered to make coffee, bring cookies, set up chairs. In these tasks I discovered a sense of community. People drank my coffee, ate my cookies, sat on the chairs I'd arranged in rows or in circles. My life intersected with theirs in the smallest, most ordinary of ways, and it felt simple and good. I averted my eyes around men, distrusting them, distrusting myself; for the first time in my adult life I went more than a week without sex. The scars on my arms hardened into shiny pink tracks. I still met with Hannah once a week. Sobriety was a jigsaw puzzle, and she and I sifted through the pieces, began to fit them together here and there.

I still hadn't shared, as participating in an AA meeting is called. I equated the practice with voluntarily stepping into a circle of strangers armed with stones. To admit to weakness and failure, to ask for help—yes, I equated that with death.

So, with dread and admiration, I listened to others tell their stories, wondering what it would be like to cry in front of twenty or thirty or fifty people. Eventually, their need helped me to accept my own. That they could ask for help—some freely, others with obvious difficulty—no longer seemed like weakness. I wanted to comfort them. I wanted to touch them. I'd found my tribe and discovered that gratitude offered the possibility of grace.

Shortly after Christmas, craving my parents' company and the sweet-scented serenity of home, I took the bus from the Port Authority bus terminal to Hartford to visit them for the weekend. This time, both of them sat in the Pacer, offering their imperfect love; I bounded toward them, grateful. Still, my sobriety needed time to set, like a splinted bone; we were careful around one another, especially my mother. She didn't say much that weekend, but she touched me. She placed the tips of her fingers on my forearm, held her rough palm to my cheek.

On Saturday night, we rented a movie. My father lit a fire. I lay on their overstuffed couch, my feet in my mother's lap, and she tickled them like when I was nine years old. Pretending to watch the movie, I studied her face. In the golden light, her face was as soft as a child's, her grave expression aging it around the eyes and mouth but lending it a quieter beauty than she'd worn in her youth. She wore cotton two-piece pajamas printed with small blue flowers. Beneath her beribboned and ruffled collar, her neck was etched with faint rings. Life had marked her too.

In that moment I saw my mother for the first time, a woman with my eyes and smile but her own secrets, griefs, reasons. In this moment, she was just herself, and I was free to love her or not. It was my choice.

I sat up and leaned into her; our upper arms and

haunches pressed close, warm and solid. I took her hand. We kept our eyes on the movie. So did my father, but I felt something in him relax.

When you learn a large truth, it seeps through your flesh and settles in your bones so deep you almost, almost forget it. But throughout your life, it turns up again and again, like an old picture in a kitchen drawer. Sitting next to my mother, I realized for the first time, but not the last, that love is so large I would never find its core.

As any AA old-timer knows, the Pink Cloud never lasts. One morning, I woke up and it had vaporized with me on it. I was Wile E. Coyote, the Road Runner had just lured me off the cliff, and I hung in that nanosecond before my rude plummet to earth. My urge to drink had resurfaced. Scared to drink and scared not to, not knowing what else to do, I went to my regular Friday-night meeting.

Held in the auditorium of a large church in the West Village, the meeting attracted a large and eclectic crowd. Lunchbox-toting downtowners sat beside self-conscious yuppies and older men and women, anonymous and serene in cardigan sweaters. A few homeless men bummed cigarettes, waltzed with invisible partners on the church steps, drifted in and out of the ornately carved doors. Here and there, a woman knitted.

All week, I'd tried to smoke away my thirst for a vodka tonic, but it didn't help, and the power-puffing had made me ill. Every morning, I'd risen with swollen eyes, my throat raw, as if coated with steel shavings. I'd done everything I could to resist a drink, everything but admit to myself I wanted one. As the speaker ended his qualification—that's when an alcoholic shares with the group what his life was like before, with, and after alcohol—my hand shot up, urgent with need.

The moderator called on me. I rose, terrified, a cigarette between my fingers.

I spoke for maybe ten minutes. At an AA meeting, this is a filibuster; you're supposed to keep it short. I'd taken a seat in one of the last rows, as usual; as I talked, people swiveled in their seats to look at me. The weight of their understanding settled on my shoulders; I sensed their lungs bellowing softly in and out. They scented the air with their sweat and smoke and commingled sadness and joy.

I don't recall what I said. Maybe I talked about the people I'd hurt—my family, Eric, Hannah—and about the tattered shoebox inside me, my collection of old hurts, that I couldn't bear to throw away because if I did I'd have nothing. I may have talked about the refrain that often ran through my head: *Don't touch me. Don't fucking touch me.* Or how one part of me wanted to die and the other fought to get better, and I didn't know which would win.

Midway through my speech, a great wave of grief smashed against my ribs. Then another. A clot of tears rose in my throat, and I began to sob. I could not contain them; they kept tearing loose, like shutters in a storm. I covered my face with one hand and clutched a cigarette in the other, smoking through a gap between my fingers and talking, talking, tense with shame and despair and, after many minutes, a shaky joy. Eventually, my torrent of emotion slowed to a trickle, and I took my seat, giddy with pride and relief. I felt as if I had braved a terrifying amusement-park ride and my car had, finally, glided to a stop.

After that, I shared at every meeting. I uncovered my face, but kept the cigarette.

April 1991 found me five months sober and ten months past my last full-time job. To stretch my unemployment check, I moved out of my Brooklyn apartment and found a room-mate. Louise, a pretty, timid, unmarried woman in her fifties, owned a turn-of-the-century brownstone in Prospect Park, not far from my old place. It was run-down but gorgeous—twelve-foot ceilings, awash in light, furnished with antiques. My room, on the third floor, overlooked a tiny, lovingly tended flower garden overhung with grapevines. I didn't even bother to ask if I could smoke in my room. Three or four times a night, as Louise read feminist literature in her lonely bed, I tiptoed downstairs, through the kitchen, and into the garden to smoke, betrayed by every creaking floorboard.

I met Bud a few months after I moved in. An acquaintance was dating a musician who had a friend, a drummer. Did I want to meet him? Sure, I said. I hadn't yet disavowed musicians.

Bud and I met at a restaurant near his apartment, on the fringe of the East Village. Over many beers (his) and Diet Pepsi (mine), he unwadded his crumpled history. He hailed from a grit-swept, left-off-the-map town in Texas. Several years before, he had moved to the city to break into the music scene and find session work. Almost immediately, he hooked up with an R & B group with a dancing brass section and a girl singer. The money was good, and he'd toured with them ever since.

I liked his sharp sense of humor, his Texas twang, and his status in the city's music community. We sat in the restaurant for three hours, drinking and smoking, filling and refilling ashtrays—Bud smoked two packs of Marlboros a day.

A month after we met, I moved into his one-bedroom apartment, an 800-square-foot landfill of dirty clothes, empty takeout boxes, recording equipment, and beer bottles. Lots and lots of beer bottles. Lined up against one kitchen wall were literally hundreds of amber longneck empties, most filled with foul-smelling chaw. Bud also chewed tobacco, mostly onstage, to keep his hands free to play. With a plug in his cheek, his face looked puffy and hurt, as if he'd been busted across the jaw.

A few days after I moved in, Bud flew to Copenhagen for a month—the chilly Danes love the blues. The day he left, I doused the place with bleach and wrestled plastic garbage bags of bottles to the Dumpster.

With Bud gone so often—essentially I had my own apartment—I returned to the luxury of smoking my first cigarette of the day in bed. Living with Louise had forced me to hide my smoking like an idiot aunt in the attic, and to smoke unfettered by guilt was like undoing the top button of my jeans after a huge meal. I didn't move in with Bud to smoke freely, of course. I moved in because he was as close as I could get to a drink without actually imbibing. Still clueless about how one survived without alcohol, not yet sure that I could, I used our relationship to act out my ambivalence about sobriety.

For most of our seven-month relationship, Bud toured with his band. When he rolled into town, I tried to drag him to AA.

"Just one meeting," I said, with the zeal of the newly converted. "Check it out, see what you think." It was July, Bud had just returned from Copenhagen, and we were in bed, where I hoped my lecture about his drinking might be better received. Unfortunately, he was still slightly drunk from the night before. His face—normally the hue of Virginia ham—was flushed magenta. The beer on his breath smelled improbably sweet, like hay.

"Now, come on, honey, don't let's start this again. I told you before, I'm not the AA type." He groped for his Marlboros and lighter on the desk next to the bed, sending a few beer bottles, a stack of unopened mail, and a few *Modern Drummer* magazines crashing to the floor. To Bud's way of thinking, a cigarette was the prelude to sex as well as the finale. His eyes jittered through the smoke.

"You look terrible," I said.

He tossed me his lopsided smile. "I love you too." It was almost impossible to ruffle or offend him. Crushing out his cigarette, he held out one arm. I nestled beneath it. "Let's git busy." He nuzzled my neck.

"Don't change the subject," I said. "AA works. I haven't had a drink in seven months."

"And I ain't had one in seven hours. Git off it, will you?"

Untangling himself, he pulled on his jeans and headed for the kitchen. "I'm worried about you," I yelled after him in exasperation.

I heard the refrigerator open, the crack of a pull-tab. "Ahhh," he groaned contentedly from the kitchen. "Much better." He padded back to the bedroom, sat on the edge of the bed, and retrieved his cigarette from the ashtray. Bud must have smoked a trillion cigarettes in that room. Lying there was like bathing in dirty bathwater.

"It's nine thirty on a Thursday morning and you have a beer in your hand," I said. "You don't think there's a problem here?"

"I ain't got a problem when I drink. I got a problem when I don't."

"Bud," I said. "You fall off your seat in the middle of a set."

He grinned. "But I git right up again, don't I?"

9:20 a.m.

I bring my left hand—my smoking hand—to my lips, then draw it back, examining my fingers. With nothing better to do, I consider different smoking mannerisms, wonder what they reveal.

I begin with grip. Like most smokers, I use—used—the V-hold, between index and middle fingers. Too common. It divulges nothing. Maybe I'm overthinking. Still, culture likely influences grip—do Bedouins smoke like English-

men? Americans like Europeans? What might a preference for pinching a cigarette between thumb and index finger, as if squashing a mosquito, say about a person? Or holding a smoke with the ember toward the palm, the remaining fingers curved around the burning end—why the secrecy? What desire motivates a woman to clamp down on that phallic cigar, or a man to cradle a pipe? Freud could have had a field day. Does anyone still use a holder? How effete, the equivalent of a pinky ring, at most a passing phase. Ditto for holding a cigarette between the middle and ring fingers, or underhand, using the thumb and middle finger like tweezers. Maybe my rejection of these unconventional grips reveals my hopelessly practical nature.

My inhale, short and hard, betrayed low frustration tolerance and a need for instant gratification. (I had no patience for those long, meditative drags that taste of life, death, eternity.) The exhale equally hard—a blast of thin brume, with my lips taut rather than puckered in a soft O. Afraid it would hurt, I never jetted smoke through my nostrils. Strange—I have a high tolerance for mental pain and anguish, but for physical pain, zip. At twelve, still afraid of matches, I stood in the snow and lit books of them at a time. When they sputtered to life, I pitched them; their death hiss elicited in me a grim sense of triumph.

A meat-and-potatoes smoker, I never attempted a smoke ring or the celebrated French inhale, in which smoke expelled through the mouth is immediately inhaled through the nose. Did my disinterest in tricks suggest low creativity? Impatience with complex tasks? Or simply that I never learned to play? (Note to self: Purchase bottle of bubbles at dollar store. When urge to smoke hits, blow. Play, damn you.)

What I lacked in showmanship, I made up for with courtesy. Solicitous of others' comfort, I blew my smoke to the floor, the ceiling, or off to the side. But sometimes, honor demanded that I exhale, ever so gently, into the face of a contemptuous nonsmoker. Quick to anger? Problems with authority? Hell yes. But the gesture also said, You see me as a deviant who, in my selfish attempt to grow a tumor, has willfully fouled your air. Had you but asked, I would have gladly extinguished my cigarette. Now you must pay. Eat my smoke, you self-righteous twit.

I hated lipstick marks on my filters. Those coral stains were too intimate—a bra hanging from your towel rack, forgotten there for a visitor to see. Smokers who let their ash grow too long unnerved me. Mesmerized by that dangling curve of cremated tobacco, I bet against myself: It will drop off before they tap it off.

Some smokers let their cigarettes burn out in the ashtray, or snap them, still lit, into the gutter, aiming for arc and spark. Not me. I crushed my butts with gusto—ground them into ashtrays, squashed them like bugs. Extinguishing a cigarette was my showdown with and victory over death. I burned up its life, as it tried to burn mine, and when I was done, I snuffed it. Twenty times a day, I got away with murder.

After our 9:00 a.m. meeting, Gail and I walked the few blocks up Third Avenue to a coffee shop. We slid into a booth in the smoking section, dug into our bags for our cigarettes and lighters, and lined them up on the table in front of us, like loaded pistols. Our waitress bustled over— fiftyish, thick-waisted, wearing orange support hose and white orthopedic shoes. She held a coffeepot aloft like a lantern. "You ladies want coffee?"

"Please," I said. "And . . . two grilled corn muffins." A year sober, I'd started to feel guilty when I ordered only coffee.

"I'm not hungry," Gail said. Her freckles stood out on her pale face, the skin almost translucent, like the pearly interior of a shell. She bowed her head. Dark roots bled through her platinum hair.

"You okay?" The meeting had been more emotional than usual, lots of tears and raging. Perhaps its intensity had upset her. I wanted to take her hand, but she was so emotionally fragile I feared that my gesture would leave a bruise. She'd started showing up at meetings a few weeks before, swaddled in voluminous and complicated black dresses I learned later that she'd designed and sewed herself. Though she always sat silently in the back of the room, I sensed her intelligence, liked her immediately; she was like a badly wrapped gift. This morning, I'd asked her to coffee. To my surprise, she shrugged and followed me.

Gail fiddled with her teaspoon. "I don't know if these meetings are helping. I still want to get off." Although addicted to heroin, she preferred AA meetings because listening to junkies reminisce in Narcotics Anonymous meetings made her want to use.

"So what?" I said. "Of course you do. You're an addict. That doesn't mean you can't quit."

"I don't know if I want to." She scraped her ash against the lip of the cheesy tin ashtray, oily with tar.

"Yes you do. You'll get clean and go back to your fabulous Hollywood life." The child of wealthy parents, Gail had grown up in Manhattan and moved to Los Angeles to work as a lighting designer. She herself was in darkness. She'd come home to kick heroin a few months before, but couldn't stay clean for more than a few days at a time.

"I don't know if I want to go back."

"You're going back. I'll come with you," I said. "Give me a third of your salary. I'll make sure you stay clean."

"Yeah, right." She flicked me a smile, and I did reach for her hand, then—laid my palm on it, lightly, and then withdrew it.

Gail lit a cigarette. Her throat banded with each inhalation and relaxed with each exhale, reminding me of the emptiness in mine. I reached for my Newport Lights.

"Why not? To repay me, you can help me stop smoking. They say it's harder to quit than heroin, so stopping should be cake for you."

Gail's pale lips twitched. "I'm a junkie. Quitting smoking is at the bottom of my to-do list."

"Well, it's at the top of mine. I told myself I'd quit when I had a year sober."

"That's what everyone in AA says."

"I know." I blew smoke at the ceiling. "I should throw away my pack right now. So why don't I?"

"So why don't you?" She looked at me, raising an eyebrow. The dullness in her eyes had burned off like rocket fuel, and for a tenth of a second, there she was.

I thought for a moment. "Because the thought of quitting makes me sad. The kind of sad you get when you say good-bye to someone at the airport. Someone you really love." I laughed, one dry syllable. Avoiding Gail's gaze, I took one last drag of my cigarette and crushed it out.

When I looked up again, Gail's eyes held a softness I'd never seen before. As if she'd finally made up her mind about me. "*Quod me nutrit me destruit,*" she said, as the waitress bustled over with our muffins.

"What does that mean?" I asked when she left.

"'What nourishes me, also destroys me.'"

11:18 a.m.

Under my blanket, my photo album on my knees, I pore through my baby pictures of Daniel. The album—gorgeous, expensive, the handmade paper as rough and dimpled as orange peel—was a gift from Hannah, who attended my wedding to Matt. It's meant for display on a gleaming glass coffee table, but naturally I haven't pasted the photos in the book; they're just stuffed in.

I did, however, stuff them in chronological order: Daniel coming home from the hospital. Daniel screaming bloody murder facedown on his changing table. Daniel smiling through his binky. Me, spewing cigarette smoke.

Whoops—I misfiled. Holding the photo to my nose, I examine it for a full thirty seconds. I recall this day per-

fectly: Matt and I at a street festival in Brooklyn during the summer of 1992. That would make me twenty-nine. The afternoon was hot but mercifully dry; we baked, figurines in a massive kiln. Inhaling the hot oily sweetness of funnel cake, dizzied by driving soca and lilting reggae, I was as happy as I knew how to be.

But there's something not right about my expression. Something that makes me uneasy. Staring down the camera lens, I raise my chin defiantly, as if egging an unseen adversary to take a shot. My eyes look like someone just blew them out. My right eye, anyway; my left is hidden by a thick stream of smoke. What other parts of me did that smoke obscure? The fearful part. The self-hating part. The loving part. All those parts, intersecting. I was a Venn diagram of dysfunction, exposed by Matt's artistic eye.

Then I get it: Although I'd been sober for more than a year, I look drunk. Ah, my Drunk Face. In my twenties, I wore it in almost every photo. My parents' collection of snapshots, kept in Zip-Loc bags in a small wicker chest, is proof. There I am, at parties, holiday gatherings, a rare visit home, hammered and clutching a cigarette.

My cell phone rings. "Hello?" Static crackles in my ear.

"Hey, it's your brother."

"Hey," I say happily. Although we live only twenty minutes apart, I haven't seen him in months. After 9/11, he and his wife—a platinum-haired knockout from Sweden—decided to leave the city. Lehigh University hired him as its design director, and they bought a crumbling house in the crumbling city of Easton. One of their neighbors is a crack

dealer. For months, I called to invite them to dinner, the movies, to my in-laws' parties, but finally stopped. I've come to accept Kurt's absence from my life, and love him from a distance as best I can.

"Hold on. You're breaking up." I clank to the back door and sit on the top step, shivering under a gunmetal sky.

"What's all that racket? Is that the chain? Mom told me you chained yourself in the house to stop smoking."

"Yeah. It's sort of an experiment." Reflexively, I reach for my cigarettes, before I remember.

"That's totally insane," he says with admiration. "So what do you do all day?"

"Sleep. Cry. Watch stinkbugs crawl across the living-room ceiling."

"How's not smoking?"

"Like not breathing."

"I hear you. I stopped for like two months, but then I started again."

He fills me in on his life. He's still with the band he joined in New York City; they're playing at CBGB's next weekend. Their house is sucking them dry; fixing their sagging front porch will cost them almost twenty thousand dollars. They don't know if they like their new lifestyle.

"We may go to Sweden—bum around for a while, figure out what we want to do," Kurt says.

"Are you painting?"

"I fool around a little bit."

Sometimes, I want to lock my brother in his studio and not let him out until he produces a painting that astonishes him. Without thinking, I say, "One day, the pain of not painting will outweigh the pain of doing it. Then you'll paint because you have to."

Silence on the other end of the line. I'm embarrassed that I've spoken so plainly. His painting is none of my business.

"Maybe I don't want to paint at all, but I can't give up the idea that I should."

"Maybe." I'm surprised by his candor.

"Listen, I have to go," he says. "I have a meeting in ten minutes."

"All right, hon. I'm really glad you called. Love you." I don't ask when we'll get together.

"Love you too. Hey."

"Hey what?"

"We should get together soon. I'm sorry we haven't come around."

"That's okay," I say, surprised. Kurt never talks like this.

"We're just so busy with the house, and I'm terrible about returning calls. I don't call you, I don't call Mom, I don't call my friends in New York. I don't return emails. I don't know why. I just don't want you to think I don't care."

"Forget it." But I won't forget this poignant exchange. "Bye, love. Take care of yourself."

"Later."

I push End on my cell and stare into space. For most of my life, I believed that my brother had little use for me. Why did I think he didn't care? Or that Mom and Dad didn't, for that matter? An addict's view of reality is as twisted as a strand of DNA. Nicotine doesn't distort perception the way alcohol does, but it certainly blunts it. I feel certain that if I'd talked to my brother with a cigarette in my hand, I

*would not have felt his love for me. Nor would I feel this
compassion for him, this new awareness of his vulnerabil-
ity, an emotion I unfairly stripped from him before he was
ten years old.*

*I look at my hands. Rough skin, stumpy fingers, short
nails, the better to type with. My brother and I each began
life with two of them. As babies, we must have used them to
explore the world's sensory feast—bananas and dirt, sand at
the beach, our mother's lovely face. But at some point, we
stopped reaching. My brother is a painter who can't bear
to paint. I live life one-handed, using my left hand only to
smoke. I offer Daniel and my husband one-armed hugs,
half-embraces that betray my ambivalence at inviting them
into my life and my fear that loving them means losing
myself. A one-handed reader, I turn pages with the right,
smoke with the left. I even drive with one hand, courting
accidents as I fumble for and light my cigarettes.*

*I wonder what it will be like to drive with my hands at
ten and two, as my father taught me. To wrap my son in
both of my arms.*

In August 1991 I rejoined the pornerati, landing a job at the
men's magazine *Gallery*. Having lost touch with my hard-
living porn posse, I looked forward to making a new,
equally intemperate circle of friends. That hope quickly fiz-
zled, however: my colleagues were as square as Batman's
jaw. Occasionally, we gathered at a sleek, trendy bar for *one*
after-work drink, me swilling Diet Pepsi, as usual. After one

round, everyone but me went home to their sweethearts—one editor was married, one engaged, and one sweetly faithful to a steady girlfriend. None of them smoked, of course. I'd write a few dirty letters ("I never thought this would happen to me . . ."), then trudge outside, alone, and light up in front of the building.

I also met Matt. The first time I saw him, he was behind his closed door, in the dark. Bent over his light box, he moved a loupe over a set of color transparencies, carefully, methodically, like a physician checking for broken bones. The managing editor rapped on his door, then flipped on his light. Matt straightened and blinked.

As we were introduced, he smiled, his eyes not quite meeting mine. I extended my hand. After a beat, he reached for it like you reach for a car-door handle on a hot day.

Although Matt was not my type, I was strangely drawn to him. Short and slight, with wide blue eyes and cheekbones that soared like a cathedral ceiling, he reminded me of a beautiful child caught in a waking dream; I pictured a pair of tiny wings folded softly beneath his shirt. Charmed by his gentle, goofy sense of humor, I sought him out, and we became friends. I wandered to his office to play with his desk toys. He cornered me in mine, talking comic books and movies until I had to edge out backward. But something about him touched me, worked patiently at my knotted heart. A loner, he rarely mentioned friends or family; he had an orphanlike quality, as if starved of touch. From our conversations, I gathered that he spent most evenings and weekends at his drafting table, drawing. Light and color, paper on which to capture them—these were all he needed, or seemed to need.

Each morning, on my desk, I found whimsical little doodles he'd left there the night before. Every afternoon, we ate lunch in the park a few blocks from the office. After a month, I had that shimmering-soap-bubble feeling that precedes falling in love. When he told me that he'd lost his aged parents within a year of each other—he was an orphan, after all—I wanted to draw his head to my breast.

A year sober, I also wanted a new kind of life, and a love as solid and secure as a brick house. Weary of men with upside-down lives, I saw Matt as an antidote to those chaotic unions, a man with whom I could join the world. We'd go to movies, hang out in bookstores, trade sections of the Sunday *Times* over bagels and gourmet coffee. I pictured us wandering through weekend street fairs and skipping through Prospect Park, our wicker picnic basket overflowing with apples and Brie and crusty baguettes.

Only one thing stood in our way: Bud. But he was gone, and I was lonely.

At lunch, I talked to him about Bud, pouring out my doubts, probing for signs of interest. Looking into his eyes, as sweet and blue as the frosting on a child's birthday cake, I saw a man who would care for a woman as lovingly as a family man tends his lawn.

He confided in me, too. Eight months before, his wife, whom he'd met at art school in Chicago, had left him after five years of marriage.

"What happened?" I asked. He lifted his palms helplessly, his smile like a sunlit wave.

One afternoon in the park, I asked if my smoking bothered him. It didn't seem to—he'd never once wrinkled his nose or flapped his hand when I lit up—but I wanted to be sure.

"I'm used to it." Carefully, he rewrapped the uneaten half of his sandwich. "My parents smoked."

"Both of them?"

"Yep. Chain-smokers. They smoked in the car with the windows rolled up. You know, in bad weather, or when the air conditioner was on." His voice held that strange quality of patience—or perhaps resignation—characteristic of those who have spent their lives in a haze of other people's smoke.

"How awful." I pictured him at nine years old, his face pressed to the back window of a station wagon, fading into a toxic fog. His hands sliding down the glass.

"It was pretty bad. I think that's one of the reasons I don't smoke."

"Didn't you ask them to at least roll down a window?" When I was growing up and my mother dared to light up in the car, the rest of us were on her like orangutans on a minivan in a drive-through safari; we screeched until she flipped her cigarette out the window.

"Sure I asked," said Matt.

"What did they do?"

"Turned up the air conditioner."

Over time, smoking became a third, shadowy partner in our relationship.

Consider the implications of being in a committed union. You fight, make love, open your chest and display your soft, glistening innards. You argue about who will mail the bills, even trot out, to your utter shame, the tired debate about the toilet seat: up or down? Eventually, like it or not, you meld together, become one. Right?

Not always. For me, smoking was a dependable boundary to erect when I felt angry, uncertain, or afraid, which was most of the time. With a cigarette in my hand, I could tolerate my self-doubts and flaws. Without one, they proliferated like malignant cells. Deep down, I didn't believe that I deserved a kind, decent man like Matt. Smoking allowed me to live with that knowledge.

But there was another reason I didn't open up to Matt. My anger frightened me—look how it had already warped my life—and smoking helped me snuff that rage. Why alienate Matt with my issues and my anger when I could, with a flick of a lighter, so easily dispense with both?

For the seven years Matt and I were together, I kept him on the other side of a wall of smoke. He breathed in all my unspoken loneliness and anger and shame. Secondhand smoke for a secondhand addict.

In my previous relationships, I could play the good woman whose bad men bloomed in the warmth of her love. My relationship with Matt was calm, placid, untarnished by rage or turmoil. Which was what destroyed it, of course. But in the beginning, his love felt like the sun on my hair.

On a raw Friday night in November, the buzzer rang. Damn lowlife scum, too wasted to remember their keys. I crawled out of bed—my arms and ribs prickled with gooseflesh, Bud's landlord was cheap with the heat—buzzed in the anonymous and inconsiderate tenant, and shuffled back to the bedroom.

I'd stayed home from work, drifting in and out of a feverish sleep. My nasal passages felt packed with concrete; the glands in my neck seemed the size of walnuts. But my real dilemma was whether the eight cigarettes left in my pack would last the night. I could call the Chinese place on the corner if I got hungry, but no one delivered cigarettes. To get a pack, I'd have to shower, apply makeup, and flirt with the Arab who ran the corner deli, a prospect too exhausting to contemplate. Screw it. Eight should do it, if I took a few Xanax.

I'd just crawled back into bed when someone knocked. I groaned, pushed off the covers, and shuffled back to the door. There stood Matt, dripping, clutching a large paper bag. My first thought was, *God, I look like hell.* My second: *I can send him for cigarettes.*

"I won't stay long." Shifting from foot to foot, he thrust the bag into my hands. "I knew you were sick, so I brought you some stuff."

"That's so sweet," I said, touched. "Come in. Don't get too close." Setting the bag on the counter, I lifted out two cans of chicken-noodle soup and a quart of orange juice. My eyes welled up; illness brought out the infant in me.

"How did you know where I lived?" I reached into the cupboard for glasses. "You want some juice?"

"No thanks. You told me at lunch once. You said Bud's last name, too."

The juice burned my raw throat like fire. "I did?" Of course I did. I'd been waiting for Matt to make a move for a month now, was ready to hand him my life. I knew he thought he would simply heat me some soup and fade into the night. Not if I had anything to say about it: I was sick, not dead. But first things first.

"I hate to ask, but could you do me a huge favor and get me some cigarettes?" I asked. "There's a deli right around the corner. Would you mind?"

"Should you be smoking?" he said doubtfully.

"Well . . . I'm not smoking much," I lied. "Please? Newport Lights. Three packs." I didn't know if I'd be getting out tomorrow, either.

"Sure." I handed him a ten. After he'd gone, I lit a cigarette—I could afford to squander one, now—and plodded to the couch.

Forty minutes later, I was still waiting. Had he gotten lost? Mugged? When the buzzer rang a few minutes later, I swung open the door and cooed: He held a pizza.

"I thought maybe you'd be hungry." He set the box on the counter.

"I can't believe how sweet you are." I didn't ask about the cigarettes. Hopefully, he'd tucked them in his jacket pocket.

"And these." He removed three packs of Newport Lights from the roomy leg pocket of his cargo pants and handed me my change. "The pizza is my treat."

He would never make a move; it was up to me. I gathered him in my arms and kissed him. We didn't leave the apartment until the following night, and he didn't complain when I lit up in bed.

A week later, I moved out of Bud's apartment, leaving a note sticky with guilt, and rented a tiny apartment in Brooklyn. Matt kept his place in Jersey City. Six months later, we rented a place together in Brooklyn Heights.

I don't remember asking if I could smoke inside. But I know that I did.

Unlike the other men with whom I'd been involved, Matt treated me with tenderness, even reverence. He sketched me nude, wrapped in a sheet of smoke, as I lay on my Goodwill couch with a cigarette in my hand and an ashtray by my side. I watched his eyes move from my body to his rough newsprint pad, his charcoal-smudged fingers making such tiny, tentative, feathery strokes. When he turned the pad around, I saw myself, blurry around the edges, indistinct, caught in the process of becoming. As if his drawing were really a photograph that he had just immersed in developer, and he was waiting to see, again, what he had seen. For a time he saw the best of me.

A year of writing dirty letters was enough. The following summer, I left *Gallery* to accept a position at a downmarket woman's magazine, a print version of *The Jerry Springer Show*. I edited stories on how to attract a man, what to do when he cheated, and how to get over him if he dumped you. Eight months later, the editor sat me down in the conference room to tell me that things weren't working out. I'd known that the first day. The magazine made *Lowrider* look like *The Atlantic Monthly.* As far as I was concerned, I was still writing pornography

For the next seven months, I collected unemployment checks and circled the want ads in the *Times.* I snagged interviews for jobs I wanted—an alternative weekly paper needed a reporter, a well-known humor magazine an editor—but was never called back. Thankfully, the managing editor for trade magazines devoted to floor coverings and snack foods didn't call, either.

Then I heard from an editor at Rodale Press, a publisher in the small town of Emmaus, Pennsylvania. She was looking for an associate health editor.

I'd never heard of Rodale until I saw the ad in the *Times,* and I researched the company before I sent my résumé. Rodale was named for its founder, who had preached healthy living long before Euell Gibbons filmed his first GrapeNuts commercial. The company published *Prevention,* a respected consumer health magazine, and health books that were written by staff writers and sold through the mail. I didn't expect a response, and had applied only to prove to unemployment that I was actively seeking a job.

After setting up an interview with Maureen, the editor who would be my boss, I hung up, perplexed. Why would Rodale want to hire a former smut peddler? It made no sense. But a week later, mindful of my unemployment check, I boarded a bus in the Port Authority terminal for the two-hour ride to Emmaus.

I met with Maureen, the president of Rodale's book division, and its executive editor. Throughout the five-hour interview, I prayed that one of them would suddenly throw his feet up on his desk, pull an ashtray out of a drawer, and companionably offer me a smoke. Alas, my prayers went unanswered, and I went into withdrawal. By the time the office manager drove me back to the Charcoal Drive-In, the local diner that doubled as a bus terminal, I was trembling with need, and lit up before her sedan took a right out of the parking lot. Sucking greedily, I relaxed. They'd never hire me. Surely they'd smelled the smoke on my freshly dry-cleaned suit.

Two weeks later, Maureen called. "We'd like to offer you the position. Thirty thousand to start." Muzzling my shock, I thanked her and said I'd call back in an hour. Hanging up, I slid to the floor in the kitchen, my back against the warm radiator.

I'd be a fool not to accept. It was time to face facts: I would never be an editor for *Glamour* or *Self,* never have an office in the Condé Nast building. I'd searched Manhattan for a job, and the only one offered—a good one too—was out of state. It seemed the work of Providence. Opportunities tend to arise when you are ready for them, and I was ready. Terrified, but ready.

That night, I pleaded for Matt to come with me. "You have to come. Sooner or later, Rodale will need an art director." We'd been together two years. Sober people—normal people—settled down and had children. It was time to take our relationship to the next level.

The next morning, I called Maureen and accepted the job. She gave me my start date—the Monday after Thanksgiving. Three weeks. I hung up, lit up, and shed a few frightened tears. I'd lived in New York for almost ten years, and I could not imagine a life without Indian food and subways and my AA friends. Plus, I'd have to drive. Shit.

3:37 p.m.

Hunched over my computer, I surf the quit-smoking Websites. The posts from recent quitters practically throb with agony. Those with more clean time cheer them on. And so it goes, post after post. Millions of people all over the country quitting, crying, raging, wracked by cough and constipation. Sneaking cigarettes, smoking like Turks for a day or a week. More crying, confessing on the board, soaking up support, trying again. This is a nicotine junkie's circle of life.

From one post, I learn something new: Alcoholics prefer mentholated cigarettes. Can this be true? From my first cigarette, I never smoked anything but. Trying to corroborate the claim, I check a medical database of thousands of biomedical journals—I use it all the time at work—and find one study conducted in 1960. Hardly scientific proof, yet I feel intuitively that it is true. Maybe alcoholics crave that dry-ice freeze with which menthol bathes the lungs and throat. To me, nonmentholated brands taste like dirt and their smoke swirls uselessly in my mouth. They don't deliver that icy burn in my chest, like I've swabbed my lungs with VaporRub.

A bit later, I stumble across an essay on Salon.com—titled "I Am a Smoker"—that answers the nonsmoker's petulant query: Why do you smoke? The writer flips her witty responses like a carnival knife-thrower. (My favorite is, "Because parachuting is ostentatious.") I'm inspired to draw up my own list.

Because no matter how long and hard you jog, in the end you will die. Because it helps me think. Because it keeps me from thinking. Because today is uncertain and tomorrow, questionable. Because screaming would be rude. Because it's a way to hold my own hand. Because it gives me a reason to leave the room. Because it's low-carb. Because life needs a mute button. Because I don't know how to knit. Because where there's smoke, there's fire. Because smoking giveth and it taketh away.

The last item gives me pause. What does smoking giveth me, exactly? Comfort. Smoke eases, smoke soothes. Just like alcohol did, until it didn't. I wonder where Gail is now, if she managed to stay clean. If Bud still cracks open a beer at nine in the morning. If David still sips martinis in the luxe hush of uptown piano bars.

I know what happened to Celeste. The last time I saw her—before I met Matt—we hadn't talked in almost a year. As always, though, she stayed in my head, emitting faint pings like the black box in a downed jet. With the evangelical fervor typical of AA newcomers. I'd called her out of the blue to invite myself over and stage my own little healing meeting.

Celeste answered the door in a long T-shirt and underpants. She trilled hello, ever the actress, and pulled me close.

My nostrils twitched. She smelled like the inside of a Halloween pumpkin past its prime, when it starts to collapse in on itself. In my arms, she felt as light as a balsa-wood airplane and just as ready to soar.

"Come in, come in. You look lovely," she said in her BBC-announcer voice, and waved me in. I stepped into a Hieronymus Bosch painting: dark labyrinthine clutter. She'd draped a towel over her one small window.

"It's a bit of a mess," she said, and dropped a foot-thick pile of the Times from the sofa to the floor; it fanned at my feet. She settled on the couch, patting the space beside her. Her T-shirt hiked up. Several small bruises dotted her thighs.

"So tell me absolutely everything," said Celeste. "Are you seeing someone?"

"Nah." I hadn't come to talk about Bud. "How about you? Still with Ricardo?" She'd been with Ricardo, a hustler, on and off for the past ten years. When his older lady friends grew bored with him, he drifted back to Celeste and her monthly check. He'd stay a month, beat her up, and disappear again.

"Not right now." Her voice clicked shut like a gymnasium door. She lit an Eve from a pack on the cluttered coffee table. Her hand tremored almost imperceptibly, like an eyelid twitch.

Her degradation was breathtaking, literally sucked away my ability to speak. What could I have said, anyway? I couldn't tell her she looked great, or ask about her job, or congratulate her on a promotion, or even ask if she'd seen a good movie lately. I had to do something, so I lit up, too.

There we were, two alcoholics, one dying, huddled around the smallest of fires.

"Get this," I said. "I stopped drinking. I'm in AA. Can you stand it?"

"That's wonderful, darling." Celeste rolled the ember of her cigarette against the edge of the ashtray, scraped off the ash.

"I thought we could go to meetings together. Hang out again. I know you've done the AA thing, but maybe this time it will stick. You have me now. We have each other."

She smiled like a mourner at a post-funeral reception. "I don't think so. It's too late."

"Quit the drama. It's never too late." I'd heard that in AA. "And stop talking like the Queen Mother."

She stubbed out her cigarette, avoiding my eyes. "Julia. I have bad seizures. Sometimes I can't get to the bathroom in time. I just want it to be over."

I wanted to slap her. "So you're just going to sit in your apartment and die. Just give up and fucking die."

"Now who's being dramatic?"

"Pack some stuff. I'm taking you to the hospital."

She held up her hand, mad enough to drop the accent. "Fuck off. Just go." Alcoholics always say that.

"Oh, shut up. You know you want me to stay."

She smiled her smoky little smile then, tipped her chin, slanted her eyes. "I do." She put her head on my shoulder and snuggled next to me.

I heated her a can of soup I found in the cabinet over the stove. I took out her garbage. I persuaded her to take a shower. We watched an afternoon movie, holding hands.

When she fell asleep, I kissed her forehead. Then I gathered my things, let myself out, and returned to the world.

I don't remember how I found out. I know I called a few months later because her black box had stopped pinging. A recording informed me that her number was no longer in service. Alarmed, I asked about her around the rooms. Finally, someone who knew someone who knew someone gave me a man's telephone number.

"When did she die?" I asked. I felt sick and dizzy, like I'd rolled down a long hill.

"Three weeks ago. Cerebral hemorrhage. The guy in the apartment below hers complained about a leak," the man said. "The landlord let himself in and found her in the shower. I came by the next day to check on her and he told me."

"You're her friend?" Thank God you had a friend. One friend. "How did you know her?"

"She wandered into my home group a few months ago. I tried to look out for her, but she was too far gone. She was a good girl. A sweet girl."

Maybe there was silence. Maybe in my grief and stunned surprise I thought, You are gone. You no longer walk this earth.

"I have some of her stuff at my place," the man said. "It's all boxed up—I'm sending it all to her parents—but you're welcome to come by and take something. To remember her by."

I don't recall his name or face, but I remember that I chose a small tortoiseshell barrette. I keep it with my jew-

elry and Daniel's baby teeth in a small gold-lidded box from
the Museum of Modern Art. It's meant for baby-fine hair.
Celeste's hair, like her life, was sparse.

A deep ache engulfs me, followed by a sharp pain. I
cover my eyes with one hand and start to cry, hard. What
could I have done to save her? Was there anything I could
have done?

I sob and sob. I can't stop. I see her in that coffin of an
apartment, alone. I remember my anger when she told me
she was just waiting to die. What I construed as typical
alcoholic self-pity was acceptance. She was right. It was too
late.

More sharp pains, like cold liquid on a bad tooth. I
cover my face and weep for her. Her pain had always been
too much for me to bear. I was wrong to expect her to
bear it.

Why did Celeste die and not me? What was the difference between us? She tried to kill herself with alcohol and
succeeded. My suicide is a work in progress. If I continue to
smoke, my head could explode like hers. Smokers die of
strokes all the time. Some of them must crumple in the
shower.

Then I lift my head and stop crying, my wet eyes staring
at nothing.

I know why she died and I didn't: because I was loved
and she was not. Even before I stopped drinking, I knew
that the world was populated by people who loved me: my
family, Hannah, David. Decent men had tried to love me.
Except for the man who had befriended her in the last

weeks of her life, Celeste had no one. No one thought she was special. No one cared if she lived or died. What she had in place of love was oblivion. What I have in place of oblivion is love.

I can understand why she gave her life away. I have no right to squander mine.

DAY 4

7:12 a.m.

"Three days," I say to John. "Seventy-two hours without a cigarette."

We've finished our French toast and bacon and I'm curled on the couch, wrapped in my furry blanket. I feel good. No cravings. My sadness has broken like a fever. The synapses in my brain are firing again. John hasn't filed for divorce. Still, I'm wary. I've been here before, many times. Thrown down my cigarettes like a pair of crutches—it's a miracle!—only to take them up again a few days later.

"This better work," I say. "Because if it doesn't, I swear to God I'll have my lips sewn shut."

John clasps my foot under the blanket. "You can do it, hon. Think of how happy Daniel will be. Remember last week when you asked me to buy you cigarettes on the way home? He saw me bring them in. Boy, he gave me hell." He squinches his eyes and pushes out his lower lip, imitating my son's outrage. 'Cigarettes! You bought cigarettes for my mom!' I felt so bad."

"*My guy,*" I say. "*I miss him.*"

"*It is a little too quiet around here.*"

"*I have to admit, though. It's been a nice three days without Nickelodeon or the Cartoon Network.* No Johnny Bravo. No Jimmy Neutron.*"

"*No hide-and-seek with the couch cushions,*" says John. *My guilt spreads like spilled milk. Hide-and-seek is Daniel's favorite game, and I hate it. I want to draw with my son, read him stories, conduct science experiments with him at the kitchen table, our heads touching over a microscope. He wants to drag all twelve of the couch cushions onto the floor, build a fort, crawl inside, and make me look for him.*

When he was four months old, we played our first game of peekaboo, that rough draft of hide-and-seek. I loved watching him extinguish the world—my beaming face— and find it again. We played this game until, at four, he discovered the cushions. At first, he would slip under them while they were still on the sofa. At five, he began pulling them off to build his fortresses, calling, Find me, Mommy! Find me!

Now, when Daniel takes the first cushion from the couch, I am flooded with a sense of guilt so strong that I want to run screaming into the street. I can't bear looking at the exposed frame, on which are now scattered at least a quarter-cup of Cheerios and popcorn kernels. I can't stand the way his pleas filter through the cushions. My son is suffocating and I'm to blame. His game enacts the great shining terror of my life: that when I chose to leave my marriage I damaged my son, perhaps irreparably.

That's why, when he breaks out the cushions, I stand by the coffee table, my arms at my sides, my heart pounding its struggle between love and despair.

Find me, Mommy! Find me!

"Did you like hide-and-seek?" I ask John suddenly.

"What?" After two years with me, my non sequiturs still addle him.

"When you were a kid. I'm trying to figure out why Daniel likes it so much. Did you like it?"

"Well, yeah," he says, as if I'd asked, Do you like sex? "Didn't you?"

"Not really. It was boring to hide in someone's tool shed or whatever. I couldn't wait to hear olly olly oxen free."

"Olly olly what?"

"You know. What the kid who was It yelled to call in everyone else at the end of the game." I don't tell him that sometimes I didn't even wait for the call and just snuck home to watch TV. I wonder if, without knowing it, my son already has learned the lesson I've lived by: Hide behind a wall of smoke and no one will find you.

"Hey," John says. He holds up the chain and waggles his eyebrows. "Commere, little girl."

"Pervert."

He snaps the lock around my ankle, gathers his brief-case and keys. I kiss him good-bye from the couch; I just can't deal with clashing and clanking. "Call me if you need me," he says, and is gone.

Another ten hours to fill. Silence fills the room like poison gas, dispelling my good mood. Irritated, I shift my weight, which rattles the chain. Its sound is rich and soft, like hundreds of quarters spilling onto each other, but God, it never lets up; I just want it off.

Maybe John is still warming up the car. If he is, I'm telling him to spring me. I crane my neck to peer out the front window, but the Jetta is gone. My internal gyroscope spins crazily. Maybe I should pop a second Wellbutrin to speed my return to sanity.

A car drives down the street, a blur against the dusty lace panels in the computer room, its tires hissing on the wet asphalt. It halts at the stop sign, then speeds away. I never thought the sound of a stranger's retreating car could make me feel so alone. My mood plunges further, aggravated by my bedraggled state. I haven't showered, my hair is limp, my face bare of makeup. My old glasses sit askew on the bridge of my oily nose. Ordinarily, I subscribe to the philosophy of Fernando, the suave talk-show host created by Billy Crystal on Saturday Night Live: *It is better to look good than to feel good. Today, however, I neither look nor feel* mahvelous. *I am alone in my house, on my street, in this city, the state of Pennsylvania, the nation. If I looked out my window I'd see the earth falling away from me, a whorl of blue and white, a snow globe displayed on black velvet.*

On impulse, I pick up my cell phone on the coffee table and call Matt. "Hey," I say when he answers. "This will sound weird, but I want to know if you play hide-and-seek with Daniel."

"What?"

"Do you?"

"Why?"

"I was just thinking about the way Daniel likes to hide.

*The way he likes small spaces. Did you know he begs me to
let him sleep in his closet? It's like this special thing I let him
do on the weekends. He covers the floor with his stuffed
animals, I throw his blanket over him, and he loves it. He
sleeps there all night. So do you? Play hide-and-seek with
him? Just humor me."*

"Well, no," he says, finally. "He never asks to play it
here."

"Huh." *I'm jealous that Matt doesn't have to play and
ashamed that I'm jealous.*

"Okay?" Matt says. *He means: Can I go now?*

"Am I a good mother?"

*Another non sequitur. Through the cell, I can feel the
struggle in him. I don't know how he feels about me now.
I'd like to think that he's forgiven me a little, that he knows
that I loved him the best I could and that I still do.*

"Yeah," Matt says, finally. "You are a good mother."

I exhale slowly, grateful, relieved, ashamed.

The Friday night before Thanksgiving 1993, Matt and I
left Brooklyn forever in the old Mercury Sable that my
mother sold me for a dollar. As we headed over the
Queensboro Bridge, I swiveled in my seat and watched the
city lights recede through the rear window, my throat
aching with tears. Like sobriety, this move suspended me
between past and future, apprehension and hope; I sailed
between them, an aerialist in free flight. I rolled down the
window, admitting that dark night, and smoked one ciga-

rette after another, clutching each like a roller coaster's safety bar.

We arrived in Emmaus late and drove directly to our apartment—the first floor of a duplex covered with light-blue aluminum siding, hastily rented the weekend after I accepted the job. We parked on the scrubby grass, like rednecks. Caught in the Sable's headlights, a child's bicycle lay forlornly on its side. Our new landlord, the dour old woman who owned the duplex, had mentioned the young family on the top floor.

We unlocked the door to our apartment, crossed the threshold, and looked at each other, unable to believe what we'd done. The place was horrendous—three cramped, dark-paneled rooms clotted with the odor of stale cooking grease. A previous tenant had papered the bedroom with lavender unicorns cavorting under pastel rainbows. We'd known about the mythical beasts, of course, but in the dark, they'd turned sinister. The next day, I hid them with lace panels from Kmart.

Our apartment—a couple hundred yards from my office, I wouldn't have to drive after all—stood twenty-five feet from an active railroad track, one of dozens that zippered Emmaus to the wider world. Others might have been disturbed by this proximity; I saw it as a plus. On Monday mornings, Matt took the 6:00 a.m. bus into New York and stayed in the city all week. At night, alone with the unicorns, I let the trains lull me to sleep. Each night, at least one passed by. At first, I would hear its doleful whistle from miles away. Ten minutes later, warning given and gone, its thunderous presence filled my room, its horn the sound of archangels, some trumpeting, some clanging pots and pans.

I missed New York desperately. At night, in my dreams, I sat at a table in Nightingale's Bar on Thirteenth Street, watching Bud play, or strolled down Broadway, deep in conversation with Jerry Seinfeld. On the weekends, I pined for the Indian food in the East Village, the nightclubs, my pornographer pals with whom I'd shared so many beers, cigarettes, secrets.

Where were the smokers, anyway? Not at Rodale. Devoted to the art and science of clean living, the company had banned smoking in its offices since the mid-1980s. Maybe that explained why no ground-out butts fouled the parking lot or the packed dirt around the entrances of the charming old brick building that housed the book division. Rodale was Eden. Its employees biked and jogged on its campuslike grounds, lifted weights in the company-run Energy Center, lined up for free blood-pressure checks and cholesterol screenings and—in the spring and summer— tended vegetable gardens in company-provided plots. I took zero advantage of the company's largesse. Most smokers don't run or bike, and I'd killed every plant I'd ever owned. I was a stranger in a strange and relentlessly healthy land. With its abundance of light and space and fresh air, the Rodale campus stood in stark contrast to my dark, cramped, secret self.

Another smoker might have said, I'll smoke when and where I damn well please. Not I. Surrounded by fresh-faced marathoners at *Runners World* magazine, earnest soy eaters at *Prevention* and *Backpacker*, I just couldn't light up in front of my colleagues. Why not just tattoo a swastika on my neck? I truly believed that they would more quickly forgive my dirty-letter-writing past than my smoking, a classic example of projection. My attitude toward cigarettes had begun to change even before I arrived at Rodale. At thirty, I'd smoked for more than ten years and—to paraphrase an old Camel ad—was smoking more and enjoying it less.

Oh, there were still those few golden cigarettes: the first of the day, the heralded postcoital ciggie, the leisurely smoke in the bathroom as I dressed for an evening out. The summer cigarettes on the beach, lit with wet pruned fingers and extinguished in the sand next to my blanket. I still viewed a cigarette as a friend, but an unreliable one, the kind whose name made your mother's mouth pinch up like the knot on the end of a balloon. The Bad Influence you drop, with relief and regret, after the car crash or the bust. Cigarettes linked me to a past that I preferred to forget, and if I didn't want to march down Rodale's Road to Wellville, I did want to know where it began.

Determined to master my new environment, I extended myself and quickly made friends. I'd honed my social skills in three years of AA meetings, and the young singles and couples in the book division—like me, imports from other states and starving for diversion in this one-pizza-parlor town—were eager to expand their social circle. My house morphed into Party Central—I hosted movie nights, Super Bowl parties, dinners.

Of all my new friends, I liked Caroline the best. A writer several years older than I, with cheekbones you could slice cheese on and chestnut hair that unfurled down her back like a flag, she and her husband, Gerald, arrived at Rodale from Washington State, where she wrote features for a small weekly newspaper. During the week, she churned out chapters on athlete's foot and chapped lips, and worked on her fiction at night. Weekends, she and Gerald invited Matt and me for dinner—they loved to cook—or we'd hang out with them and a few other couples our age.

My new friends were smart, accomplished, and, mostly, believers in the Rodale mission. Nothing like me, in other words, and fear of exposure tormented my days and haunted my nights. Ironically, only nicotine eased it. I sat in my office, biting my cuticles, surrounded by bright industrious people, and wrote about vitamin supplements and vegetarianism, counting the seconds to my next cigarette break.

Even so, I lived in constant fear that Maureen would discover my secret vice. I pictured her nostrils flaring with suspicion, and then uttering the four words closet smokers most dread: "Have you been smoking?" Intense, filament-thin, and a brilliant editor, Maureen was standard-issue Rodalian—runner, skier, consumer of salads, company woman. But she was kind—patiently rewrote my wretched prose, assured me that I'd soon learn to write in the cheerful, punchy Rodale style—and I wanted her to think highly of me. That meant I had to be someone else, or at least appear to be. It also meant that I would endure any amount of inconvenience and absurdity to smoke without her finding out. Which I did. I never walked a mile for a Camel, but I did wade through thigh-deep snow for Newport Lights.

The winter of 1994 pounded Emmaus into the ground. As I recall, at least a foot of snow fell each Wednesday, but Rodale didn't do snow days. Even if it had, I had no excuse not to show up; I could see the back of the building from my front window.

So every Wednesday, I dug myself out and trudged to work until the snowfall continued for, in my opinion, too fucking long. I stopped shoveling. When Matt arrived back in Emmaus on Friday nights, he was not in a shoveling mood, either. The snow piled higher and higher. We pretended it wasn't there.

The thigh-deep expanse of snow that blocked my walkway made it difficult to enter my place to sneak a smoke. But not impossible. Every hour of every workday, all winter, I slipped out of the office and headed home, leaving my coat in the closet so as not to arouse suspicion. Not in the smoker's closet, either. Rodale actually had segregated closets. It was a Jim Crow kind of thing, and it aroused in me a grim and furious anger. So like a cat who sneaks a pee in her owner's bed, I hung my coat in the nonsmokers' closet, fouling the outerwear of the good and decent people who eschewed tobacco.

I paid for my little act of rebellion, however. Coatless, in cowboy boots—to buy a pair of Totes would be to concede defeat to the snow—I slipped and slid through the plowed parking lot, the wind whipping, my teeth clacking—*shit! Cold!* When I reached my yard, I plunged into my snow-covered walkway like a Labrador retriever into a marsh after a downed duck, trying to step into the holes I'd made the day before. I got inside, closed the front door behind me, and, closing my eyes in relief and rapture, lit up on the couch behind the tattered tablecloths I'd used as curtains in Brooklyn. For five minutes, I could let down my guard, become the cherry ember on the end of my cigarette, flaring with each pull, fading with each exhalation.

Then I brushed my teeth, spritzed myself with Lysol to mask the odor of smoke, and waded back to work. Of course, you never get rid of that stink. It clings to smokers like ivy to brick. I don't know who I thought I was fooling.

In the spring, tired of sneaking around, I outed myself, lighting up occasionally, uneasily, around my colleagues at the local bar after work. They drank alcohol in moderation, as *Prevention* advised, and over one or two beers discussed compost heaps and marathons. I chugged Diet Pepsis, nodding and smiling and trying to ignore my body's distress signals: Need cigarette *now*.

I learned to assume a certain expression when I lit up, meant to convey both concern for the air quality of others and mute, cringing apology. I thought of it as my Smoker's Face and wore it for the next ten years, my Decade of Apology. I apologized to my coworkers for smoking. To my husband for the affair that ended our marriage. To a man who loved me for breaking his heart. To my son, in silence, for not being the mother he deserved. To myself, for picking the absolutely wrong man and trying to make him love me. I kept making that face, and eventually it froze that way.

10:38 a.m.

Experts on smoking cessation advise smokers to write down their reasons for quitting, and to read the list aloud several times a day. Please. Has reason ever stepped between a smoker and his lust for nicotine, a tornado that leaves him in regretful, pathetic ruin? I've attempted this exercise more than once, written about wanting to avoid terrifying diseases, of loving my child, my partner, life itself. But the words just lay there on the page, as limp as a flag on an August afternoon. I couldn't feel them.

I'm willing to try again, however. I am prepared to go to any lengths to make it this time, lengths that extend beyond my pessimism and this seventy-two feet of chain. So I sigh, dig through my purse for a pen, and start a list on the back of our unopened gas bill.

I want to quit so that I'll never again burn a hole in my car upholstery. Graceless from birth, I trip over cracks, smash my grocery cart into the only other one in the aisle, and drop cigarettes between my legs, or in the gap between driver and passenger seat, entirely too often. My Jetta is pocked with small burns. (Fortunately for me, I've never dropped a cigarette in John's Sebring.) Juggling ember, forced to choose between flesh and upholstery, I've always sacrificed the latter. Quitting will allow me to avoid the dilemma entirely.

I'd like to end my abject apologizing, too. As a girl, I watched as smokers lit up anytime, anywhere. Ashtrays dotted every doctor's waiting room and elementary-school teachers' lounge. Guests on Dinah! *and* The Merv Griffin Show *lit up without asking. You could smoke in the mall. Parents sent their kids for cigarettes, giving them an extra quarter for a treat—maybe a pack of candy cigarettes. (They tasted like Pepto-Bismol, but when puffed a dusting*

of powdered sugar created the effect of smoke.) Now, smok-
ers must constantly affirm nonsmokers' right to fresh air. I
support courtesy—Emily Post couldn't have been a more
considerate smoker than I—but in recent years my man-
nerly behavior has degenerated into groveling. Quitting will
liberate me from my ceaseless cringing.

I'm running out of room, but, after a pause, I squeeze in,
I want to see Daniel grow up. I hadn't planned to write
that—don't need to, that particular reason is burned into
my heart—but the list is incomplete without it. Please, God,
burn it in a little deeper.

Time for a midmorning movie.

Channel surfing, I come across The Towering Inferno,
the 1974 disaster flick about a skyscraper that catches fire,
trapping its occupants on the top floor. I can't believe my
good luck. Inferno *is the cinematic equivalent of Cheez*
Whiz, a movie made for days off. Onscreen, a woman in a
pastel evening gown opens a door. Flames leap at her like a
pack of wolves. With my luck, a similar disaster will befall
me. A gas leak, perhaps. I imagine the conversation at my
front door.

Fire Chief: There's a gas leak down the street, ma'am.
You'll have to vacate the premises.

Me: Well, the thing is . . . can't you just fix it? I'm kind
of stuck in the house right now.

Fire Chief: No, ma'am. You'll have to evacuate your res-
idence immediately. Come with me.

Me: Do you have a hacksaw?

No time for that—move, lady! My neighbors are already
outside. Still chained to the radiator, I rattle across the street

to join them, clad in my dingy bathrobe and a pair of John's white tube socks. Splendid.

I return to the movie. More people jumping to their deaths, or cowering from the smoke and flames. The scene evokes images of 9/11. I've tried many times to imagine the desperation of those who jumped from the upper floors of the Twin Towers, the unbearable heat and smoke, the terror that drove them. Far more fortunate were those able to hide from the heat and flames, thereby cheating death.

Hiding from fire. Hiding to escape death.

Smoking to escape death.

I smoke to flee death.

At first, the notion seems counterintuitive. Until I recall all those times I believed that I would die if I could not smoke. The cause of death: being trapped in the moment in which I found myself. More often than not, I lit up not to intensify the pleasure of the moment, but to wrap the past and the future in shimmering bows of smoke. Stealing into the future, I watched myself walk the dusty streets of Morocco, take my parents' hands as they lie in hospital beds, skydive from 15,000 feet. I smiled as Daniel swung his own giggling infant in the air. Retreating into the past, I held my newborn son again, ordered a martini with David, tangled in sour sheets with men whose names I don't remember, their faces hanging above mine like stars. Most of the time, though, smoking suspended me, a specimen encased in Lucite, at the moment I pressed my thumb against the lighter's sparkwheel and radiant plasma gave way to flame.

I smoked for pleasure, of course I did. But my prime

motivation was to escape those small daily deaths. I lit up when my kid was driving me crazy and the hours dripped like saline in an IV line. When my boss was a bastard. When, in the middle of the night, a man I loved had not come home. I sat at the kitchen table and smoked for hours, and when I looked into the bathroom mirror, I didn't recognize myself, white-faced, ready to kill, to die.

I used to think, smoke or die. Now it's quit or die. At this moment, I'm not certain that I can. My desire to smoke was factory installed, bred in the bone. It wouldn't surprise me to learn that I emerged from my mother's womb asking for a light. Within a month of my first cigarette, I was smoking a pack a day. The odor of an unlit cigarette, that sweet tobacco smell like dirt before rain, sustained me. The weight of a new, unopened carton under my arm, against my chest, reassured me. I forgave cigarettes everything, those burn marks in my Jetta, the endless abject apologies. I loved cigarettes from the moment we met, but that love is long gone, has turned to desperation, to anguish.

I think what I am saying is that I have fallen out of love.

In a 1974 paper titled "The Smoking Habit and Its Classification," tobacco researcher Michael A. H. Russell wrote, "There is little doubt that if it were not for the nicotine in tobacco smoke, people would be little more inclined to smoke than they are to blow bubbles or to light sparklers."

Nicotine, the primary chemical that acts on the brain, is

the *sine qua non* of cigarette addiction. But there's more to ciggies than nicotine. Tobacco smoke, a venomous vapor of toxic gases, liquids, and solids, comes in two varieties. Mainstream smoke is inhaled and exhaled by the smoker and, alas, by nonsmokers. Sidestream smoke wafts directly into the air from the burning end of the cigarette.

Mainstream and sidestream smoke contain thousands of additives. These include:

- carbon monoxide, which prevents the blood from carrying oxygen through the body. Some studies suggest that sidestream smoke contains three times as much carbon monoxide as mainstream smoke. In heavy smokers, it reduces the blood's capacity to carry oxygen by as much as 15 percent.
- hydrogen cyanide, which reduces the body's ability to transport oxygen. The Nazis used a form of hydrogen cyanide, Zyklon-B, in their gas chambers.
- formaldehyde, a class-A carcinogen. The primary ingredient in embalming fluid, this chemical is pumped through the veins of the recently departed to retard the process of decay.
- ammonia. The process of adding ammonia to increase the oomph of nicotine—called freebasing—is similar to the method used to heighten the effects of cocaine.
- tar, the particulate matter that smokers inhale when they draw on a lit cigarette. According to one source at the University of Pittsburgh, smoking a pack a day coats the lungs in about a pound of tar a year. So in a strange way, smoking causes weight gain.

A year after Matt and I moved to Pennsylvania, Rodale hired him as an art director, and we moved out of the apartment with the unicorn wallpaper and into a pretty little row home in Allentown. Soon after, we announced our engagement. We'd been heading in that direction anyway, and decided to make it official. We shopped for a ring; Matt's face glowed with love and pride as he slid the square-cut ruby ring we'd chosen together onto my finger. Finally, sobriety's gifts were spilling into my lap like the prizes in a piñata: a promising career, a loving man, good friends. Our lives spread out before us like a thousand acres of fertile land.

Six months after the wedding, I was pregnant. We hadn't been trying, and since my menstrual cycle was about as reliable as a magazine horoscope, my condition took me some time to notice.

Many pregnant women develop an aversion to certain odors, including cigarette smoke. Not me. I smoked through my first month without queasiness. My only symptom was an overwhelming fatigue that made me fall violently asleep as soon as I got home from work and compelled me to spend entire weekends in bed.

"I think you're pregnant," Matt said.

"Nah," I replied, lighting up between naps. "I'm just working a lot."

On a Sunday night in February 1996, after I'd slept for thirty-six hours, Matt drove to CVS for a home-pregnancy test and held it out to me. "Do it," he said.

To pacify him, I retired to the bathroom and peed on the stick. Minutes later, the plus sign blazed a triumphant pink.

Oh, shit.

I wasn't sure that I wanted to be a mother, but erring on the side of caution, I shredded my cigarettes, not trusting myself not to pick them out of the trash. The next morning at work, I shared my news with Caroline, who leaped from her desk and threw her arms around me. By the end of the week, I was so in love with this tiny seed of a being inside me—the Cheeto, as Caroline christened him, *him* because I knew it was a boy—that giving up cigarettes was painless.

It's amazing how your sense of accountability kicks in when you learn that you're bringing another life into the world, how, no matter how bedrock your addictions, you find the strength to place the needs of the new life you carry before your own. During my pregnancy, when I thought of smoking at all, it was fondly, the way you remember a lover who was all wrong for you but whose memory, with the passing of time, makes you shake your head and smile. But I'd found another love, another way to fill myself up. The comfort I'd derived from cigarettes seemed a cheap imitation of the peace I felt as my son floated inside me.

Daniel was born in mid-October 1996, on an afternoon when the sun poured through the autumn leaves like molten gold. Terrified, I delivered him in two great pushes, my mother on one side of me, Matt on the other. The nurse held up a mirror so that I could see him fight his way out of me, but she'd taken my glasses, so his entrance into the world was lost to me.

My mother saw, though. She said that his arms were

wrapped around his body like two small wet wings. Halfway out of my womb, they unfurled and stretched, his hands curled into fists, his eyes squinched shut, his lips puckered with the force of his effort to be born. The nurses weighed him, performed their tests, swaddled him, and handed him over like a package. His head was the size of a large orange, his brown hair as fine as the down on a woman's forearms.

I was overwhelmed; my son was a tiny god, I his hapless attendant. My mother stayed with us for two weeks to "help." She brought her bleach and her scrub brushes, cooked for us every night, and tried, in her way, to comfort me. Looking at my pale, strained face, she'd urge, "Go take a nap," but of course all I heard was "go." In my exhaustion, I mistook her comfort for contempt: She didn't trust me to keep my son alive. When Daniel cried, we raced each other to his newly painted room, its walls adorned with animal plaques, pigs and rabbits and dogs. Whoever got there first plucked him from his crib and held him triumphantly to her breast. If we crossed the finish line together, Matt took Daniel and we faced off like lions over a kill. After a week, I wanted to strangle her.

One night, Daniel squalled louder than I'd ever heard him, furious with need, and just like that, my milk came in. I put him to my breast. As he started to nurse, a piece of me slid into place with a solid *thunk*.

But every night, he cried. Cried and cried and cried, starting promptly at six and ending at ten. "Colic," the pediatrician said. Matt and I took turns balancing him on our forearms, cupping his screaming face in our palms, bouncing him. We strapped him in his infant seat and sat him on top of the warm, humming dryer. Nothing worked. I never slept for more than two hours at a time. I began to hear his screams in my sleep, but when I jolted awake and dragged my beat-up body from my bed to peer into his crib, he was out. Between my lack of sleep and his constant screeching, my nerves were shredding like a hunk of Parmesan across a grater.

"You know something? I'm beginning to hate him," I said calmly to Matt at five o'clock one morning, minutes after Daniel had finally squalled himself to sleep. We sat on the edge of the couch, staring dully at the sunrise, which was unbeautiful, unmiraculous, simply the commencement of another forty-hour day.

"Don't say that," said Matt, his blue eyes dark with reproach.

"I'm just being honest."

Daniel howled on schedule until he turned three months old. Then one evening, just before six, our eyes met. He regarded me gravely. And I swear to God, his eyes went soft, turned liquid with empathy, and he did not cry.

I lean forward on the sofa to watch my son, asleep in his baby seat on the floor. Daniel is three months old, beautiful, strong, alert. When he smiles, his fat cheeks bunch up, hiding his eyes: a Buddha in Huggies. He's an intense baby. He even sleeps with intensity. His eyebrows knot in what looks like concentration, and his mouth, the top lip adorned with a nursing blister, suckles softly.

We played this morning, as we do every morning. I laid him on our bed and dangled my necklaces so he could reach for them. I put on a James Taylor CD and danced around the living room with him in my arms. I nursed him. I talked to him, sliding my voice up and down like a flute to make him smile. I will repeat these activities again today and tomorrow and the day after, and yes, I love him, but I'm lonely and miss my work and my friends and keeping my breasts in my shirt once in a while. I long to hear an adult voice other than my own.

Caroline comes by as often as she can, and a few of my friends from work stopped over last week, but seconds before they rang the doorbell, Daniel spit up on my shoulder. I met them at the door spattered with baby puke. They oohed and aahed, but stayed only fifteen minutes.

It's 1:00 p.m. Matt is at work. From this point, my day will slide toward its end like a bead of sweat down my back. The refrigerator hums. Time has stopped. I think I am going crazy.

Daniel's head jerks and he throws out his arms, spreads his tiny fingers wide. I know what this is—the startle response. *Or is it?* I dial the on-call nurse at ABC Pediatrics, as I do every day.

It's Julia Hansen again, I say. I'm sorry to keep calling, but he's doing it again. The startle thing. I just need to make sure he's okay. Is he okay?

The nurse is an older woman, and kind. She tells me, again, that he's fine, and is he sleeping? Can you take a nap, rest a bit?

I know I'm wired; my eyes burn. Before she left, my

mother told me to sleep when Daniel sleeps. Matt tells me. Caroline tells me. I want to, but I can't. What if he dies while I'm asleep? I watch, will his every breath.

I think, I can put him in his infant seat and sit him outside the bathroom door while I take a shower. Then we can go to the mall. For a moment, my heart lifts. Yes, we can leave this house. I finally got my license the week before he was born, after not having been behind the wheel in ten years. Last week, I strapped him into his car seat and drove him to the pediatrician for his well-baby visit. I felt absurdly proud, as if I'd manned the space shuttle.

Then I think, no. Taking him to the mall will expose him to germs and if he gets sick, he will die. Also, if I carry him upstairs, I'll need to carry him downstairs, and he could sail from my arms like a slippery fish. They should make tiny football helmets for newborns. I think, maybe I can make one, and I realize that I am deeply disturbed.

I am afraid and trying to keep my fear at bay, but it's hard, I'm so tired, I feel like I'm doing this all wrong, and something is, is, *missing*. It comes to me instantly, the clouds in my brain part and I can almost hear the celestial choir: cigarettes. *Of course.* If I had a cigarette, I could carry Daniel to the back door in his infant seat, step outside into the crisp December air, light up, and feel better. I'd be me again. Cigarettes would grant me safe passage to a distant land called Normal. My normal, as opposed to everyone else's.

It's been almost a year since I shredded that pack of cigarettes, and until this moment, I didn't know how much I missed smoking. Now my loss is evident, and everywhere.

There are no cigarettes on the kitchen counter, where I'd always kept them. No ashtray on the back porch. No way to measure time in the only way I know: Eight hours equals nearly a pack of cigarettes.

I look at my son; he sleeps peacefully. My heart floods with love, overruns its banks.

I can't smoke again. Ever. My mother has told me this. Matt has told me this. I know they are right. Only bad mothers smoke, like Mrs. Winegar, the slatternly mother of my childhood friend Margaret. If I smoke, my son will grow up like Margaret did, grimy, smelling of urine, snot caked under his nose. He'll set fire to our dog while I sit at the kitchen table in a stained bathrobe, flicking ashes into a coffee mug.

I want to be a good example to him, a paragon of health, but I've made my choice. There is no choice. I've seen myself on the back steps, lighting up, inhaling, sending my smoke to heaven, my fear and anxiety vaporizing like a meteor. I can almost feel the relief of it, feel time lurch and buck, its cogs whirring, and start to move again. To let go of that vision would leave me stranded here, alone, and that can't be good for Daniel. I'll be a better mother if I smoke. I'll never light up in the house or in the car. I'll never let him see me with a cigarette. I'll hide my smoking from him. He'll never know.

I won't smoke today or tomorrow, but I know I will smoke again, and this knowledge makes the rest of this day, and the days to come, bearable.

I lie back on the sofa and close my eyes.

3:57 p.m.

Along with a few hundred books, the wall-to-wall, built-in bookshelf in the computer room holds mementos from my New York life, including my collection of religious figurines. I started acquiring them in the mid-eighties, when I idly peeked into two shopping bags someone had put out on the curb across from my Brooklyn apartment. They held two identical statues of Saint Bernadette, one a foot tall, the other reaching my knees. How pissed off with God do you have to be to kick your plaster saints to the curb?

I haven't looked at them in a long time. They kneel, palms pressed in prayer, faces turned to heaven, eyebrows raised faintly in that seemingly patented look of supplication. Rosary beads hang from their wrists. They wear the same simple gown; veils cover their hair. I used to have their purity. At the age of three, my mother has told me, I'd played the Virgin Mary, wandering solemnly through my grandmother's house with a paper napkin on my head, my palms kissing, my eyes cast down.

Like me, these saints have seen better days. Paint flakes from their gowns and faces. Their plaster noses are chipped. A lot of good their prayers did them. The only reason I know that they represent Saint Bernadette is that the name is carved in the plaster at their feet. What is she the saint of? What's her beat? I rattle over to the computer and Google, "Saint Bernadette." My search turns up over forty pages of entries. I scan the screen. Over and over are the words "patron saint of affliction." How appropriate.

For me, smoking is both comfort and affliction. I don't know which cigarette upset that balance, which was the first to exact more pain than pleasure, but I must have smoked it after Daniel was born. I was still young. I still had my breath. My face hadn't yet begun to sag—it's thought that smoking damages the structural protein in skin that gives it its elasticity. I couldn't see the damage.

I resumed smoking when Daniel was almost a year old, on a warm summer night in my backyard with Caroline. My friend's marriage was splintering. She loved Gerald, but had no desire to pass her life in a small town, writing about bowel health and bee pollen. Her desire to write novels had become impossible to ignore, but the thought of hurting her husband caused her anguish.

That night, after I put Daniel to bed, we sat at the picnic table and wrestled with her dilemma. An on-again, off-again smoker—she'd been off since I'd met her—she'd started smoking again, Marlboro Lights. Pulling on smoke sharpened her already prominent cheekbones. Her elegant nervous fingers tapped out cigarette after cigarette, then crushed them out half-smoked. I'd thrown out all my ashtrays, so she stubbed them out on the picnic table and lined them up, two, three, four nice long butts.

I thought, what a waste.

To bum a cigarette seemed natural and inevitable. "Just one," I said.

"Julia, don't do it. Please don't do it."

"One isn't going to kill me."

No, the 75,000 or so after that one would do it. I bummed for two weeks, and then was back to buying car-

tons. Matt was furious. My mother launched her nagging campaign, pleaded long, loud, and often on the phone, via email, in person, until I had to fight my urge to grab her shoulders and shake her until her teeth rattled. But although poked and prodded by guilt, I felt as complete as when I carried Daniel inside me.

One night after work, Caroline showed up at my house without cigarettes. She looked different. The light in her eyes had returned.

"You quit?" I asked, apprehensive.

"Cold turkey," she said. And she'd made up her mind; she was leaving Gerald. I felt betrayed. I'd thought we were going to smoke together at my picnic table forever. She moved into an apartment in Allentown and I didn't see her as much anymore. I had my child; she had her fiction. Three years later, she left Allentown to become a writer. I stayed and became a mother who smoked in the house.

War and smoking go together; watch any John Wayne–era war movie. There's usually a scene where a group of soldiers encircle a gut-blasted buddy. Trying to comfort his friend, one of them places a cigarette between his lips. The wounded soldier inhales hungrily, gratefully. He dies, of course, but peacefully, sent to glory under the soothing ministrations of tobacco.

It's been said that soldiers in the field value cigarettes above food. "If you can't send money, send tobacco," George Washington wrote to the Continental Congress in

1776. Asked what America needed to win World War I, General John Pershing replied, "tobacco as much as bullets." Cigarettes blow smoke in the face of terror, sharpen the senses, blunt unimaginable stress and anxiety, evoke civilization in brutal conditions. To smoke is to return, however briefly, to normality.

Hard-core smokers—the true nicotine addicts—are soldiers, too, fighting invisible enemies like fear and doubt and anger and self-destructive urges they don't understand. Smoking creates wartime conditions, psychologically speaking. Like alcoholics drink and gamblers bet and compulsive eaters gorge, compulsive smokers light up to cope with shortages of spiritual fuel and wounds opened by the emotional shrapnel they take and inflict. When I had an affair with a colleague and moved out of my house for six months, taking my son with me, I smoked like a soldier, for comfort and courage and strength. You don't search your soul in the middle of a battlefield. Cigarettes helped me make it out alive.

Tom came to Rodale from Texas. He'd worked as a feature writer at a prestigious paper, had won awards. Tall and balding, with a long, angular nose and eyes the color of glacial ice, he possessed an appealing intensity. Smart and funny, worldly and well traveled, Tom wasn't the road not taken. He was a thousand of them, winding and rutted and beckoning.

After a few months, he began to accompany me on my cigarette breaks. We talked about writing, politics, our marriages. Eventually, we talked more often than I smoked, spending hours in each other's offices. His eyes were the entrance to a forest. I walked in.

Even for a consummate hider, there was no hiding this. Sick with fear and regret and a mad desire to flee my marriage, I told Matt what I'd done on a July afternoon, three months before Daniel's second birthday. That night, we put our son in his crib and cried together. The next, friends of ours took Daniel so we could talk. Matt must have called my mother earlier that day, however, because that night I picked up the phone and she was already screaming. I took the phone into the mudroom, which opened into the backyard, and sank to the floor. Matt followed and stood above me, unmoving, like a dog beside its dying owner. I lit a cigarette, my hands shaking so badly that I could barely touch the lighter's flame to its tip.

I finished my cigarette and lit another, and another, and another. I needed them to anesthetize me, and they did. I didn't feel my mother's fury or my husband's pain or the horror that was pounding on the locked door of my heart, screaming to be let out. But I couldn't smoke enough to step outside that moment, to stop time. Dusk kept encroaching, and the sun kept melting into the sky, which bled purple and orange and finally, mercifully, went black.

The evening air wafted through the screen door, moist and sweet—I could just smell it through my smoke and the napalm. In *Apocalypse Now*, Robert Duvall loved the smell of napalm in the morning. He should have smelled it that night.

Finally, her rage spent, my mother spoke. "If you and that man hurt Daniel, I'll kill you," she said. "So help me God."

I found a three-room apartment, small but clean, five minutes from the house, and signed a six-month lease. Matt and
I agreed that, in that time, we'd get counseling and decide
whether we could salvage our marriage. If not, I'd take the
house because I could carry the mortgage on my salary.
Barely.

Once a week, we saw a therapist, but it wouldn't have
mattered if we'd met with Dr. Phil himself. I'd already
decided. All I could give Matt now was time to vent his grief
and rage, and a silent promise that when we parted I would
not be with Tom. That promise secured my freedom. I
would have paid any price to be free—from what, I didn't
know.

It's Saturday afternoon, a week since I moved back into
the house and Matt moved into his apartment. Daniel is
back in his old room, taking his nap. While he sleeps, I
wander from living room to kitchen and back again like an
Alzheimer's patient, and indeed, I can't remember how this
all began.

I can't call my mother. I can't call a friend. Ashamed of
what I've done, I have withdrawn from everyone at work.
All people know is that I've left my husband. Caroline is
gone. She calls from New York, but it's not the same; I'm on
my own with this and I'm not doing well. I am trapped in
turmoil of my own making and there is no escape except
for cigarettes, each one a key under my tongue.

I wonder what Tom is doing. Something fun, probably.

He's not afraid to go places, do things. He called this morning wanting to take me and Daniel somewhere. How about the Please Touch Museum? The Philadelphia Zoo? I thanked him and said, I can't. I have shattered my family like a teacup, deprived Daniel of a family unit, and every time I see Tom I am painfully aware of this.

If I told him, he would try to understand. He knows the value of patience. I need more time. Matt needs more time. He buys my son, whom I haven't allowed him to meet, books and toys, a little Texas Rangers baseball cap, which he bought when he drove—*drove*—to Texas, which might as well be Mars.

I can't even drive to Sesame Place. All week, I was determined to make the trip, even though it meant an hour of highway driving. But this morning, after I strapped Daniel into his car seat and drove up Tilghman Street past the supermarket and the Kmart, I could not make the right turn onto the entrance ramp of the Pennsylvania Turnpike. I drove past it and turned around and drove home again, and we played in the backyard instead. Correction—Daniel played. As he rolled his Tonkas through his sandbox, I smoked, careful to stay far away.

I want to present my son the world with a flourish, like a birthday cake. Instead, I flick lighters, turn cigarettes in my fingers, examine the glowing ember beneath the ash.

I am thirty-six years old. I have to quit, but not tomorrow. Tomorrow is the bright future you invoke as you decide, in a tenth of a second, to order the bacon cheeseburger instead of the grilled fish. Tomorrow shines in the distance of today as a porch light glows reassuringly at the end of a dark road, but smokers know it for the lie that it is. When tomorrow comes, there is only need that clamors to be met and never is. The more I smoke the less I enjoy it but the more I seem to need it.

I wander into the kitchen and light up at the table, pushing aside the construction paper and colored pencils and the big plastic container of glitter. Before his nap, Daniel and I made macaroni pictures. In the middle of gluing elbow pasta to cardboard, however, the enormity of what I've done punctured my consciousness like a nail, triggering self-hatred so strong it brought me to my feet.

I kissed Daniel's glitter-covered forehead. I'll be right back, sweetie, I said, and headed for the back steps. Thirty seconds later, he clambered out of his seat and padded to the battered screen door, calling, Mommy? Mommy?

He knew where to find me. I always hide in the same place: on the back steps, a Diet Pepsi in one hand, a cigarette in the other. I hide in plain sight, staring out over my small yard, the few cramped feet of my universe.

4:36 p.m.

Just found this, by the poet Elton Glaser. It exquisitely captures the life and death of a single cigarette and the pleasure and pain of smoking.

SMOKING

I like the cool and heft of it, dull metal on the palm,
And the click, the hiss, the spark fuming into flame,
Boldface of fire, the rage and sway of it, raw blue at the base
And a slope of gold, a touch to the packed tobacco, the tip
Turned red as a warning light, blown brighter by the breath,
The pull and the pump of it, and the paper's white
Smoothed now to ash as the smoke draws back, drawn down
To the black crust of lungs, tar and poisons in the pink,
And the blood sorting it out, veins tight and the heart slow,
The push and wheeze of it, a sweep of plumes in the air
Like a shako of horses dragging a hearse through the late
  centennium,
London, at the end of December, in the dark and fog.

I broke up with Tom in 1999, over Labor Day weekend. We'd made vague plans to get together on Sunday, but I didn't call. I didn't want to see him. By then, I was so toxic with guilt and shame that I could barely function. Daniel was with Matt, visiting his cousins in Queens. I spent the weekend alone, lying on my bed, watching television and smoking.

I was hiding again, but Tom found me. He walked in my unlocked door, stormed into the living room, and screamed at me for not calling.

I took him all in—his Hawaiian shirt, the flip-flops on his feet, the delicate toes, the bared teeth under his mustache—and something inside me, something hard like a fist, unclenched. I understood everything: his rage at how I'd marginalized him, his grief that we were never going to work, my regret that I'd hurt him so cruelly without meaning to. I understood that we were over.

A week later, just to make sure, I browsed the personals on AOL and picked out the man who would destroy me, as I had destroyed him and Matt.

A few months later, Tom took a job in another state. He left Allentown on my birthday. I called to say good-bye, but he was right, there was nothing to say. I felt that peculiar lightness in my chest that means your sadness is beyond words.

I still feel it when I think of Tom. He deserved better than me, a woman who hid on the floor of his car when we drove through Allentown. I will say this, though: I never smoked in his house.

7:18 p.m.

John is in the kitchen making a snack when I call Daniel. Matt must have known it was me, because my son answers the phone, the usual cartoon sound effects—bing! bang! sproing!—in the background.

"Hello." His voice is small and husky. I'm always surprised by how much younger he sounds on the phone.

"Hi, sweetie. Are you having fun at your dad's?"

"Yup."

"It must be like a vacation, being at your dad's during the week. I'll bet you've been eating pizza and playing video games every night."

"Uh-huh."

I am momentarily out of conversational niblets. Then I think of him hiding in the couch cushions, calling to me. So I take the plunge, I go in looking for him.

"You know why you're not at home right now, right?"

"I am at home. I'm at my dad's."

I wince. "You're right. You have two homes, one here and one at Daddy's. You know why you're home there, though, right?"

"Because you're quitting smoking," he says. I explained this to him on Sunday night, before I drove him over to Matt's, minus the whole in-shackles thing.

"You understand why that's important, right?"

"Because if you don't stop, your heart will turn black and you'll die," he says. My black heart stops for a second, then resumes beating.

"Exactly," I say. "And—and I just want to remind you why you're not here right now. It's because when people stop smoking, they get cranky and I've been really, really cranky. If you were here, you might think I was mad at you, but I wouldn't be. I'd be cranky because I want a cigarette so bad."

"You're always cranky," he points out helpfully.

"Well, I know. I'm sorry about that. I'm not a very patient person. I get very . . ."

". . . frustrated," he finishes for me. How does he know that word? "Like when you yell at people in the car when

you're driving. You stick up your middle finger," he says, savoring his words like gummy worms. I can tell that, to him, the act of raising that digit to heaven is a gesture so glorious that he can just barely conceive of it.

"Right. Frustrated. And when I get frustrated, I'm not mad at you, honey, it's just the way I am. I was frustrated before you were born." I know I'm rowing out to deeper waters than he can swim in.

"Mom."

"Yes, sweetie?"

"Can I stick up my middle finger when I'm a teenager?"

My eyes fill. He's so much like me. I'm caught between shame and pride.

"Maybe," I tell him. "When you're, like, fifteen. Or maybe fifty. But listen. I don't care all that much about you sticking up your middle finger—I mean, I do, you shouldn't do it. But what I don't want you to do, ever, is smoke. Because it kills you. You're right—it turns your heart black. That's why I'm trying to stop. That's why if I ever catch you with a cigarette, I will make you eat it. Then I will tickle you until you pee your pants and swear that you'll never smoke again."

He roars with laughter; lost him at the word "pee."

"So. If I don't smoke, you can't, either. That's fair, right?"

"Yup."

"Okay. Let me ask you," I say. "Let's say you're in sixth grade. Or fifth grade. Or tomorrow. You're on the playground. One of the big kids offers you a cigarette. What do you say?"

"I'll say, I don't smoke, you stinky teenager." For some reason, Daniel despises any kid over the age of twelve.

"Excellent. And Daniel."

John comes in from the kitchen, puts his snack on the coffee table. A Seinfeld *rerun is on, but the TV is on mute, so I know he can hear me.*

"When you come back to Mommy's house, let's play hide-and-seek. Only this time, can I hide, and you find me? I know you like to hide and have me find you, but sometimes it's fun to be the one who seeks. Okay?"

"Okay."

"I love you, Daniel."

"Love you too," he sings, and we both hang up.

Olly olly oxen free.

I jump from the couch and head for the computer.

"What?" John says, munching hard pretzels and drinking Guinness.

"Nothing." Taking a seat at the computer, I type the phrase into Google and get only a few hits. Of the several admittedly sketchy possible explanations, the best is that the phrase is a little stew of French and German: Allez, allez in kommen frei.

Allez *is the imperative form of the French verb* aller *(to go). In kommen frei is, for reasons not given, a phrase common in old Dutch/German New York, meaning "come in free." In my mind there's only one possible interpretation: Everyone goes free. The game of hide-and-seek is over.*

DAY 5

9:17 a.m.

I woke up wanting a smoke. Three hours later the craving still lurks, a buzzard perched in serene and awful patience. Ignoring it hasn't helped, so now, worrying a link of chain between my fingers, I conjure the Perfect Cigarette to test my resolve.

I sit on my back steps on a sunny Saturday morning at the end of May, the summer spooled out in front of me like a bright wheeling kite. Nearby, someone is frying bacon. Our cherry tree's heavy blossoms adorn the lawn like pink rosettes on a birthday cake. John and Daniel are asleep; this fresh new day is mine alone. I light up, inhale deep. The back of my throat tingles like a sunburned shoulder under a cooling film of Noxema. By some alchemy, the combination of menthol and hazelnut coffee produces the flavor of an After Eight chocolate.

Enjoying my make-believe smoke, I am the kind of happy you are at seven, when you stick your head out the window of a speeding car, open your mouth, and shut your eyes.

Why? Why do I love what makes me sick? My life is a toxic garden—men the silver bells, alcohol and razor blades the cockle shells, my cigarettes the pretty maids all in a row, twenty to a pack. As the song goes, they hurt so good. Pain and pleasure, the yin and yang of addiction; one cannot exist without the other. Nor can I separate one from the other. I must dilute the former with the latter the way a dealer cuts cocaine with talcum powder. For me, refusing pleasure— good food, nice furniture, any creature comfort—bestows a perverse kind of pride.

A memory rises like a low-hanging moon. Before John and I married, my Rodale coworkers threw me a bridal shower—ambushed me in the conference room—and pre-sented me with a gift certificate to a ritzy day spa. The idea was that, as a stressed-out bride-to-be, I should treat myself to some outrageous indulgence, like a rose-petal massage or an almond-milk bath. Although fraught with nerves and fatigue—John and I were organizing the wedding our-selves—I never redeemed that certificate. When I found it months after the wedding, in a pile of papers, I stuffed it way down into the trash can. As coffee grounds stained the pretty rose-hued envelope, I felt a grim satisfaction tinged with sadness.

I am trying to change. Now I take pleasure in spoonfuls, like medicine—a square of chocolate here, a Saturday-afternoon nap there. John eggs me on. In fact, it was he who tempted my inner Puritan to Obsession—the scent, not the noun.

On our first Christmas together, John handed me a slim

box wrapped in thick, expensive gold paper. As I tore it open, my greedy enthusiasm wilted: perfume. I hated perfume. It reminded me of my mother, who is aggressive with her scent—it hits you like a fur-wrapped fist. Out of love, however, I smiled at John, uncapped the heavy egg-shaped bottle, and held it to my nose. A whiff of opium den lavished my nostrils. "Mmmm," I sighed, and rolled my eyes to heaven. John beamed. My show of rapture over, I returned the bottle to its box. When we took down the tree, I retired it to the cabinet above the toilet.

One night a few months later, I stepped out of a bath, feeling ungainly. I'd recently quit using the injectable contraceptive Depo-Provera—the Shot, it's called. My hormones had gone haywire and I'd gained almost ten pounds. My misery knew no bounds; my inflated breasts and hips horrified me. Dripping on my bath mat, a towel wrapped around my thickened body, in need of a comfort that a cigarette could not provide, I remembered the Obsession.

I opened the cabinet and removed the bottle. Uncapped it, shy as a bride. The liquid was the color of the cognac I'd sipped alone in chilly apartments twenty years before. Cognac was my winter spirit; it warmed like a Dickensian fire. Now, all I had was perfume.

I hesitated, then misted the air and stepped into the fine spray. Its scent, so different from smoke, was a veil of silk that floated lazily, like a feather from the ceiling, to rest softly on my shoulders. I smiled in delight, my hips forgotten. A rainbow shimmered in my chest. For a few seconds I was drunk again, reeling from orange blossom and sandalwood, *vanilla and spice. At the time, I didn't know the word's Latin etymology—per, meaning through, fumar to smoke.*

My mother stocks her bathroom with enough perfumes and fragranced soaps and lotions and bubble bath to scent a harem. Hawaiian ginger mingles with eucalyptus, rose and lemon and lavender glycerin soaps glow like stained glass. I used to sneer; my mother's perfumery didn't change the fact that life was harsh and comfort an illusion. Now I understand her will to pleasure: Like faith, it allows you to go on. And I know that, no matter how seductive, a cigarette is to pleasure as a slap is to love.

A Marlboro Red perched on his pillowy lower lip, Rick leans back on his bar stool to check me out.

"Gorgeous." His tobacco-colored eyes smile into mine.

Rick is gorgeous too—tall and slender, with a full head of black hair. Not pretty-boy gorgeous. Pickup-truck gorgeous. He has that blue-collar allure, the look of a man who can fix a transmission and bag a six-point buck. His long nose could have been broken in a bar fight. A goatee covers his weak chin—his only flaw—like an unconvincing lie. It's his eyes that capture me, though. His tobacco-colored eyes.

When I stumbled across his photo on Love@aol.com a week ago—at three in the morning, I can't sleep when I'm between relationships—I thought he'd make a perfect Mr. Right Now. He'd keep me away from Tom, who is still pleading with me to come back three weeks after our breakup. I don't want to; I'm still hemorrhaging inside. Resuming our relationship would kill me. But I am fragile and Tom persuasive. I emailed Rick before I could change my mind, attaching a photo.

Now, in the bar's cool pleasant darkness, among the crush of young men sipping dollar drafts and plying pretty girls with frothy drinks, I am falling in love. So much for Mr. Right Now.

Rick orders another lager—his fifth; I'm counting. The bartender slams a mug in front of him. Rick drains half in one pull, then reaches for his pack. He lights up like a cowboy at a campfire: head cocked, one hand cupped protectively around his flame, squinting against the smoke. Rick smokes even more than I do. He smokes like the devil. I reach for my pack, and he's right there with his lighter.

"I didn't think you'd answer my email," I yell over the AC/DC on the jukebox.

"Why not?"

"I'm five years older than you. I have a three-year-old. I thought for sure one of those would scare you off."

"I don't scare easy." He waggles his heavy eyebrows at me. He could charm a batch of homemade cookies from a church lady, yet I sense darkness in him. I want to swan-dive into it.

"So you're a writer," he says. "I'm impressed." His eyes look like they've just been stirred. "What do you write?"

"Well, I just coauthored a book on sex and relationships for women."

"A sex book for women, huh?" He grins.

"And relationships." I'm sliding like a house on a rain-soaked hillside. He is definitely coming home with me tonight.

He complains bitterly about his job—he installs and repairs heating and ventilation systems. After promising him a promotion, his boss gave it to a colleague. "Shafted me, basically," he says, draining his beer and signaling for another. "I am so out of there." His long, slender fingers *tap-tap-tap* the bar's polished surface. His hands haven't stopped moving since he walked in.

He hunts deer and wild turkey. He carries a handgun in the glove compartment of his pickup. "A Ruger," he says proudly.

"Wow." I've never met a man who owned a firearm. "Why?"

"Why a Ruger?"

"No, why a gun?"

"For protection."

I want to ask, "From what?" but I just say, "Oh," torn between admiration and alarm.

He voted for Ross Perot in the 1992 election.

"Oh, come on, not Ross Perot," I say. "Not fucking Ross Perot." It's a red flag, but I forgive him. At this point, I'd forgive him anything.

He's just broken up with his girlfriend. This I can relate to. We talk about what has happened to us, what we've done. Our confessions bring us closer. I tell him I'm putting the mistakes of the past behind me. He says he wants to do that, too, and I believe him.

Rick's out of cigarettes. "Time to hit the machine." He gestures toward the bar's front entrance. "Need a pack?"

I check my supply—eight left, a gas gauge on E. "Whatever brand of menthol they have." I reach for my purse.

"Nope. On me." His smile is like a dare. He has drunk at least six beers and his eyes are still as bright as polished stones. He has that look in his eye, though. That falling look that tells me I have him. He has me too.

Which is why, when he returns bearing cigarettes, I tell him about Daniel. How funny my boy is, how sweet. That he is the most important thing in my life. That after all Daniel has been through, he needs stability and I won't introduce him to a man unless he plans to stick around. It's too soon for this, but I need to say it out loud.

Rick grins. "I love kids," he says. "A lot of my girl-friends had them."

"A cigarette is the perfect type of a perfect pleasure," observed Lord Henry Wotton, the witty hedonist in *The Picture of Dorian Gray*. "It is exquisite, and it leaves one unsatisfied. What more can one want?"

I wanted Rick, cigarette-pale and Virginia Slims-long, my attenuated object of desire. Our turbulent two-year relationship, bookended by chaos, began three months before Y2K and ended three months before 9/11. Rick was the father who had abandoned me, penance for destroying my marriage, the embodiment of my alcoholism; in him, I recognized a kindred, self-destructive spirit. Together, we symbolized the volcanic force of addiction, he in his active phase, I in my dormancy.

Rick grew up poor and wild in Indiana, a high-school football hero who'd sliced through the cheerleading squad like a combine through a cornfield. He had refused a scholarship to a prestigious university to stay in his hometown, taking and quitting menial jobs and raising hell. Charming and manipulative, he danced from woman to woman like a flame and consumed them, leaving only cinders behind. Eventually, his job-hopping led him to Allentown.

Rick had wanted to be an architect, and throughout our relationship obsessed about his dream house: an A-frame in the woods, furnished with the best of everything and so private he could, as he said, piss off the front porch. I longed to live with him in that airy, sun-washed place. Swamped by his dark allure, hooked on our intense sex and his occasional moments of tenderness, I tried to follow him into that dream. It nearly killed me.

Like nicotine, Rick acted on me fast—made me dizzy, like the first cigarette after a three-hour flight or a bout of the flu. I ached for his kiss, his touch. By the time I discovered his past, packed with black deeds, I was hooked with a desperation that bordered on, and occasionally crossed into, insanity. I thought, he'll never do those things to me. Just like a two-pack-a-day smoker thinks: Cancer? It will never happen to me.

But I did get cancer. Cancer moved his possessions into my house and slid an engagement ring on my finger.

A toxic relationship sweeps over you like floodwater, only the water never recedes. After the honeymoon period,

Rick turned cold and controlling. Desperate to please him, I handed over my life, and my son's, like a set of car keys and let him drive. He said movie theaters were dirty; we didn't go to movies. He refused to wear condoms, I went on Depo-Provera—the Pill was out, I was over thirty-five and smoked. He wanted to spend Easter Sunday at a shooting range, that's where we went. I told my mother, who had invited us for ham in Jersey, that we had other plans. Wisely, she didn't ask what. But standing beside him on that bleak April morning, watching him squeeze off rounds into a target tacked to a hay bale, I thought, *This is not right.*

Longtime smokers know the feeling of lighting up, hoping in vain to recapture the pleasure of those early satisfying smokes. Rick inspired in me that same frustrating, ungratified hunger. Frantic for his affection and attention, I clung to him; he called me a nagging bitch, and I believed him. We cycled rapidly: explosion, reconciliation, a day of sweetness and mind-blowing sex, explosion. I could not imagine life without him. I fantasized that he would die so that I could escape him. I don't know why he didn't leave. Maybe he loved me in his way; maybe the thought of leaving scared him too.

Life became a haze of work, smoke, and battle. After I put Daniel to bed, we'd sit at the kitchen table, smoking, me pleading for him to understand why I couldn't move back to Indiana with him as he wished. These were half-a-pack fights, at least, and our cigarettes more eloquent than our words. We brandished them angrily, blasted smoke in each other's faces, ground them out in disgust.

"Don't you get it? I can't take Daniel away from his father," I'd shout, lighting my fifth cigarette that hour, my lungs screaming for mercy.

"Don't give me that," he'd sneer, misunderstanding me. "You could if you wanted to. Take Matt to court. Women always get the kids."

Eventually, my desperation fermented into a rage that swirled around me like our commingled smoke. He never extended himself to Daniel, would have me consider his needs before my son's, never offered me attention outside of bed. I suspected other women. Long after I'd gone to bed, the bright chirp! of AOL's Instant Messenger function sounded from the third floor, where we kept the computer.

As our relationship deteriorated, my smoking intensified. Each cigarette was a portable therapist, a suicide hotline, a self-help book I lit instead of read. When our relationship blew apart, cigarettes helped me through it, like relatives at a funeral.

The end came when he wrecked my Saab. He came in late one Friday night, smiling nervously like a husband whose wife has just noticed stripper glitter on his shirt. "I love you, baby," he said, and led me outside to show me the crumpled driver's-side door. I'd paid off my car only three months before. I kept calm until the next day, when he added that he'd canceled the Saab's collision insurance without telling me; he'd wanted to lower our premiums, which had doubled because of his accidents and tickets. My love for him began to burn and curl like paper under a match.

One night a few weeks later, I climbed the stairs to the third floor. Rick hunched over the computer, smoking, ignoring me. I stood beside him, my knees jittering, loving him, fearing him, knowing it was him or me.

I blurted, "I want you out of here," and waited for my house to burst into flames and sink into the earth, like in the horror film *Carrie*. I always believed Rick would be the one to leave, that I'd never be able to let him go. Even after all the tears and screaming fights, actually doing what I'd long contemplated terrified me.

I gave him a week to move out and drove to my parents' house with Daniel, white-knuckling it all the way. When I came home to my empty house, my heart torn away like a shirt pocket, he was gone. I returned my engagement ring to the jewelry store where Rick had purchased it. The jeweler gave me only half of what he'd paid.

Actually, what I'd paid. The morning he bought the ring, he could put only a small portion of its cost on his credit card, which had reached its limit. That afternoon, fluttering his eyelashes, he'd asked if we could put the remainder—$4,000—on my Visa.

I paid for my own engagement ring.

Rick was the Last Cigarette. The one you smoke before you quit forever, the poignancy of its demise and your impending loss filling you with grace. The one that makes you sick to your stomach but tastes so good you don't stop until the filter burns your fingers. The one you love the best. I put Rick in me and I needed him and he sickened me and I loved him and we burned fast and then I sighed and crushed him out.

A few months after Rick moved out, I found a new place to smoke at work. The Bunker was a back entryway into the grand Main Building, where the book division had moved its operations five years before. Designed to impress, all air and sun and soft curving lines, the Main Building boasted lactation rooms for nursing mothers and a large cafeteria that served low-fat, fiber-rich entrées prepared with organic produce. Employees who felt the urge to pray or meditate could visit the kiva, a small, round, determinedly nondenominational room furnished with benches and inspirational books and a dry wishing well into which the spiritually inclined placed coins. I liked to imagine the secular types filching them for cappuccino.

The Bunker connected the Main Building to the customer service department, a small, squat, windowless structure as dark and industrious as an ant colony. Dubbed the Bunker because the entrance was hidden by a short concrete tunnel, it was the perfect place to smoke. Before, I'd had to trek through the Main Building to get to the customer service department, and smoke outside the door that led to the parking lot. Smoking in the Bunker was more efficient. I simply exited through the main entrance, crossed a short parking lot, and lit up, hidden behind a protective shell of concrete.

The Bunker was also my thinking place, and I had a lot to think about. Rodale was changing. We were hearing rumors about a "new direction." Consultants strolled the carpeted halls, asking questions. I watched from the sidelines with interest. By 2001, I'd started to feel like I was writing the same book over and over. Eat more fiber, walk every night after dinner, melt your stress in hot water and scented bubbles. Everything I wrote was designed to relieve this or soothe that, but there was no relief for what I had, no supplement or herb to blot out my awareness of my many failures—as a mother, a partner, a writer—that had taken over my mind like weeds in a vacant lot.

2:10 p.m.

I wind the chain over my left hand, loop after loop, the way a boxer wraps his hands before he dons his gloves.

So far today, I have retrieved and opened the mail. Cleaned the kitchen. Called my mother, who didn't answer. Ignored the basket of clean laundry that John carried up from the basement this morning, which sits on the rocker next to the fireplace. Watched TV until I fantasized about emptying a .44-caliber handgun into the picture tube, Elvis-style. One more talk show, and I will strangle myself with my chain.

Time to bother my husband. Picking up my cell phone, I punch in John's work number. He answers on the second ring, in the coffee-achiever voice he reserves for the office.

"Hey, sweetie," I say. "How's it going?"

"Hi, hon. I can't talk. I'm about to go into a production meeting."

"I'm just calling to let you know I'm bored."

"Are you wanting a cigarette?"

"Not right this second. I did have a few weak moments

today, probably because I have nothing to do. When you smoke, you can always light up."

"Did you fold the laundry?"

"That will burn five minutes. Maybe ten, if I fold really slow."

"Well . . ." He is helpless. "Just hang in there. You'll get through. Hon, I'm sorry but I have to go. See you around six." Click.

Shit. I clickety-click-click over to the basket of laundry, upend it onto the coffee table, and start sorting.

My body has broken nicotine's spell. My mood has stopped spinning like a pinwheel in the wind; the fog in my brain has burned off. But the buzzard is still perched in the tree. I miss my cigarettes, the solid feel of a new pack in my hand, the rasp of my lighter's flywheel, the disreputable odor of smoke. The party is over. I think of a baseball field, of an old man snapping off the thousand-watt flood-lights after a night game, section by section—thwunk! thwunk! thwunk! Such terrible finality. When I stopped drinking, my desire for alcohol switched off like a radio. That won't happen with smoking. Though I despise ciga-rettes, I'll mourn them forever. Enjoy, in memory, that Per-fect Cigarette.

Smoking used to make me feel so good. Like this dream I had once. In it, I flew above a great mysterious city; employing the peculiar logic of dreams, I recognized it as Moscow. Though it was after midnight, people thronged the narrow cobbled streets, wandering through an open-air bazaar. I streaked high above the crowd, legs together, arms tight to my sides, a graceful purposeful arrow seeking a tar-

get. Below me, the onion domes of the city's cathedrals glowed, as if lit by unseen bonfires. Merchants in stalls hawked fruit, jewels, cloth, fish, live chickens for sacrifice. Strange music coiled in my ears, blending with the faint bleating of sheep. Oily perfumes filled my nose. Hanging there in the sky, I trembled, expectant, waiting for my life to change.

Once, smoking made me feel like that dream, fully alive. Once, it turned the world into a carnival at night. A great gaudy moving show unfolding under a canopy of neon, the kind of lighting that makes everyone look like they've eaten bad clams. Cigarettes were the whirring generators that kept the whole spectacle moving like a line of spinning plates. To light a cigarette was to strap myself into my ride: my life, only bigger, brighter, better. In this carousel of light and sound, the hissing void closed. Grief whirled away too fast to feel it. I lost myself on that glittering midway. My life in smoke was as beautiful as the neon-lit Ferris wheel, sus-pended in its ocean of night like a luminous neon jellyfish. I never wanted that life to end.

But the carnival moved on, its night promises broken, and you can no more hold on to a cigarette's pleasure than cage air. Such sublimity, such treachery: What one cigarette bestows the next will undo. Smoking is punishment and reward, abuser and best friend, venom and medicine.

I snap a pair of John's jeans to release the wrinkles. Something he said when we first started dating floats into my head. Newly in love, walking hand in hand by Blue Marsh Lake, we shared what we wanted from life. He said, "I just want to matter to someone." I've never forgotten this plaintive, plainly stated desire for love, because it was all I ever wanted too. I just never knew it.

I think of my family and Daniel and John and Matt, the wobbly circle of love we've drawn together. Life is the drive to connect. To trace other people's hearts like routes on a map, to let them trace yours, to lead one another to where you began and where you want to go. To make these perilous journeys with the road singing under your wheels. My smoking was a missed exit, the Lockup the culmination of my life in smoke. The chain has told me the rattling, ringing truth.

Many religions honor the purifying power of smoke. It moves only upward, a symbol of our hunger to reach heaven, or communicate with the beings who reside there.

Catholic priests swing censers, which emit fragrant veils of smoke that symbolize the prayers of the faithful wafting up to God. Vedic Hindus worship red, two-faced Agni, the smoke-bannered god of fire—"He waves the red smoke that he lifts above him, striving to reach the heavens with radiant luster." The Vikings placed their slain warriors on flaming longboats. The souls of these dead heroes streamed toward Valhalla, Hall of the Slain, to feast and fight and drink for all eternity.

Holy smoke, indeed. Even the sulfurous smoke from hell streams up.

To Native Americans, tobacco was sacred, a gift from and a conduit to the gods. Its smoke evinced contact with the supernatural world. All tribal languages have a word for tobacco: *asema, chanee, kinnick kinnick, tsalu.* The Iroquois believed its smoke carried their prayers to the Great Spirit. The Hopis equated it with the clouds that delivered rain. The Cherokees used its smoke to divine the future, good or ill according to which way the wind blew the vapor.

Longfellow immortalized the sacred pipe, or *calumet*—peace pipe, in white-man lingo—in his epic poem *The Song of Hiawatha.* Native Americans still practice the pipe ceremony today. While it differs among tribes, it shares common elements and meanings. The pipe is a portable altar, and the tobacco smoke—drawn into the mouth and released, rather than inhaled into the lungs—facilitates prayer. In a typical ceremony, the bowl of the pipe is filled with tobacco with the left hand, which is closest to the heart, and lit. A puff of smoke is offered to the Great Spirit, Mother Earth, and each of the four directions—north, south, east, and west. When the smoke is drawn through the stem, the breath of the Great Spirit enters the body. The smoke drifting from the bowl is the breath of prayer.

To consume conflagrant toxin, passing it through the cooling chambers of the lungs and mouth, and discharging it again, is a most personal offering. A way to demonstrate one's devotion to one's gods, or demons, beyond all doubt.

I plunk Daniel in his car seat and tuck Miko, his stuffed raccoon, into his hands. Planting a kiss on his forehead, I slam the passenger door of my new Jetta and settle in the driver's seat. "We're going to Mom-Mom and Pop-Pop's," I say over my shoulder, and turn left out of the day-care parking lot.

Rodale is on summer hours—it's Friday, just past noon. We're supposed to work until two, but I want to beat the traffic. To get to my parents' house I have to drive one hour on the highway and to do that I must take a Xanax. Which I did, fifteen minutes ago. I am afraid, but there is no man in my life to take the wheel.

It's been thirty-two days since Rick left. I'm counting. I keep a calendar on the kitchen counter next to the phone. Every morning, I cross out the day with a thick Sharpie marker. That big black X is my life. Rick is gone. I want to blow up the world, but I have to take care of Daniel. During the day I try to work. After work I take Daniel to the park for ice cream, we play Don't Break the Ice and Don't Spill the Beans and I smoke myself into a state of temporary sanity.

I am up to two packs a day. I can't eat and have lost ten pounds. To burn off my stress and rage I run an hour a day, six days a week, and smoke until it hurts to draw breath. My throat is raw and my eyes swell and my stomach fizzes like peroxide on a cut. I run to the toilet and heave, my eyes open, but nothing comes up. When I'm done I light another cigarette, but I'm too sick to smoke it so I hold it, just hold it.

Two hours later, I pull into my parents' driveway next to the Saab, which I sold to my father for eighteen hundred dollars the week after Rick left. He still hasn't fixed the crumpled door. My head tightens with rage. That bastard

Rick. That car cost me four hundred dollars a month for five years. I pay it off and he wrecks it. Crashes my car, my whole fucking life.

My parents and their German shepherd, Rocky, burst out of the house and down the steps. "Daniel!" my father cheers through the window, and my son whoops with delight. As I release him from his car seat, my father picks him up and swings him in happy circles.

"You look terrible," says my mother.

"Thanks, Mom."

"How much are you smoking?"

"A pack a day." She doesn't need to know the truth.

"Jesus Christ. You've got to quit. You have Daniel now."

"I know, Mom. I will."

"When?"

"When I'm ready."

"When will that be?"

"Please. Just. *Stop.*"

But I know I'm off the hook for tonight. When I'm home, we fight on Saturday mornings.

I'm the last one up, as usual. Pouring a cup of coffee, I glance out the kitchen window. Daniel holds a hose, my father guiding his hands. They are watering his gorgeous garden and occasionally spraying Rocky, who bounds around them. My father bends and places his mouth to Daniel's ear, his huge hand cupping my son's shoulder. Age has mellowed him. Not once have I seen him jab his fork into Daniel's arm to silence his chewing. Not once has he told me that only a loser would pine for Rick the Hick, as he calls my ex.

Fishing my cigarettes from my purse on the kitchen counter, I take my coffee outside. My mother sits on the bench right outside the back door, already frazzled and glowy from the heat, watching Daniel and my father at play.

"Morning." I take a seat on the steps across from her. The warm breeze caresses my bare arms; I smell the tomatoes in the garden. The sun filters through the fat green leaves of the huge old maple. My parents' house is a peaceful, welcoming place to fight.

I light up, close my eyes, knowing what's to come.

"Do you need to smoke the minute you roll out of bed?"

"Mom."

"It's ridiculous."

"*Mom.*"

"No," she continues, ignoring me. "I'm your mother and I have a right to say what I think. You've got Daniel to think of now. You *must* quit smoking. When are you going to quit?"

"I don't know, Mom."

"When?"

I feel a *ping!* in my head. It's finally happened. My brain has thrown a rod.

"Get off my back," I snarl. "My life is a fucking nightmare. How about some compassion? How about asking how I feel?"

"I know how you feel. It's time to get over it."

"Thanks for your support, Mom."

"I'm supporting you by telling you the truth. You and Rick were wrong for each other. You got rid of him. You did the right thing. The strong thing. Suck it up, get over it, move on."

"You don't get it—"

Her brown eyes, ringed with milky gray, sting like a slap. "I get it. You're eating yourself alive over a drunk. A loser. You've always picked losers, but you've always been a fighter. Can't you fight now?"

"Why do you think I smoke, Mom?"

"Why do you?"

"It helps me."

"Helps you what?"

"Endure," I say, after a pause.

"Endure what?"

"Life, Mom. To live my life you need endurance, don't you think?"

"What a bunch of shit."

"Mom, I haven't had a drink in over ten years. Isn't that enough? Must I give up everything? Smoking is all I have."

"What do you mean, all you have? You have Daniel. You have your work. You have us—a family who loves you, as imperfect as we are."

"I know, but that's not what I mean." Then I think, *What do I mean?*

"So explain it to me."

My throat is a fortress and tears are invading, a hot

charging army. I don't know how to tell her that you pick the comfort that completes you. Some people run marathons; some people drink. Some people meditate; some shoot heroin. And some people smoke. I can't explain why I'm not soothed by yoga or bubble baths or pedicures, the meager rewards I dispense to faceless readers like aspirin. All I know is that when I smoke the world dissolves for five minutes and I need those five minutes, will risk my life for them. My mother's voice fills the crater of silence between us.

"Julia, I want to comfort you. I've always wanted to comfort you. But you've pushed me away since you were a little girl. You were always so deep inside yourself. You seemed so self-contained. I thought, well, maybe she doesn't need me. Still, just in case, I kept trying to reach you, and I never could."

I consider this. Remember scuffing my shoes three feet behind my family on our walks. Her face a half-moon at my door.

"Now you're grown, and you're still pushing me away," she continues. I can't look at her. "There's nothing I can say to comfort you. But let me tell you something: It's not just you anymore. You have a child who needs you. I see how Daniel runs to you at the end of the day. How he holds you when you put him to bed. How his eyes follow you around the room. He needs you, and damn it, you are responsible. Whether you want to or not, whether you think you can or not, you must respond to his needs, and you can't do that if you're dead. You are obligated to live. For him.

"I know you love him, but how much? Enough to live? What's it going to be for you, Julia—live or die? Because you have to choose. You've been working up to this choice for twenty years. You going to choose to smoke? Fine. Smoke yourself to death. But while you're here, fight. And show your son how to fight. Don't push Daniel away like you push me away. You're breaking my heart. Don't break his."

She touches my cheek and goes inside. I watch the plume of smoke from my cigarette spiral lazily into the air.

Live or die.

3:46 p.m.

I have to get away from this chain. This metal leviathan that wants to drag me to the bottom of its black crashing sea.

I rattle to the closet by the stairs and pull on my puffy green coat, the color of a week-old bruise, and the first pair of shoes I see, the L.L. Bean knockoffs with the rubber chain-tread bottoms. Chains everywhere, even on my shoes.

I sweep through the living room like a queen. This chain can't stop me. Nothing can stop me from breathing fresh cold air. I stride through the dining room, through the kitchen, into the mudroom that opens into the backyard, grimly ignoring the racket at my heels.

Looking out the window, I scowl at my bedraggled yard. Leaves from our cherry tree and small grape arbor are everywhere, a wet brown blanket covering our lawn. John raked last weekend, but they just keep falling. The tiny cement patio, the picnic table, and the barbecue grill are strewn with burst grapes, their puckered skins oozing green jelly.

Always, I am the bad neighbor who refuses to mow her lawn until the grass is ankle deep, who lets the crabgrass take over and the molehills multiply. My neighbors are used to my abomination of a yard, wouldn't raise an eyebrow if I put a rusted-out Bonneville on blocks.

Then I met John, who was to the mower born. A month after we met, before the leaves dropped, John walked my small yard like a gentleman farmer. "Next spring, we'll till the yard and replant the grass," he said. We?

In March, he rented a tiller and turned my lawn into a mud pit. He poured grass seed into a manual spreader; it blew through the air like chaff. He watered the mud twice a day and covered it tenderly with straw, to keep it warm.

"It looks horrible," I'd volunteered.

"Be patient, hon," he'd replied. "You're always so impatient."

Just as he promised, the grass sprouted, a timid, tender green. When crabgrass pushed up beside it, John drove to Kmart and returned with spray bottles of poison. He brought his Hedge Hog from home and trimmed my bushes. He ripped away the dead ivy that crawled down the side of my house and over my dining-room windows.

I stood watching him, smoking, shifting my feet. "What can I do?" I asked.

"I got it, hon," he said, and kept working. I fetched him tumblers of diet iced tea.

Another leaf flutters from my cherry tree. That's it. I'm going to rake the yard. Right now.

In my coat and robe, I yank on the mudroom door until it gives way—it sticks in wet weather—and step outside. The chain catches in the hinges. Shit. I lift it and guide it out the door and down the tiny path that divides my lawn from my neighbor's. She might be inside, watching me, but so what? She screams at her three small daughters from morning till night, horrible things I can hear when I put my ear to my living-room wall. I'd say we're equally disturbed.

In the garage, which John has also tidied, the rakes hang neatly on the wall. I remove one from its hook and turn to face my yard.

I start under the cherry tree. The leaves are wet and heavy; raking them into a pile isn't easy. When the tines pierce them they release the pungent smell of decay, rich and spicy, an odor I find oddly comforting, like the smell of one's own sheets. Rudely unearthed, spindly long-legged spiders and ugly bugs the color of iron skitter away like dark thoughts in daylight. Beads of sweat gather between my breasts and trickle down my sternum, but it feels so good to move, to breathe this cold air. This is what it feels like to be normal. I'm just raking my leaves like a good neighbor.

As if on cue, my other neighbor, the Stepford Wife—sweater twin set, Dorothy Hamill haircut, no makeup—pulls open her garage door. She married money and bore two polite children who could model for the Gap. Her propriety is like salt; it draws out my shame. I never could bear for her to see me smoke. I'd be out on my front steps and, hearing her front door open, hastily stub out my cigarette and try to step inside before she saw me. Unfortunately, she

*caught me many times. Their yard is kept up by a lawn ser-
vice. Naturally.*

*She chirps, "Hello!" and waves cheerily. I wave back
and lean casually against my rake to hide the chain. She's
maybe fifteen feet from where I stand, the chain just out of
her field of vision. Oh, God, what if she comes over to the
fence to chat? The thought is horrifying yet amusing, like
picturing an old woman tumbling down a flight of stairs. I
stare down at the leaves as if deep in thought until she takes
off in her SUV.*

*I start raking again, make another pile. A blister blooms
in the web between the thumb and index finger of my right
hand, but I keep at it, my hair in my eyes, my arms burning,
until little piles dot the yard. The Stepford Wife has disturbed my equilibrium; I am no longer raking leaves but my
shame and sadness and fear, emotions I spent years analyz-
ing so I wouldn't have to feel them. But they weigh me
down, like this chain. They're heavier, in fact. This forty
pounds around my ankle is nothing.*

*I was born in chains, condemned to drag my self-hatred
clanking behind me until I work myself free. This task will
take a lifetime. So far, it has involved psych wards and
smut magazines and AA meetings. Now it involves love,
stronger than this chain but no less cumbersome. I think I
am finally strong enough to bear its weight. Which is why
I'm chained to my dining-room radiator. I shackled myself
for love.*

*I fetch our plastic trash bin with the yellow sticker that
reads Yard Waste Only and move from pile to pile, scoop-*

ing each into the can on the tines of my rake. The Novem-
ber light is fading, the sky the color of ash. Stowing the
rake in the garage, I pull the leaf-stuffed bin to the side of
the house, listening to the steady rush of traffic on Ott
Street.

As I start up my pathway, the motion-detector porch
light blinks on. I stop, caught. My blister throbs. Here in
imminent darkness, I feel as soft and shimmery as a summer
memory.

Well-meaning folks are constantly regaling smokers with
stories of someone they know who, after smoking two
packs a day for thirty years, ups and quits, just like that.
They're driving down the highway, puffing away, when they
suddenly throw their cigarette out the window and never
smoke again. Or they pray, and lo and behold, their compulsion to smoke dissolves like a morning dream.

More often, however, smokers struggle—the average
smoker quits five times before kicking the habit for good.
After caving in numerous times, they finally get it: They'll
quit only when they're ready to let go. Successful quitters
are like toddlers who graduate from bottle to cup; quitting
is a natural step in their development. John was my letting
go, the beginning of my break with smoking.

I sensed John's gentleness the first time we met. About a
month after I started seeing Rick, he and John went to a
concert in Philly. On the way home, Rick wanted to intro-

duce his friend to his girlfriend. At one in the morning. I opened the door and Rick only partially obscured the large man behind him. John's mass underscored his quality of permanence. At 300 pounds, standing just under six feet, he was as immutable as a mountain or prime numbers.

Despite his weight, I discerned his classic features; in profile, he looked like a Caesar on a Roman coin. Calm shimmered around him like a gasoline rainbow. He asked for a glass of water and sat on my sofa while Rick and I kissed in the kitchen.

We met again six months before Rick and I split, on a double date. By then, I wondered what a man like John saw in my boastful, obnoxious fiancé. John recently had broken up with his common-law wife, so we fixed him up with my friend Susan. The four of us met at a restaurant and when I saw him, I'm quite sure I gaped. He'd lost at least sixty pounds. Although still husky, he was undeniably hot.

Rick talked to Susan all through dinner. By then, I loathed him and turned my attention to John. We talked about work and music and our kids—he had a twenty-one-year-old daughter named Tiffany. Our conversation warmed me, as if he'd wrapped me in fleece.

I called John the day after my breakup with Rick, sounding like an old See and Say toy whose string got pulled too many times. He listened to me sob for two hours. We kept in touch through the summer, and I slathered myself in the balm of his kindness. By the end of August, when I thought of him, I got that glow in my stomach, like a bellyful of stars, that tells a woman there's potential.

I asked him out then. He agreed once I eased his conscience about dating me—I was his friend's ex-girlfriend, after all. We drove to Gettysburg National Park, where Confederate General Robert E. Lee made his bloody three-day stand against the Union army. John walked me into an empty field and told me the story of Pickett's Charge. How 12,000 Confederates stepped out of the woods behind us and walked in perfect formation straight into enemy cannon. I could not comprehend their bravery, their magnificent hopeless grace. He introduced me to Tiffany, a beautiful girl, quiet like her father, with the same smooth brow and calm eyes. But her mouth was her own, always curved in a Mona Lisa smile.

In the following months, I spent a lot of time in the Bunker searching my charred soul about whether I truly cared for John, or whether he was simply a link to Rick. It took me about 4,000 cigarettes to conclude that I loved him.

John never nagged about my smoking, had accepted it as part of the package. The oldest of six, he'd grown up in smoke, like Matt. Three of his siblings smoked, as did his father. John had never even held a cigarette; like my mother, he ate. But he was bull-strong. On Tuesdays and Thursdays, while Daniel visited his father, John met me at Rodale's gym and we worked out together. His back was river broad, his calves like footballs.

Two months after our first date, John went to Las Vegas for a week with a friend. "Bring me back a tumbleweed," I joked. I'd never seen one, but I liked the way they looked in westerns, their aimless flight driven by whistling prairie

winds. I'd read somewhere that after atomic-weapons test-
ing in Nevada, tumbleweeds were the first plant to regrow
at Ground Zero.

The day he returned, John visited me in Allentown. "I
have a surprise for you," he said, and handed me a wrinkled
grocery bag. I lifted out a tumbleweed, big around as a soccer ball and bird-skeleton fragile.

He'd been driving to Hoover Dam when he saw a whole
field of tumbleweeds bouncing along the side of Highway
93. Parking his rental car on the side of the road, he jumped
a guardrail, skittered down a steep hill of dust and loose red
rock, and ran alongside the tumbleweeds until the wind
stopped long enough for him to catch one. Then he brought
it home to me.

I still have that tumbleweed—it's just dust now. I can't
say I decided to quit smoking the moment I looked inside
that paper bag. What I can say is that when John handed it
to me, he passed a test I didn't even know I'd given. He had
listened to me. He had wanted to make me happy. I felt as
if he'd placed his large cool hand over my sad burning heart
and held it there until it calmed.

Late one Thursday night in September 2001, I wheeled a
huge plastic receptacle, courtesy of the cleaning lady, into
my office. The rumor of layoffs was again sweeping Rodale's
book division, and I was cleaning out my slovenly office—
untouched since I'd moved in—to get a head start on my
imminent unemployment.

I opened my large, three-drawer file cabinet, groaned, and pulled the receptacle closer. It all went: folders stuffed with research from books I'd written, old page proofs, three-year-old business cards from various conferences. My out-of-date nutrition textbook. Old memos and sales figures. Five-year-old magazines. Gone, gone, gone. The job took two hours. I went out for a cigarette twice, boldly lighting up in front of the deserted building.

Before I left, I took down the quote taped to my door— *The American Dream: Life, Liberty, and the Purchase of Happiness*—and turned to examine my office. One box sat on top of my filing cabinet, ready to go out to my car. *Bring it on,* I thought.

As it turned out, the company declined my invitation. Two weeks later, I walked into my office, which still smelled faintly of Formula 409. My phone's message light blinked red. I punched in my code and heard the editorial director's soft voice telling me not to worry. An hour later, human resources called the other staff writers into the conference room and told them their positions had been eliminated. I didn't realize what had happened until my stunned colleagues started to wander the halls, quiet as birds in the rain. Three of us kept our jobs. Fortunately, those let go seemed more relieved than resentful, so our survivors' guilt didn't last long.

That night, I identified the feeling that had lain in my gut all day: disappointment.

"Why didn't they lay me off?" I asked John later as we watched *South Park.* He'd been spending Tuesday and Thursday nights at my house.

"Hon. You kept your job. How can you turn that into a bad thing?"

"The thought of writing another book about weight loss makes me ill. I know I sound ungrateful. I don't mean to. I'm burned out, I guess."

"What about that new book you're supposed to do?" I'd been asked to ghostwrite a big, splashy book for a well-known doctor. The assignment was a new challenge; instead of writing the usual research-heavy, direct-mail tomes, I'd interview one person and write in his voice. I knew I should be flattered: The higher-ups had awarded me a plum assignment and a vote of confidence. But somehow, it didn't seem that way.

I sighed. "I'm slightly excited."

"You can't be slightly excited."

"Yes I can." I pulled my hand from his. "Don't tell me what I can and can't be."

Only than did I realize that I'd wanted to lose my job—had looked forward to it. Not because it was so terrible, but because I'd be forced to attempt what I most desired and most feared: using my own voice, my own words. Writing for me. But now, that wouldn't happen.

"Well, your editors must trust that you'll do a good job," said John, attempting to soothe me. "They're telling you they value you. That should make you feel good."

"I guess."

5:47 p.m.

The inside of my lower lip is bleeding. I didn't even know I'd bitten it until the taste of rusty nail filled my mouth and I ran my tongue over the gash.

Deprived of cigarettes, a smoker must chew. All my life I've gnawed pencils and splintered the tops of pens. Joe, my first therapist, twirled plastic coffee stirrers in his mouth, his tongue a muscular pink acrobat. Kojak, the white man's Shaft, tucked a sucker in his cheek. In the early episodes, he chain-smoked cigarillos. But when Telly Savalas kicked the habit in real life, Kojak hit the lollipops.

I pass my tongue inside my lower lip, fighting the urge to clamp down. Birds fly; monkeys fling feces; smokers chew. But come on. Would a hard-ass like Kojak really be sated with lollipops? When Daniel offers me a Dum-Dum from his stash, I crunch through it like the owl in the old Tootsie Pops commercials who decides it takes three licks to get to the center. It's hard to believe a man who chain-smoked cigars, even skinny ones, had more restraint than I.

Maybe Kojak sucked lollipops because gum didn't work. Maybe, like me, he stuffed five sticks into his mouth at once and chewed all day, unable to stop, until his intestines filled with hard gas. Maybe he chewed his cheek on the way home from the precinct in his Skoal-colored Buick Regal, and when he got there he sat on his couch, his lollipops fanned out in front of him like a losing hand, cursing himself, his weakness, his thin-shelled confections.

I know this much—Kojak never gave a thought to how

he'd ended up on that couch. He never backed Stavros or Crocker into a desk and told them the story of his first cigarette. But he had a story, like me, like anyone who's ever equated smoke with breath. Cops and soccer moms, firemen and middle-aged homemakers, high-school kids and the homeless who look for butts in the gutter, celebrities in Star *magazine, nurses who come to their patients with smoke on their breath. I'd love to hear their stories, fish out every detail.*

I'd ask: Tell me about your first cigarette. Did you sneak it out of your mother's purse? Your father's pack? Did you smoke it alone, or with a friend? Of course you coughed and got nauseous, but did you also know you were falling in love? Did you think yes, this is for me. How long after that did you buy or steal your own pack?

Tell me, when you held that column of paper and smoke and flame, who did you become? A better version of yourself, or someone different? Think in archetypes: the Glamour Girl, the Sophisticate, the Outsider, the Tough Guy. Whoever you were, I know you were lovely. Or elegant, dangerous, untouchable, in control.

Tell me about the cigarette you can't forget. Did you light it outside the door of a one-night stand, after a breakup? On the front steps of a church at a funeral, saying excuse me, excuse me over the knees of weeping family, as I once did? War veterans, tell me about smoking to numb your terror of being blown to bits. Tell me, grandmothers, about puffing Viceroys as you dusted under the doilies on your dresser. Workaholics, what besides the quest for success makes you chain-smoke at your laptop far into the night? Tell me, someone, why we must wind ourselves in ribbons of smoke, as if binding up invisible wounds.

Describe the first time you tried to quit. Did you last an hour? A day? Six months? How long did it take for the voice in your head, the smoker in you, to whisper, Loser. You used to smoke and drink and dance all night. You used to discuss the meaning of life. *Now you pay your bills on time and fall asleep before* Saturday Night Live. Smoke, you loser. Shut the fuck up and smoke and die without a word of complaint.

Perhaps you quit after all. Did you cherish your last cigarette? Revile it? Did you smoke only half, or down to the bitter filter? Does its memory hang in your head, crowned in light like a painting at the Louvre, tempting you?

Tell me what I need to hear: that the most beautiful moments in life are those in which you do the thing you believe you cannot. That in those moments of struggle you can be born again. That you become the person you were meant to be, authentic, perfectly yourself, and that the air you breathe belongs to you, free and clear.

John steps through the front door. I bound from the couch, rattling like change in a tin cup, and kiss his cold cheek. My lip throbs.

"*Did you make dinner?*"

"*I'm sorry. I got busy.*" *I sit on the coffee table and extend my ankle. John drops to one knee and twiddles the lock.* "*Doing what?*" *he asks as the chain drops like a guillotine blade.*

"*Just thinking,*" *I say, dragging the chain into its corner.*

"*Couldn't you think and cook at the same time?*"

"*I'm sorry. We can make pasta. That's quick.*" He follows me and we begin our dinner pas de deux, moving across the stage of our kitchen—refrigerator to pantry, pantry to cabinets, cabinets to stove.

"*What happened to your lip?*" He touches the gash with his index finger.

"*A misguided attempt at oral gratification. When Lockup ends, I'm buying a pacifier.*"

"*I hope you're joking.*" He opens the refrigerator and removes the hunk of Parmesan, the giant jar of Prego.

"*Nope. As Malcolm X said, by any means necessary.*" I place our battered pasta pot in the sink and fill it with hot water. With my back to him I can ask the question that's been gathering at the back of my mind all week—actually, for months now.

"*Has it ever occurred to you that you eat like I smoke?*" I ask, placing the pot on the burner. He's regained about thirty pounds since we've been together.

John sighs and leans against the kitchen table.

"*It's the same thing. Smoking and eating.*" I turn to face him. He's staring into the dining room.

"*I hadn't thought about it.*"

"*Well . . . maybe you could.*" I gather our plates and silverware, set the table.

"*Hon. I don't think about things like that. I've been heavy most of my life. I've accepted it. You just go ahead and connect your dots and leave me out of it.*"

"*Sweetie, I'm not trying to hurt you. I'm just saying.*"

"*Well, stop saying.*"

"*Okay.*" I wait for our silence to warm again.

Day 5

The water is just about boiling. John moves toward the stove; the actual cooking is his domain. He reaches for the box of pasta.

"How much do you want?"

"None for me. I'm having a Healthy Choice."

"For crying out loud," John mutters.

"I know."

DAY 6

9:17 a.m.

John was called into the plant at 6:30 this morning to start up some new machinery, leaving me to shackle myself. I marveled at his trust until I realized that he'd taken the keys to the Sebring, stranding me at home. Perhaps to atone for his treachery, he brewed me coffee before he left. As I sip my second cup, my cell rings.

"Where were you? I thought maybe you'd hung yourself with that goddamn chain." It's my mother.

"Har har. My skin looks too good. You should see me. I look ten years younger. Okay, five."

"Are the little puffs under your eyes gone?"

"Yep. My laugh lines are better too. They're definitely not as deep." She squeals happily. The younger I look, the younger she can pretend she is. She loves it when we talk skin and makeup like college girls.

Then her voice thickens with suspicion. "Are you still wearing that white lipstick?"

"It's not white, Mom. It's pink."

"*Well, it's awful. You should wear a darker shade.*"

"*I've told you a million times, Mom. Dark lipstick makes the lines around my mouth more noticeable. It makes me look like a basset hound.*"

"*Don't be ridiculous. They're little folds, they're nothing. I had them when I was thin.*"

"*So you've said. Thanks for passing them on.*"

"*Next time you come home, we'll go to Boscov's and I'll find you a lipstick you'll love.*"

My mother is a cosmetics-counter bully who pressures me into buying twenty-dollar lipsticks with names like Brown as a Berry or Mohave Desert. I try them on as the Estée Lauder or Lancôme ladies beam lipsticky smiles of approval. Cosmetics-counter strumpets. Like politicians running for reelection, they'll tell you anything you want to hear. Back in my parents' gray minivan, I slide open the mirror on the passenger's-seat visor, pull up my drooping cheeks with my fingertips, scowl as they fall. Then I wipe off the new couleur or rouge—that's French for pricey lipstick—on my palm, slip the new tube into my mother's purse, and reapply my pink (white?) lipstick.

"*Mom. Why should it matter to you what color lipstick I wear? Does it reflect on you in some way?*"

"*I'm not saying you have to wear red. L'Oréal has some beautiful neutrals. Rose, mauve . . . When are you coming down? We'll pick it out together. You'll love it. You'll see.*"

"*Mom, if we continue this line of conversation I will be forced to shoot you in the head.*"

"*Okay, okay. Don't get mad.*"

"*I'm not. Just keep your makeup tips to yourself. Or send them to* Allure *magazine. Okay?*"

Silence. One, two, three . . .

"*Anyway,*" *my mother says, her tone a tuft of pink cotton candy.* "*When does Daniel come home?*"

It's time to bail. I'm not getting into Matt's filthy apartment and the cat shit with her again.

"*Listen, my landline is ringing. It might be work. I'll call you tonight, okay? Love you. Bye.*"

I close my eyes. Breathe in through the nose, out through pursed lips, imagine Mom as a yipping Chihuahua in a sequined sweater. Reaching into my purse for my compact, I hold its tiny mirror to the crease on my left cheek that runs like a trough from my nose to my mouth. There's one just like it on the other side. My lines. Her lines. Maybe she's right about the lipstick. I don't know. Why don't I know? How is it possible that I still get tangled in her like a crab in a net? Damn her. After forty years, I should know my own face.

I sure know hers. As a girl I divined it each morning like a shaman casting bones, decoding the configuration of her mouth and eyes: Who is she today? I still read her face— everyone's face—for clues on how and who I should be. My identity is a house of cards, always one trembling second from collapse; I've learned to hold my breath. Still, I often feel vaporous, adrift. Like smoke. Cigarettes are something to hold on to. Were.

In some sense, I wasn't born the day I slid from my mother's body. I gestated in rooms of smoke and gasped my first breath the moment I lit that first cigarette.

Actually, even before that. How old was I when I decided

that smoking made you a grown-up, free to live your own life, to make your own luck? That when you lit up, glittery stage sets were pushed into place around you and suddenly you were shaking your booty on a strobe-lit dance floor? In the magazines I paged through at home, the pediatrician's office, the school library, smokers were portrayed as Somebodies, every woman a starlet, every man a finger-snapping stud. Of course, I could never be one of those kicky Virginia Slims women, who wore haute couture and self-assured smiles. I felt more affinity with the Marlboro Man.

I haven't thought about him for years (ever, really), but now I see him galloping through sunlit grassy plains, blue-veined mountains, snow-crushed landscapes. In my memory, he doesn't have a face. He doesn't need one. It's enough to see the brim of his Stetson, the tip of his cigarette, one raw, chapped palm curled protectively around a match. He was me. I was him. I followed him into paper-and-ink vistas and rode behind him, my arms around his waist, into blood-orange sunsets.

I was a child, but I knew that he grieved, like me. That if he met me, he would accept me as a kindred spirit. I'd help him brush his horses, clean the clotted muck from the crevices in their hooves, wrestle syrup-eyed calves to the dirt. I understood, too, that Marlboro Country was not a place, but a state of being. For me, those open spaces didn't suggest an America lost or quickly vanishing, but the possibility that I, lost and quickly vanishing, might find my way there and, like my melancholy cowboy, live as an outsider, proud and stoic and alone.

Alone.

My God. I believed in Marlboro Country. Me. The woman who discusses the subtext of cereal ads on Nickelodeon with my son and fantasizes about blowing up Wal-Mart. Those atmospheric landscapes burrowed into my brain like pinworm larvae and hibernated until the day I entered that liquor store in D.C. and pointed to a pack of Benson & Hedges Menthol Lights 100s. (Even my love for the Marlboro Man could not dissuade me from my taste for mentholated cigarettes.) That pack gave me the only sense of myself I could feel, an identity I could see, taste, hold in my hand.

The writer Ambrose Bierce described opiates as "an unlocked door in the prison of identity. It leads into the jail yard." I could say the same for cigarettes. Only in my case, the door led to Home Depot and seventy-two feet of chain.

I quit smoking in January 2002, four months after my first date with John. Like my pregnancy with Daniel, this quit was unplanned, ostensibly accidental. Upon reflection, however, I think I'd been preparing for months. The chaos of my past was receding and, cautiously optimistic about my future, I had begun to entertain the possibility that I might, maybe, possibly, some day quit. John and I were already discussing marriage; he loved Daniel, played with him, disciplined him. He even took Daniel, along with his sixty-year-old father, John Senior, to a World Wrestling Entertainment show in Philadelphia, an event from which I was blessedly excused. Even Matt felt comfortable around

John. In one of those surreal arrangements that make sense only to commingled families, my ex-husband came to my house on Christmas Day to watch Daniel open his gifts and eat prime rib two seats away from my almost-fiancé. My happiness made me feel softer, rounder, as if I'd gained needed weight.

To spare my nerves and my son, I decided to quit on a Daniel-free weekend. That Friday night, John and I did what we often did when Daniel stayed with Matt: We worked out at Rodale's gym, then spent the weekend at his place, an hour southwest of Allentown.

At some point during the drive, I pulled out my Basics and lit up, holding my cigarette out my window, open only a sliver to keep out the cold. The pack was almost at the end of its life; mashed nearly flat by my wallet and keys and checkbook, it held just two bent cigarettes. Normally, I would have asked John to stop at the next convenience store or gas station so I could stock up for the weekend. Instead I sat silently as we sped by one, then another. Dread smoldered in my bones.

Then I remembered the nicotine patch in my purse.

I always kept my patches on my kitchen counter where I could see them and pick at my smokers' guilt like a ragged cuticle. For some reason, however, I'd stuck a patch in one of my purse's zippered compartments, the way a teenage boy keeps a condom in his wallet, just in case. I dug it out and studied it. In the glare of oncoming headlights, I saw that its child-resistant sheath was scuffed, its edges frayed. I tried to imagine it coming between me and my desire. It seemed unequal to the task.

I decided to make those two cigarettes last the night, until John and I made love and went to sleep, and slap on the patch in the morning. When I woke up, I peeled the patch—which smelled vaguely minty, like an old woman's liniment—from its shiny protective backing and pressed it onto my right upper arm. That night I bought a two-week supply. On Sunday morning, I pasted one on my left arm and went from there.

For eight months, I hardly missed smoking, mostly because I enjoyed the fuss people made when I told them I'd quit. People cheered as if I were an astronaut in a ticker-tape parade. I waved away the praise with false modesty, hiding my doubts, praying that I wouldn't have to appear, cigarette in hand, in front of those same people in the not-so-distant future.

As the months passed, my anxiety dissolved, like a Sucrets on the tongue. No longer did I light up and wonder if *this* was the cigarette that would give me cancer. I could look my son in the eye again. I felt more like June Cleaver and less like a crack addict.

As a stroke victim relearns the simplest actions of life—to speak, walk, brush his teeth—I learned to drink my Diet Pepsi and coffee, work, end a meal, make or receive phone calls, lie in bed after sex without a cigarette in my hand. To distract myself from the intense emotions that accompanied life without nicotine, I invented a game of describing how they felt without the anesthesia of smoke. Anger was being unable to reach orgasm; loneliness, a boulder rolling across the mouth of a tomb. Tears made me a virgin bride, shy and undressed. The game allowed me to connect the first few dots of an internal picture of myself that didn't include a white cylinder in the foreground.

The game also marked my first attempt to find my writer's voice. I played it a lot at work, where my craving for a cigarette was strongest. I'd come to dread my job. Since the layoff, I'd had little to do, and the book I was ghostwriting didn't change that. I adored the doctor—I'd affectionately dubbed him Donahue M.D., an homage to his considerable charisma—but he constantly missed his deadlines. He'd call me while running through airports, en route to medical conferences, telling me that he'd get to the copy I'd emailed him tomorrow—two days, max. The slow pace of our work maddened me. Sometimes, I had to bite my arm when I talked to him on the phone. Once, after a late-night phone conversation with him in my office, I roared with frustration and pounded my desk. Five minutes later, the puzzled VP of publishing, who'd also been working late, knocked on my door. "Everything okay in here?" she asked.

Good ghostwriters must forfeit their own voices; they're a bit like submarines, descending into the head and heart of a stranger for the duration of a project. But silencing my voice made it unruly. It wouldn't shut up about its desire to write books that didn't involve diet and exercise. I still questioned my talent, but as the months crawled by, desperation eclipsed my doubts. The editorial and marketing departments had begun an ongoing debate about their vision for Donahue M.D.'s book. Each time it changed, I had to rewrite Chapter One.

A smoking woman is a hungry woman, using nicotine to blunt appetites that she believes are too frightening or subversive to feed. I'd used smoking as a choke chain to train my desires, those snapping Dobermans, to heel. Now they could breathe. At night, I lay next to John, unable to sleep. Awakened from my tobacco coma, I felt like an adolescent again, urgent, flushed, hormonal, the hot wet breath of longing in my ear. Staring at the ceiling, I felt my heart pound desire's cadence: *I want. I want. I want.* It was a start.

The day I quit, I was in the best physical shape of my life—115 pounds, 15 percent body fat. I had Rick to thank. During our breakup, I'd lived on cigarettes and Diet Pepsi, dropped ten pounds, and channeled my anguish into a workout regimen that rivaled marathon training. Six days a week, I hit the Rodale gym for an hour of hard running on the treadmill. Afterward, I staggered across the polished wood floor to lift free weights, which hardened the skin on my palms just below my fingers and exuded the comforting smell of sweat on metal. I exercised ninety minutes minimum, while smoking up to two packs a day.

Even after I fell in love with John, I kept up this punishing routine. Pushing my body to its limits made me feel impenetrable, like dense jungle undergrowth. Nothing could get through, Rick and all my other enemies would tangle and die in thick knots of liana and strangler figs. Two months after my last cigarette, I hadn't gained an ounce. I gloated.

January passed into February. I wore my gauntness like

a flashy cocktail ring, stripped to muscle and bone, proud that I was always cold. In the morning before I got out of bed, I ran my fingers down my sides, traversing the sharp ridge of ribs, the jutting hipbones.

At the Rodale gym, I changed into show-offy Spandex and headed for the row of treadmills that faced a mirrored wall. As I ran, my elbows bent at my sides, my eyes began their tour of me. They slid over my shoulders, cut from endless sets of military presses, to the cords of blue vein over my biceps—small, female, but dense from lifting thirty-pound weights. *See Julia run.* Though the flat bricks of my abdominal muscles were below the mirror, I felt them flex above my hips, my strong legs. As my feet pounded the treadmill deck, I chanted my spiteful mantra to Rick, to the rhythm of my wind: *Every step is one step farther from you.*

I ran until my heart threatened to burst, then stepped into the shower on trembling legs, my head as silent as deep space. I had conquered my body.

Then I went off Depo-Provera.

I received my last shot in December 2001. My next was scheduled for mid-March 2002. I skipped it. Luck had taken me this far.

A week later, I was sure I was pregnant. My breasts doubled in size and fairly steamed, as hot as baked potatoes. My nipples hurt so badly I cried; I had to shower with my back to the spray. After two weeks, I couldn't zip my size-five jeans. In three weeks, I developed an uncharacteristic craving for sugar. Not chocolate. Not ice cream or cake or pie. Domino light brown sugar, soft and pliable as a breast in its polyurethane bag. For weeks, baffled, I spooned it right out of the bag, sucking the grains until they liquefied on my tongue.

Depo defies the guiding principle of weight management: Calories In, Calories Out. No calories in; except for brown sugar, I had virtually stopped eating. Hundreds of calories out as I continued to run and lift in a desperate bid to stop the gain. Still, I put on a half-pound or more a week. My body had gone haywire, had been breached like the walls of an ancient city, and the loss of control terrified me.

By the end of the summer, I'd gained twelve pounds and weighed more than I ever had in my life. I stopped going to the gym. Fuck it. I was fat, and I was going to stay fat.

John and I began to have fat fights. "Look at this," I'd cry, grabbing my waist in my two hands, shaking it at him in frustration.

John sighed and drew me against his chest. "Hon, you were too skinny before. I like your body better now. I love your ass."

"Which means that my ass has gotten fatter."

"No, it has not," he said with Christian patience. "You're built like a woman now. You're soft. You have curves."

"I don't want to be soft. I don't want curves." To be soft was to be weak, assailable. I stepped on the electronic scale again, which I'd carried from the bathroom to the kitchen to show him my shame. It flashed three times and handed down its sentence: Sweet Mother of Christ, 127.5.

"Hon, get away from the scale."

"This is Rick's fault," I cried. "That fucker."

"That's it. I'm not listening to this shit. You're not fat.

You're not even close. If you need me, I'll be mowing the lawn."

I stood there for a minute, staring at the eighty-dollar scale at my feet. Then I picked it up and hurled it against the wall.

Centuries ago, smoking did not lead to heart disease and cancer and emphysema, but to imprisonment and flogging and decapitation. Similarly, the antismoking movement was not a made-in-America campaign, but spans centuries and continents.

In 1492, Rodrigo de Jerez, a Spanish explorer who sailed with Columbus, picked up the smoking habit from the natives in Cuba. When he returned to his hometown, jetting smoke from his nose like Blake's Great Red Dragon, he frightened the townspeople, who believed him possessed. The Inquisition threw him into prison. When his jailers finally let him out, seven years later, everyone's lips were wrapped around pipes. Go figure.

According to some accounts, in 1633, Sultan Murad IV of Turkey wandered the streets of Istanbul in disguise, begging passersby for a smoke. The charitable souls who offered it were either gutted on the spot by Murad's own scimitar or dragged away for execution. He had smokers hung. Beheaded. Quartered between four horses. Thrown into cages and deprived of food and water until they died. To the east, in Persia, two merchants caught selling tobacco were force-fed milkshakes of molten lead.

In the early seventeenth century, the first czar of the Romanov dynasty, Michael Feodorovich, declared the consumption of tobacco a capital offense and set up a Tobacco Court to enact penalties. Offenders were whipped and castrated; their noses and mouths disfigured; given all-expenses-paid, one-way trips to Siberia. And these were for the first offense.

In time, the punishments became less corporeal, though no less definitive. The invention of the cigarette-rolling machine in the 1880s enabled the mass production of cheap cigarettes, propelled tobacco to heights of popularity, and jump-started the modern American antismoking movement.

From the start, these crusaders adopted the metaphor of bondage. This, from an antismoking tract published in 1883: "He who has once formed the [tobacco] habit is ever after a slave. How often and painfully the slaves of this degrading habit desire to break their chains, but alas, in vain! It has a fascination and compulsion which they cannot resist." From the 1889 pamphlet *Tobacco: Its Use and Abuse* by one Reverend J. B. Wight: "Such is this tobacco-slavery, and it numbers among its victims more persons than were ever captured in war in Attica or were brought from Africa in ships."

Congress enacted the Volstead Act—Prohibition—in 1919. Having ousted Demon Rum, the Temperance Movement set its sights on The Little White Slaver. By this time, however, the antismoking movement had lost steam, and World War I weakened it further. The Red Cross and the Salvation Army distributed cigarettes to soldiers. Medics offered cigarettes as painkillers. According to one surgeon,

"As soon as the lads take their first whiff, they seem eased and relieved of their agony." In 1900, 2 percent of Americans smoked cigarettes. By 1930, 40 percent did.

The antismoking movement ebbs and flows. Right now, it's flowing. As of 2005, nine states banned smoking in all workplaces, including restaurants and bars. Legislation was pending in many more. Even tobacco-producing states have succumbed. In one of its last acts of the 2005 session, the Georgia General Assembly approved a bill that bans smoking in most indoor workplaces.

Studies conducted in some cities suggest that the bans already have benefited public health. Few smokers argue the point. Still, a handful of smokers will always maintain that smoking is not a cause of illness, but a cure for the most debilitating disease of all: life.

Among the true believers was Sir Walter Raleigh, the sixteenth-century English explorer, poet, and scalawag who organized the colonizing expeditions to America. A pet of Queen Elizabeth I, Raleigh was beheaded for treason by her successor, King James I. Some historians speculate that James—who so despised smoking that he published a 1604 screed entitled *A Counterblaste to Tobacco*—possibly held a grudge against Raleigh for introducing the weed to Britain, an action he may have deemed as treasonous as conspiring to kill him.

At his execution on October 29, 1618, Raleigh was allowed the equivalent of a Last Cigarette—a Final Pipe. Having enjoyed it, he asked to see the ax. Running his thumb over the blade, he said, "This is sharp medicine, but it will cure all disease."

12:24 p.m.

To peel or not to peel. At the kitchen counter, I debate whether to strip the plastic sheet from a low-fat macaroni and cheese entrée. The decision isn't as simple as it seems. According to the Nutrition Facts label, this small plastic dish contains forty-four grams of carbohydrates. The bad kind, of course. The white-death, refined-flour carbs that go straight to your ass like the nose of the neighbor's dog.

I weighed 130 pounds this morning. Every time I quit smoking, I fill with water like a cheap canoe. But my stomach is growling like a cornered cat—those long, whining rumbles—and I want my mac and cheese. Only seven grams of fat, but so good, even if the sauce is the color of raw chicken skin. I prefer the prison-jumpsuit orange of the Kraft stuff. As a kid, I'd crack open a box and, with a wet finger, savor the powder straight from the packet.

But forty-four grams of carbs . . . I return the box to the freezer. The average smoker gains six to eight pounds after quitting. An eight-pound gain would bring me, at 5 feet 2, to almost 140 pounds. An untenable, unbearable number. The QuitNet message board's Weighty Matters forum is full of anguished posts from formerly svelte female smokers. They counted every calorie, stepped up their workouts, and gained anyway—10, 15, 25 pounds. This can't happen to me. Literally, it cannot happen. I won't be able to take it.

I rattle back to the couch and curl my palm around the fat that rings my waist. Now that I've quit smoking, this roll will grow. What metabolic treachery is occurring in my cells at this moment? Maybe I could smoke five cigarettes a day, just to keep me away from food.

No, damn it. If I smoke, I'll die. But if I stop, I'll get fat. Not much of a choice.

I declared war on food early. Closing my eyes, I am ten again, standing on the scale in my little-girl underwear and new platform shoes. The nurse fiddles with the counterbalance. I hold my breath, scared but not knowing why. "Eighty pounds," she announces brightly. I stare at my shoes—burgundy leather and suede, with laces thin as licorice whips. My mother bought them for me the week before. Somehow, my pride in them is gone.

The doctor sweeps in, scribbles in my chart, and informs my mother that I am "pudgy." I hang my head in humiliation; I know what that word means. It means fat. Fat pig. "Shoo her outside," the doctor says to my mother. "Watch what she puts in her mouth."

Inside our green Impala, I cry, pinching the hateful flesh on my thighs. "He's full of shit," soothes my profanity-loving mother, smoothing my hair, but she is beautiful—the most beautiful mother ever—and she lies. I am hideous. To punish myself, I only pick at the Kentucky Fried Chicken that she sets on the table that night. My mother eats one piece of crispy skin and two hard-boiled eggs. The next morning, stuffed down in the trash, I find an Entenmann's coffee ring, its gooey center ravaged. Its dry carcass reminds me of an image I remember from Wild Kingdom: a gazelle torn apart, its innards ravaged by a lion, baking in the Kalahari sun.

Here is a partial list of things I don't eat: potato chips,

Value Meals, Little Debbie's cakes, pasta, white potatoes, white rice, cookies, pizza. When I want to eat these things, I smoke. I eat the greasy cheese off a slice of pizza and smoke, dig the cookie dough out of the ice cream and smoke. All night, I imagine the crust lying in the garbage, the doughless ice cream in the freezer. To me, food is to be mastered, and cigarettes erase pain. One is lost to me, leaving me alone, unprotected, with the other.

Now that I'm fat against my will, I love to watch people eat. Incredible as it seems, most people experience food as a friend, a pleasure, rather than an enemy to be vanquished. They dig into oozing plates of nachos, groaning platters of cheese fries, enormous slabs of chocolate cake as if it's their right. I eat chicken breasts, egg whites, oatmeal, but Depo weight defies logic and Atkins alike. Without cigarettes, I will gain even more. I've shoved my clingy workout clothes in the back of my top dresser drawer and stopped working out. There's no payoff. As a health writer, I've waxed rhapsodic about the emotional rewards of a brisk walk. I am a hypocrite. A fat hypocrite.

John thinks I'm fine the way I am. What does he know? He is a compulsive eater. It makes a crazy kind of sense. Waitresses place groaning platters before him, which I watch him enjoy with fascination and dread. Smoking and overeating are rooted in the same sickness, the inability to control your body's urges or master that burning need for comfort. So you give up and give in, knowing that the thing that comforts you will kill you in the end.

Some disgruntled employees play computer solitaire or surf porn during business hours. Others bring a shotgun to work and kill their colleagues. In 2003, I devised my own form of revenge—part corporate sabotage, part *cri de coeur*—which I enacted each day in the cafeteria. Returning my tray and dishes after lunch, I bypassed the tubs of gray dishwater meant for the flatware and dumped my dirty utensils into the waist-high gray trash barrels.

By then, my lunch table had dwindled to three or four people from the old days. Mary had been fired. Martin and his wife had moved to Indianapolis to get his master's in public health. Kathy, buried in work as usual, ate lunch at her desk. My main companions were Tammy, an editor around my age, and Donna, a copy editor in her late forties. A chubby, reserved Southerner, Tammy had worked at Rodale almost as long as I; we often lingered at the table, reminiscing about the old days. Donna was a Rodale lifer, simple, imperturbable, who wore thick glasses and a perpetual sweet, squinty-eyed smile. They had witnessed my rebellion before. Sometimes, however, editors and designers from other departments joined our table. When my utensils landed silently on the mountain of salad greens and crumpled napkins and chicken bones, they cut their eyes at each other like poker players—*What the hell is she doing?*

Enjoying the highlight of my day. Because my assignment, while I waited for Donahue M.D. to deliver copy, was to cobble together material from the company's published books to create new ones. The practice is called repurposing—breathing new life into old books, updating information and giving the material a fresh spin. I patched together a weight-loss book. A menopause book. A walking book. I sat at my desk and knew in my heart that I could not possibly come up with another way to tell readers to eat more fruits and vegetables.

Then, I did.

Go on a produce safari: Bored with bananas and broccoli? Take your taste buds on an exotic getaway. On your next supermarket run, stalk the produce section for these tasty tropicals.

Starfruit: Tart but refreshing, this chartreuse-hued fruit tastes like a combination of lemon, apple, and pineapple. For a simple but elegant dessert, slice thin and toss with sugar, berries, and champagne.

Guava: Sweet and fragrant, this smooth-fleshed fruit looks like a green apple on the outside, with bright-pink flesh that tastes like pear and strawberry. Ripen at room temperature until they're yellow and fragrant, then enjoy.

Jicama: A homely but crispy-sweet tuber, kin to the sweet potato. Cook them like potatoes—bake, boil, mash, or fry.

Taro: Dubbed the potato of the tropics, this starchy, nutty-tasting tuber is the main ingredient in the tra-

*ditional Hawaiian dish poi. Try pureeing taro with
coconut milk.*

I wrote things like this while my colleagues edited block-busters. My situation was *Seinfeld*ian. I was Elaine Benes, pitching the Urban Sombrero to J. Peterman.

To be fair, the editors assigned me these books not out of malice, but habit. As part of the old guard, I'd produced dozens of them, and could churn them out quickly. So I smiled, and wrote them, and at one o'clock each afternoon, sailed my flatware through the air like a third-grader lofts a paper airplane.

In my own defense, before I turned to such petulance, I tried the proactive route. I requested meetings with my executive editor and tried to convince her of my value to our team. *I'm energized by the new opportunities at the company. Onboard with its new mission. I hope you'll think of me for new and challenging projects.* She listened and smiled and nothing changed.

Until the Thursday morning before Labor Day weekend. She summoned me to her office and said she'd decided to kill Donahue M.D.'s book.

"We'll find something else for you to do," she said, poised and polished in her expensive suit. "Something fun. We have lots of exciting projects in the works."

Her words glittered in the air like Charlie Bucket's Golden Ticket. Now I could trash those five versions of Chapter One on my hard drive. I wanted to rise from my chair and do a little end-zone dance in front of her.

As the day wore on, however, I started to worry: What if they changed their minds? I wasn't convinced I was off the hook. Sure enough, when I returned to work on Tuesday, my in-box contained an email: They'd decided to give Donahue one last chance. I went out to my car and cried. Chucking my flatware would not appease me now. I'd have to buy a shotgun. I could not face that book again. If they insisted, I'd quit and wait tables at the Emmaus Diner.

Or quit and write something else. I'd write an exposé of Depo, investigate its controversial history and health effects. I'd persuade some fading fifty-something celebrity to team up with me to write *The Menopause Monologues,* a book I'd proposed two years ago. I'd let John support me and write health tidbits for *Ladies' Home Journal* until Daniel turned eighteen, then stick my head in my oven. The future was wide open. I sat in my car for ten minutes with the windows rolled up, perspiring, the steering wheel pressing a dent into my forehead. Then I said fuck it.

At some point, every quitter stalls at the intersection of Fuck It and Don't Give a Shit. You're stranded in the questionable neighborhood of your own head. It's been a bad day and it's getting dark. *You just don't have the energy for this right now.* You are so tired, sick of your kids and your well-meaning spouse and you're fat and your job—your whole life—is a joke and sitting in that intersection, cars whizzing by, passersby tapping on your window—*need some help? No, I'm okay*—you crumble inside like an old New England headstone. You place your top teeth square on your lower lip, that hissing *F* surging from your depths, and then you do it, force that poisonous air trapped inside you through your teeth: *ffffffffuck* it. And it feels so good to let go, to stop pretending. To be exactly who you are: a smoker.

Fuck it. I drove to the CVS a few blocks away and bought a pack of cigarettes. I didn't open it, though. I stuck it in my glove compartment.

I huddle on my back steps in my purple bathrobe, sipping coffee. Daniel is dressing for school. Twelve feet away, John flips pancakes, the sweet smell of batter heavy in the crisp September air.

I didn't sleep well. Last night, as John and I watched TV, I kept looking out the front window at my car, half-expecting to see a dim light inside the Jetta, from the pack glowing like kryptonite through the chinks in the glove compartment. Every time I looked, I thought: It's not too late. I can open the pack and shove the cigarettes down the garbage disposal.

This morning, however, I rose before the alarm sounded, brewed coffee, and crept outside in my bare feet, ashamed but defiant, to retrieve the pack. I haven't had a cigarette, not even a furtive puff from a butt, since January, but today I will smoke. I've worked myself into a rage about Donahue and nothing matters but regaining my equilibrium, feeling myself again. When I look into the mirror I don't recognize this woman with the heavy breasts and uncertain eyes. She used to be a girl with a hard body; promotions fell into her lap like ripe plums. Now she's just another woman with her back to the cliff of middle age. I need something to keep me grounded like sandbags weight an air balloon. A cigarette can do that. It can keep me from snapping my tethers and sailing away.

I have to hold out until John leaves so that he won't smell the smoke. Alcoholics can chew gum, bulimics have their Lysol, but the odor of just one cigarette hangs around like the last drunken party guest.

The pack is in my left pocket, the green Bic in my right. I thought I'd disposed of all the lighters in the house, but a few nights ago, I'd found this one and pushed it to the back of the kitchen's junk drawer. Buried it, really. This morning, I'd curled my fingers around it as I would my son's hand.

As I sip my coffee, my neighbor opens her sliding-glass door and shuffles down her driveway toward her dark blue Taurus. Martha lives across the alley with her aunt. She looks to be in her late twenties, wears big plastic 1980s-style glasses, a man's dark blue parka, and a blue ski hat pulled low over a face like a fist.

I don't wave. On occasion, Martha stalks up and down the alley beside my house, muttering. She screams at my neighbor, Chris, a yardwork addict who's always mowing his lawn or blowing leaves, to keep off her property. She threatens Daniel and Chris's six-year-old son, Jacob, when they ride their scooters in the alley. I can't believe that her aunt and the Pennsylvania DMV allow her on the road. As a nod to propriety, however, I clutch my robe more tightly around me, push my knees together, and lower my head to hide my aging face from the sun.

Martha eases her bulk into the Taurus and speeds off. I sip my coffee, cold now, and consider the day ahead. It is not promising.

Fuck cancer. Everyone has to die of something. When my chest X-ray shows the tumor—wispy, like a pulled cotton ball—I'll get in my car and drive off the road like Willy Loman in *Death of a Salesman*. When I think about cancer, which is frequently, this is the death I imagine. I can't think about Daniel. Cigarettes come first. That's the truth.

I rub my thumb along the side of the Bic.

"Breakfast," John calls.

I stand. The Bic falls from my pocket, bounces down the steps, and skitters across the cement path. I squat to retrieve it and my robe gapes, exposing me from sternum to thigh just as the Stepford Husband speeds by in his BMW. He waves.

I step into the kitchen. The air is fragrant with love and pancakes.

"I put those frozen blueberries in," John says, handing me a plate. "I think they got good."

Usually, I thank God for this calm, sturdy man. But right now I resent him, his pancakes, his certainty, his incomprehension of the need coiled in my guts. Thirty minutes, tops, and he'll be gone.

When he comes home, I will meet him at the door with a cigarette. I will be ready to meet his eyes, to watch their disappointment flicker like the light of a TV in a dark room.

One midwinter afternoon, after my post-lunch smoke, I picked up my afternoon mail. Mixed in with the clinical journals and the studies I'd requested was a plain white envelope, the handwriting small and cramped, as if in pain. I knew that handwriting. It was Tom's.

The envelope contained a glowing review of Caroline's first novel. *You did it. Damn, girl, you did it.* I managed a smile before my face seized up like an overheated piston. Then, before I could shush it, my heart declared its desire. It said: I want to do what she does. I want to write. From that moment on, I couldn't smoke enough to forget it.

4:30 p.m.

I wish I could go back twenty years and talk to the girl I was. Tell her what happens to us, what she'll learn. Not just for her, but for me.

In my fantasy, we roll down Route 84—she's driving, I'm in the passenger's seat—in our Bug on a Friday night in June. We're in the right lane, barely doing the speed limit, a semi beside us roaring like a blast furnace. Nineteen wears black and the elderly driver's grim, straight-ahead stare. She's scared, but I'm not—this is a fantasy, after all. The wind rushing through the rolled-down windows clings to my face, my bare arms, moist and warm as breath.

"On your way to the Lit Club?"

"I hope you don't think you're hanging out with me," she replies, raising her voice over the rumbling semi. She

sucks on a Newport Light. I know how she feels, filling her lungs with cold, clean self, exhaling her fear into the dark.

"There's no point. I quit drinking ten years ago and smoking six days ago."

"How depressing. How do you survive?"

"Day to day. Like you."

The semi is in back of us now, its headlights and metal grille filling the rearview mirror.

"So you know who I am."

"Yeah. Although I don't know why you're here. It's not like you can change anything."

"I just wanted to see you again. Talk. Make fun of your driving skills. You really do drive like an old lady."

She glances at me, smirks, then turns back to the road. "We gain some weight, I see."

A car rockets past us in the left lane. The Bug rocks in its wake of wind.

"Follow it," I say.

"No way."

"Just do it." To my surprise, the speedometer's red needle trembles upward, settles at seventy-five. In the rearview mirror, the twin beacons of the semi's lights fade like morning stars.

"Wow. I didn't think you'd have the guts."

"It's your fantasy," says Nineteen, flipping her butt out the window.

We're closing in on the mystery car when the light poles on Route 84 disappear and the smooth macadam turns rough. Black night rolls back and we fly through six shades of sky, violet stained with cream, bitter reds and oranges, smoke-blue dusk, the apricot and gold of late afternoon. By the time we pull up beside the car—a white Buick convertible with fins—the sun is almost overhead. It's noon, or close to it.

I lean closer, so close that Nineteen's hair brushes my cheek. "Oh my God, it's us," I say. "Look."

No more than two, dressed in a pink romper, I stand chunky-kneed on the passenger's seat, my baby curls lifting in the wind. My hand rests on Mom's shoulder.

"We were so cute," I say. "Move back so I can see Mom. What's she wearing?"

"Black sunglasses. A red strapless sundress. Lipstick that matches her dress. Exactly. How does she do that?"

"Who else paints a room pumpkin? Her eye for color is annoyingly flawless." I peer past Nineteen for a better look at our mother. Below her sunglasses, a faint crease marks her cheek, ending at her poppy-red mouth. Her left elbow hangs out the window.

"Stay with her," I say.

We rocket side by side, as if drag racing, down a road edged by forest. The Buick rides in the lane for oncoming traffic. If this were real, we'd be dead.

Our headlights illuminate the small, sparsely needled pitch pines of the New Jersey Pine Barrens. My father drove us through this desolate region at night on our weekend trips to my grandmother's. I hid my face under my shirt so I wouldn't see the glowing eyes of the Jersey Devil watching us along with his buzzing, slithering, twig-snapping hordes—pine snakes, bats, dragonflies, flying squirrels, white-tailed deer. This fire-scarred landscape with its sandy, sour soil thrives. Some of its plant life can reproduce only when it burns. Its bogs and swamps sustain carnivorous plants—Venus flytrap, sundews—that attract and eat insect prey. Even orchids bloom here. Adapt or die. Plants just know. Humans must learn.

"This is Route 49," I say. "We're on our way to Ocean City."

"I figured," says Nineteen. She's always talking about these trips. Her voice lifts in mocking mimicry. "'Oh, we had fun, the two of us, before I married your father. Do you remember our trips to Ocean City?'"

"Do you?" I ask.

"No. Do you?"

"No." But we must have jumped the waves together, her hand strong and sure in ours. Built sand castles, watched them fall, built them up again. Stood side by side in the churning surf, trying to root our toes in the shifting sand.

Mom's right hand leaves the wheel and reappears with a wrinkled pack of Camels. She fishes out a cigarette with her painted lips. Her hand disappears again, emerges with the Buick's lighter. Her cheeks hollow, then she tilts her head and spews a stream of smoke.

"Like an Italian starlet," I say to Nineteen.

"Start one for me, will you?"

"I can't. I quit, I said. Six days ago."

"Bully for you. Then just put one in my mouth and hold up a match. If it's not against your principles."

"I think I can manage that, you little shit. Where are they?"

"You're sitting on them."

"I should have known." I extract the crush-proof box and a matchbook, pop a butt between her pink-glossed lips, and strike a match. They feel strange in my hands. Lighting her cigarette is like looking at your face in the bathroom mirror at four in the morning. It looks like you but not really, and you stand there for a few seconds trying to feel yourself, to call yourself back.

I lean forward again. Two still stands on the seat. Her face is solemn, her eyes tight shut, as if she's thinking very hard. I squinch mine shut to see what she sees. Gray squiggles crawl across an orange field. I open my eyes. Two's are still closed.

"She's scared," I say.

"Doing eighty, no seat belt, yeah, I'd say she's scared."

"They didn't wear seat belts then."

Nineteen laughs, blows a fat cloud of smoke at the windshield. "Only Mom between her and disaster. That's not saying much."

"Give Mom a break."

"Fuck you."

I'd forgotten how frightened I was. But I know this hurting girl. She is tuned to the truth like a piano. In time, she resonates. That's what saves her. Saved us.

"Tell me why you smoke."

"Tell me why you breathe."

"So you equate the two."

"Drop it," she says behind her white cloud.

"They say kids start smoking because they see their parents do it. Do you think it's true? You sat in that Buick. Do you remember?"

DAY 6

"I was two. You can't possibly remember either."

"No, but I have fragments. Impressions. The wind. The smell of her smoke. The Camel between her fingers. How she wore her youth and beauty like bandoliers of ammunition."

"Are you high? If you have coke, I want some."

"If it's possible to yearn at two, I yearned to be Mom."

"I yearn to get as far away from her as possible." She flicks ash out the window.

"I know you think so."

"Oh, I know so. I'm only here for the summer. When I graduate, I'm never coming back."

"You're a long way from done with Mom, honey. A very long way."

"The hell I'm not." Then, *"Don't tell me that. Please don't tell me that."*

"Oh yeah. She's with you every step of the way until you learn."

"Learn what?"

"That you can love her without losing yourself. Can love, period."

Silence.

"That moving beyond her doesn't mean you've betrayed her. That it's okay to live your life."

"I am living my life."

"No you're not. You're avoiding it, and you think it's her fault. But she's not the one holding you back."

"She's weak. She cries all the time, screams at Dad, drives him out of the house. She's taken a bite out of every sandwich she's ever made me. I can't fucking stand it, her

233

lipstick on the bite mark. There's nothing that's mine, not even a sandwich. Nothing of me she doesn't mark. I despise her."

"Okay, she can be a pain in the ass. As far as Dad goes, let's just say she gave as good as she got. Anyway, she didn't beat us, or get loaded and let us eat the Drano under the kitchen sink. She did the best she could."

"Not good enough."

"She's the mother we got, worse than some, better than most. But your problem isn't her. It's you. You're scared shitless because you don't know who you are. You're like this big smoking crater, and you know it, and knowing it kills you. So you cover your emptiness with alcohol and smoke and rage. Anger at Mom because she's there and will take it for the team, the team being us; it has always been us. Anger at yourself because you believe it's inconceivable to have what you want, do what you want—learn karate, play guitar, have cute, smart, nonloser boyfriends, get into a good school—you didn't even apply to Harvard or Yale because no way were you smart enough. And your mind is so dull, my God, you can't discuss Kant or read Proust, so how could you ever write poetry or novels. You settle for what you think you can get. You're this close to settling for-ever. You're sealing yourself off like a crime scene because how could anything good come to you or from you when your own flesh-and-blood father doesn't care enough to send you a fucking Polaroid of his face. You must really be a piece of shit."

"Stop." A whisper.

Day 6

"*You're a big toxic layer cake of sorrow and numbness and rage. Also, you're an alcoholic—that's a scoop; you won't find that out for another eight years. And you are on your way to believing, in error, that without cigarettes you'll deflate like Underdog the morning after the Macy's Thanksgiving Day Parade.*"

"*I'll drive us off the fucking road. I swear to God.*"

"*No you won't. I'm running this show, remember? Besides, you want to live. Quit this tough-girl act so I can tell you who you are. And I do know. I'm your future, you stupid bitch.*"

"*All right! Shut up!*"

She pulls over, the Bug's tires crunching sand. The Buick disappears up the road, its taillights glowing red; darkness is descending again. She puts her hands on her face, her face on the steering wheel.

"*Are you listening?*"

A wet sniffle. I can feel the wet on her hands, the tear sliding down her left wrist.

"*I came to tell you who you are.*"

"*Who,*" *she says dully.*

"*A star. You're a star in the galaxy of our family.*"

I just sit. Listen to the snapping of twigs, look for those glowing eyes in the forest. Wait for her to resonate.

"*I am blown apart inside,*" *she says.*

"*I know.*"

"*I'll die if I stay. But she'll die if I go.*"

"*Neither of you is going to die, okay? Get back on the road. Let's drive.*"

After another minute she lifts her head and we pull back onto the road. I don't know how to tell her that she— and Mom—are suffering the first and final heartbreak: growing up. That the antidote is time and forgiveness. She might turn mean again, laugh in my face. So I stick to the facts.

"Before I go, here's the CliffsNotes version of your life," I say. "You move to New York City and become a pornographer and make a mess of your life. You clean it up some-what—by the way, you'll meet a woman named Hannah, miss as few appointments as possible. You move to Pennsyl-vania to write health books. You get married and have a child. A boy as open as a bowl, so beautiful that he will destroy your heart every day. He is your Two, and you will teach him to buckle up. You will divorce his father and drive him and another man mad with pain, not even knowing why or how. Then you'll meet a man who will rip the heart right out of your chest, and two years later another man will take it out of your hand and put it back in. And you will, as incredible as it sounds, be happy. You'll marvel at how the most mundane moments unfold, as brilliant as the panels of a Japanese fan. And you will stop smoking because you will treasure every dull and frustrating minute of your life. That takes you to forty."

"What about me and Mom?"

"She changes. Just like you. Both of you stop needing each other like you do now. She falls away from you like a booster on a rocket. But she goes down blazing. Even at sixty, she gives a mean fireworks display."

She laughs. "Some things never change. Light me again."

I brush her windblown hair from her hungry mouth, insert another cigarette, and hold up a match.

"Thanks." She inhales, squinting through the haze. "Remember Mom smoking in the car? We sat in the back, with Kurt, and threw spitballs in her hair and whined that her smoke burned our noses. Dad in the driver's seat, flapping his hand, bitching. Hating her. Hating me. Kurt on his side of the seat, hating me too. I know they do. You might as well confirm it so I don't have to wonder for twenty years."

"They don't hate you," I say. "They're just trying to survive. Dad in his workshop. Kurt on his minibike, anywhere but home. Nick on an assembly line somewhere in the Midwest, pushing the same button ten thousand times a day. They just . . . can't deal. None of us can. Mom wandering the aisles of Marshall's. You brooding in your room. Loving our family is like waging guerrilla warfare—ambush, sabotage. But we survive. I swear on our son's head. In twenty years, we walk out of the jungle, blinking, bewildered, and find each other, and we're not enemies anymore. We're family."

We exit on Capitol Avenue. "Thank God," says Nineteen, and exhales slowly, no smoke, just breath.

"I know."

"You keep saying that. You know everything, don't you? You think that's such a great thing? To me, life is a mystery. Your life unravels exactly as it should. You don't get to know how it ends. Which is how it should be."

"I agree."

"I hate people who need an explanation for everything.

I can't find comfort in geometry, don't give a shit why the sky is blue. So just for a second, stop knowing. You've told me everything you know. Tell me something you don't."

I think for a moment. "Whether we'll ever pass on a four-lane highway. Fear is like love handles—the last stubborn flaw to melt away."

DAY 7

7:13 a.m.

Lockdown is done. John is asleep. The morning arranges itself before me in pale severity, a dowager on her deathbed. I stand at my front window, my forehead against the cold glass. Sullen with cloud, the sky descends like a winding sheet. Wet leaves glaze the sidewalk, lift and curl in the wind.

Seven days down, thirty or forty years to go.

I woke at six, my eyes crusted with gloom. I went to bed thinking I'd awaken as Snow White; birds would alight on my finger and twitter around my head. Instead, I am a character from a Saturday-morning cartoon of my childhood, a dippy spin-off of The Flintstones *called* The Pebbles and Bamm-Bamm Show. *Bad-luck Schleprock was a sniveler, a jinx. A brown cloud hovered over his head, spitting rain. This morning, that cloud followed me out of bed, waited outside the shower, and soaked me as I dressed and brewed coffee and shuffled through two hundred channels. Those activities burned an hour, but the day just keeps coming, a boxer who won't stay down.*

I don't want to smoke, but the absence of that desire unsettles me, like an unfamiliar pain. Every few minutes I run a systems check: Do I want to smoke now? No. Now? No. How about now? No. Even so, I am aware that cigarette lust could ambush me ten seconds, ten minutes, ten hours from now. Its presence lurks in the corner of my eye like a pedophile at a playground fence.

Drifting into the living room, I glare at the chain, snarled in the corner. In my peevishness it seems limp, ineffectual, its noisy malevolence spent. Have I, like a long-suffering husband cursed with a shrewish wife, learned to tune it out? Shit. The whole idea of Lockdown was to create a three-dimensional model of my addiction so compelling that it would haunt me forever—my personal Marley's ghost, piteously exhorting me to goodness. Resentment floods my mouth. The chain is not doing its job, which is to save me from myself.

All at once I tap the root of my bitter mood: From here on in, I am free to smoke and condemned to drag around that freedom every day for the rest of my life. My anxiety crests. I might make it through today, but what about tomorrow, or the next day, or the day after that?

I sit on the floor by the chain and rub a link between my fingers, all those tomorrows bumping up against me. Crowding me. Without nicotine, how will I endure the morning chaos, the demands of work and writing, my second evening shift of household chores and mothering? Which is worse—to be numbed by smoke or terrifyingly, overwhelmingly alive without it?

I am losing my nerve, disappearing into this fresh

*smoke-free air. John, wake up, be with me, make me real
again.*

*I head upstairs and stand over my husband. He lies on
his back, a fragrant felled tree. Long lashes, pale skin, each
cheek pink where the hot blood bubbles. He is beautiful. In
sleep he should wear a crown and hold a bouquet. I want
to tickle the edge of his nostril with my pinkie to rouse him,
but I can't wake him to babysit me. I head downstairs
again. I don't know what to do. What should I do?*

*I know. I should make breakfast. A nice bowl of oat-
meal to complement my new internal purity.*

*In th kitchen, feigning industriousness, I measure a half-
cup of oats into a bowl, hold the bowl under the tap, stir the
paste with my finger, and pop it into the microwave. I am a
nonsmoker. The bowl rotates on the turntable. I am a nonsmoker. I congratulate myself on my commitment to health.
I am a nonsmoker. From now on, I will inaugurate each day
with oatmeal. Its soluble fiber will gel in my intestines and
bind to excess dietary cholesterol, sending it downriver for
elimination. Clean shit, fresh start—good old-fashioned
American optimism.*

*I am a nonsmoker. I am a nonsmoker. I. Am. A. Non-
smoker.*

*Dosing my oatmeal with a dollop of strawberry yogurt,
I carry it into the living room and pick up the remote. Flip,
flip, flip. Infomercial, infomercial, local news, a Lifetime
movie I've seen at least twice. Music videos from the 1980s.
The Thompson Twins jump like fleas, strumming cardboard
guitars. I am mortified for them. VH1 Classic is like a mother
who shows poopy-pants pictures to her teen's prom date.*

Flip, flip, flip.

This is really it. No cigarettes. Ever. Suddenly, I under-stand why people trapped in blizzards stop walking and curl up in the snow to sleep forever. The car keys tempt me from the coffee table. John sleeps. CVS is just down the road.

I am a fool. How can I even consider smoking? Have I learned nothing? What did you teach me, chain?

Smoking extinguished my fear and rage and sadness the way the wind douses a flame. Smoking extinguished me. With each cigarette I tried to murder a piece of myself, to kill the ugly, unlovable, unacceptable, unbearable core of me, and if I couldn't kill it I would hide it. Deny it. Smok-ing is dark—a dark pleasure, a dark pain, the darkness under the bed, the chasm that engulfed me long before I lit a cigarette. I chose darkness, always, even in the third grade. While the girls in my class mooned over horses, I brooded over Helen Keller. Drawn to her black silent world, I read every book on her in our school library and made my mother drive me to the city library for more. I even taught myself the manual alphabet, a useless talent because no one else knew it. What would I have said, anyway? What could my fingers have revealed about the state of my sad, scarred heart?

Like Helen, I was estranged from the world, frustrated by my inability to join it, comprehend it, belong to it. While she wanted out of darkness, however, I wanted in. There was this field a few blocks from my house, filled with bro-ken bottles and soda cans and overrun with dry weeds. I'd edge my way in, close my eyes, hold out my arms in front

of me, and stumble forward, like Patty Duke in The Mira-
cle Worker. *Though I could see and hear, I ignored the
sights and sounds of the life around me: the distant murmur
of cars from the main street, a fat man mowing his lawn,
the bark of a dog from a nearby yard, a young mother
pushing a stroller. I chose to block out the world. This part
of me—that refused the light, feared the open road, dis-
guised my desires, hid from everyone who loved me—is the
smoker in me.*

*Anyone walking past would have stared at the little
freak blundering through that weed-choked field. Not much
has changed. I am still stumbling through a darkness of my
own making, but, finally, I want out. Good-bye, Oscar
Wilde, wielding your opium-laced cigarette like a scalpel.
Godspeed, Dorothy Parker, spewing blades of smoke across
the Algonquin Round Table. Au revoir flappers, French
philosophers, and rock stars. Fare-thee-well, Marlboro
Man. Long may you roam. I am not like them. Neither
genius nor beauty, I am just a smoker and my beating heart
is all I have.*

*I am weak and wide-open. I am exquisitely exposed. I
am the Visible Woman, the model made of clear plastic
that reveals the inner workings of the body. I don't want
anyone turning my heart in their fingers, but I don't want
to smoke, either. All I want is the serenity that God owes
me for quitting. Where is the fucking serenity?*

*In reply, the peal of church bells, muzzled by distance
and cold.*

During the winter of 2002–2003 I was closing in on happiness, was hot on its pink beribboned ballet slippers. Life was good except for my smoking and a virulent cold and flu season. That winter, John polished off a whole bottle of NyQuil. Daniel, who hadn't yet learned to blow his nose, popped chewable children's decongestants like Skittles. I inhaled their rhinoviruses and smoked my pack a day with nothing to show for it—no wheeze, no cough.

This exasperated me. How could I quit again if I didn't get bronchitis? I'd resumed only a few months before, and this was my Plan A—develop bronchitis, stop smoking. I'd heard that many smokers quit after experiencing the terror of breathlessness, but my hardiness was my undoing and had failed me before. In junior high, when snowstorms closed the schools, I waded barefoot into knee-high drifts, the icy wind slicing through my flannel nightgown like a switchblade. Pneumonia was preferable to the seventh grade. At twelve, I didn't know that one cannot will lung inflammation. At thirty-nine, I hoped to be the exception.

In the spring of 2003, I turned forty. It was official: I was no longer too young to die. John baked me a cake, chocolate with a fluffy mousse filling and daffodil-yellow icing. I said screw it and ate a whole piece. A month later, he whisked me away to a bed-and-breakfast for the weekend. As I pruned in the Jacuzzi, he handed me things: a bouquet of daffodils, a box of chocolates, a teal-blue wooden box. I opened it and gaped. "I paid for it myself," he said, as I jumped from the tub and hugged him, leaving my wet imprint on his good shirt.

Telling Daniel and my mother about our impending

nuptials didn't silence their duet of complaint about my smoking. John never mentioned it, though, and I squirmed in his silence. I knew that he cared. But he also understood that people who badger smokers to quit are not unlike rodeo clowns: Both live dangerously. More to the point, he knew that ragging doesn't work. All his life, he'd watched his father, a man of enormous appetites—for cigarettes, food, knowledge—smoke two packs a day. Sometimes, when money was tight, John Senior rolled his own with fingers roughened by thirty years in the steel and tube mills around Reading.

I loved John Senior and his wife Roxy from the day we met at their grandson's peewee football game. Round as planets, bundled in jackets and hats and scarves, they beamed at me, and then turned to their son. "Guess what we did today?" Roxy asked.

"What?"

"We bought our funeral plots." My kind of people.

That day, John Senior became my smoking buddy, my first since Caroline. After that, John and I often visited them on North Tenth Street in Reading, a former factory town, now a town of factory outlets. Their tiny house held equal amounts of trash and treasure. On every smoke-darkened wall hung the school portraits of their six children—the boys with long hair parted on the side, 1970s-style—and Olan Mills prints of their grandchildren. In each furniture-crammed room, boxes stuffed with a lifetime's worth of junk and memorabilla—ancient tax returns, faded Polaroids, well-worn pans that had cradled the batter of a hundred birthday cakes—towered almost to the ceiling. Open boxes of chocolate lay on the dusty coffee table, the fluted paper shells denuded of their contents by John Senior, a diabetic whose smoking and overeating amounted to two middle fingers thrust in the face of death. Roxy ate those chocolates too. Weakened by congestive heart failure, breathless and wheezy, she needed to lose weight but could not resist sweets.

It was all right. They made do with their dilapidated bodies, tolerated their occasional lurches and sputters, gentle Roxy beaming through the brume of her crotchety husband's generic cigarettes. In John Senior's world, a man could still smoke without apology in his own house.

A few years after they moved out of Reading and into their daughter Christine's place in nearby Leesport, John Senior started to cough.

"You wouldn't cough if you stopped smoking," Roxy would say, cutting her eyes at me, inviting me into her joke.

"Shut up, Rox," he'd snarl, and she would.

John's youngest brother Eric and his sisters Kathy and Christine also smoked, even though Kathy had asthma and Christine sometimes lost feeling in her feet—smoking had impaired her circulation. I remember my first Super Bowl Sunday at Christine's—we all watched the Tampa Bay Buccaneers crush the Oakland Raiders as her tiny town house filled with smoke. A miniature mushroom cloud lingered over the kitchen table where the smokers sat with their pretzels and beer. Besides Christine's kids, only three of the revelers didn't smoke: John, Roxy, and Kathy's girlfriend Susan, a bubbly, motherly thirty-year-old with a heart as big as her hips. Susan had become my closest friend even though, when liquored up, she turned sloppily erotic, knotting the stems of maraschino cherries with her tongue. I smoked on the front steps to get air. Susan, on her fifth light beer, kept me company.

Every family has a fragrance. Mine was scented with my mother's perfume and bath salts and loneliness, the Reichardts' with Crock-Pots bubbling with greasy barbecue, grape-jelly meatballs, and smoke. In their presence, my fears about seizing hearts and tar-clogged lungs seemed unfounded. How could anything bad happen to me in their company, all of us warming ourselves in the heat of our own tiny campfires? They didn't look ill, didn't cough much or bemoan their inability to quit. Like rooting for the Eagles, their smoking was more birthright than choice.

I agonized in private. Yet after my eight-month quit, I could not bring myself to try again, could not take another failure. When you resume smoking after a period of abstinence, you feel relief but also pain—not the sharp twinges of physical withdrawal, but the dull chronic ache that comes from knowing that you are a participant in your own demise. Lighting up, I imagined wavering on the span of a bridge, seconds from my last flight.

But I always went back to the numbers game. Twenty-five to 40 percent of smokers die a smoking-related death. Odds are I'd be in that 60 to 75 percent who don't. Smoking causes one of every five deaths in the United States. Most likely, that death wouldn't be mine. Probably not.

A smoker examines his breath like a motive, becomes exquisitely attuned to its subtleties. Is my chest tight tonight? Take a few deep breaths. Scan for the slightest sensation of stricture. Ask stupid questions: How does my lung capacity compare to, say, a Tibetan yak herder's, who breathes air as thin as a shell of ice on snow? That of the average out-of-shape, fat-marbled nonsmoker? Inhale. Exhale. Scan for a crackle, a wheeze, a sign of the beginning of the end.

Healthy lungs are gray-pink, the color of saltwater pearls, and shaped like an upside-down butterfly. Each lung is ten to twelve inches long and weighs about a pound—drained of blood, eight ounces. Filled to capacity, a man's lungs can hold about 6.4 quarts of air; a woman's, about 4.5 quarts. We breathe about twelve times a minute, taking in a pint of air with each inhale. That's seven quarts per minute, 105 gallons per hour, 2,500 gallons per day.

The respiratory muscles govern the rhythmic, automatic in-out-in-out of breathing. Located at the bottom of the rib cage, the diaphragm bows up into the chest like an inverted soup bowl and rests under the lungs. The intercostal muscles between the ribs—the same muscles we tear off the bone at barbecues—help the rib cage expand and contract, giving the lungs the space they need to pull and discharge air. The words physicians use to describe the process of respiration—*inspiration* for the inhale, *expiration* the exhale—fairly vibrate with meaning. Expiration connotes termination, death, decay; inspiration, divine guidance and grace.

DAY 7

Besides breath, the lungs bestow another gift: voice. Our vocal cords sit inside the larynx, just above the trachea (windpipe). When we are silent, the cords stay open. When we vocalize, however, the cords close and air exhaled from our lungs is forced through them, causing them to vibrate. Together with movements of the mouth and throat, this expelled air generates sounds stunning in their pitch and complexity—speech, shrieks, moans, arias.

We do virtually nothing that does not cause another to vibrate, are bound by breath. The Hawaiian word for family, *ohana*, translates as "people who breathe together." I've read, and have no way to prove, that our every breath contains a million atoms breathed at some time by everyone who ever lived. Theoretically, we inhale the same atoms breathed by Pablo Picasso or Genghis Khan, Wordsworth or Hitler, atoms that once formed the crust of the most ancient star or wafted through the lungs of God. Exhaling returns these atoms to the atmosphere to be inhaled by our children and, in time, theirs. We inhale the oxygen plants release as a waste by-product of their metabolism, and exhale the carbon dioxide they need, sharing the gift of life. Nature wastes nothing, not even our breath.

11:52 a.m.

Every town has a restaurant like the Allentown Family Diner. Old men drive there, at forty miles per hour, to nurse cups of coffee and escape their querulous wives. The waitresses, large of bust and hock, slam down slices of layer cake as thick as bricks, offering yolk-crusted forks with which to spear them. Its no-smoking section is an afterthought.

On Sundays, the diner swarms with the after-church crowd. The line to get in snakes out the door into the cold foyer, which holds a lottery vending machine, a crane game, and—of course—a cigarette machine. John and I are bunched between two older couples dressed for church and a couple in their early twenties. The woman holds a stunned-looking infant, stiff as a starfish in her pink snow-suit, and the hand of a toddler with eyes too old for his years. Her husband hovers by the door, puffing a cigarette. Every few minutes we all shuffle forward like prisoners in a chain gang. The man stays by the door, sheltered from his family and the icy wind. I want to shove him outside.

When John suggested that we grab lunch here before Matt brought Daniel home, I ignored my unease and said sure. Bad idea. I'm cold, I despise waiting in line, and I'm standing next to a fucking metal box filled with cigarettes. I should have stayed home, but no. John required a cheese-burger to commemorate my first day of freedom.

"We have to be back before two," I remind him, my breath unfurling like a noisemaker in the frigid air.

"Uh-huh." He eyes the crane game. I roll my eyes and hand him a buck. Nothing makes my husband happier than to maneuver a claw on a crane in a large plastic cube to grab some crummy stuffed toy made in Pakistan.

DAY 7

John feeds the machine and surveys the booty. The Scooby-Doo is a sure thing, but he's a gambler; he goes for the stuffed Eagles football player. He lines up the claw, toggles the joystick left, then right, and drops it to glory or defeat. The metal fingers close around the toy, but as the claw rises, the prize plops back onto the soft pile.

I watch him, my irritation rising like a fever. "You know these things are fixed," I say sourly. "You want a cheesy stuffed animal, I'll take you to the dollar store."

"It's not about the prize. It's about the game."

Despite my bad mood, I appreciate his inadvertent bit of zen. Until he says, "Give me another buck."

I sigh and slap it in his palm. John lines up his claw. I want to tiptoe to my room of smoke and draw the curtains, but call up my mantra instead: I am a nonsmoker. I am a nonsmoker. I am a nonsmoker.

Finally, the line lurches forward. We step into the diner's warm close odors, coffee and the morning's fried potatoes and smoke. To our left is the smoking section, filled to capacity. Flannel-shirted young tradesmen at the counter flirt with the waitresses; a few loners wordlessly trade sections of the Sunday paper. Booths of old folks and college kids spear runny eggs. The middle-aged Greek who owns the diner commands the action from the first booth, a lit cigarette burning in a glass ashtray beside him. He inhales, recognizes us, smiles. As he exhales, his smile slowly disappears, like the Cheshire cat's, into the cloud in front of him.

He looks so content. So healthy. They all do. Am I the

only smoker in Allentown who worries about breathing through a tube? What's wrong with these people? Smoking sections should be abolished, cigarettes illegal. You should have to buy them through a slot in a door, like crack.

"Smoking or nonsmoking?" asks the hostess, intruding on my silent tantrum.

"Nonsmoking." A small thrill of pride runs up my back: I love saying that. The hostess leads us to a booth, slaps down plastic menus, and pours us coffee without asking.

As John peruses the menu, I ask him what I should do with the chain. I want to keep it downstairs where I can see it, but what about Daniel?

"Do you think he'll notice?"

"John. It's a forty-pound chain. I think he'll notice. When he does, I need an answer." When I sent Daniel to Matt's, I told him that Mommy was quitting smoking, but spared him the logistics. Is it too strange to keep the chain in the living room? Will it disturb my son? I'd like to spare him the knowledge that his mother is a loon for as long as possible, just as I hope to delay breaking the news about Santa and the tooth fairy.

A waitress stops at our table, pen poised, cutting off our discussion. She's in her late thirties, broad-hipped and pale-eyed, with fine hair styled in a manner that exposes her thinning temples.

"Bacon cheeseburger and fries," says John. I narrow my eyes at him and order turkey on rye. "No chips," I add. She nods and turns with a swirl of polyester skirt.

"You don't need fries," I say.

"You'll eat half of them anyway."

"I will not." My purse rings. To my surprise, it's my father on the line. He almost never calls.

"Juuu-lie," he trills cheerily.

"Hey, Dad."

"So you're loose."

"Yep."

"Did you smoke?"

"Nope."

"I'm proud of you." My mother has told me that when I stopped drinking I gained his respect. I hear it now, in those four words.

"Thanks, Dad."

His voice turns sly. *"Your mother is still smoking, you know."* In the background, a faint cry of indignation. *"Maybe you can get her to quit—"*

I hear rustling on the line; my mother has snatched his cell phone. *"He doesn't know what he's talking about."* Her voice as tight and unyielding as a knot in Daniel's shoelace.

"Are you smoking, Mom?" I'm teasing, but she bites.

"I had one—one—the other day. Your father is just trying to piss me off. He's an ass. Do you know what he did? I asked him to put plastic over the windows to lower our heating bill this winter. So he goes to Home Depot and buys, not clear plastic, but white plastic. I now have white plastic over the windows in the computer room."

I smile at that. The computer room in my parents' house is actually a sunroom, all lush plants and comfy reading chairs. I feel her pain: her beautiful, light-washed sanctuary, dimmed by my father's willful ineptitude.

Attempting to pry her mind from his treachery, I say, "So ask me how it feels to be a free woman. The chain came off today."

"Oh, that's right. I'm sorry, sweetie. How do you feel?"

"Eh."

"Why eh? You quit smoking. You did a hard brave thing."

"I thought I'd feel more closure," I reply. "But this morning, the only difference was that I didn't lock myself up. Now the hard, boring part of quitting begins. The not smoking part."

"You don't get a gold star on your forehead for quitting smoking, Julia."

"I know, Ma." I'm lying. That's exactly what I expected.

"Is Daniel coming home today?" my mother asks.

"At two."

"When he gets home, love that little boy to death. He must miss his mommy. Listen, I have to go. We're taking your grandmother to lunch. We'll talk tonight, okay? When we have more time. And Julia."

"Yeah."

"Don't smoke. It's only life, but it's the only one you get. Love you."

"Love you too." I push End just as our waitress returns with our plates. Beside my sandwich, a mountain of chips.

"Shit!"

John puts his hand over mine. "I'll eat them."

I'd long wondered why God lifted my compulsion to drink but not my need to smoke. In 2003, I stopped wondering and started begging, crying, pleading with him to relieve me of my desire for cigarettes. Nada.

"He's not listening," I said to John one night in bed. "He wants me dead."

"Don't say that," hissed my husband. He had feared for my mortal soul since the start of our relationship, when we discovered that our styles of worship clashed like an old man's golf attire. In bed one sunny Saturday morning a few months after we met, John let slip that he was a Christian, and our meandering river of talk dropped precipitously into the treacherous rapids of religion.

"So, am I going to hell?" I'd asked, snuggling closer.

Silence. A pause, stretching out like a glimmering string of spit. I shoved him. "Oh my God. You think I'm going to hell."

"Hon, I don't know."

"You don't know. But you're going to heaven, right? You're unbelievable. This is like the Jesus Fish episode of *Seinfeld*."

"Oh, for crying out loud."

"You know, when Elaine finds out that all the presets on Puddy's car radio are set to Christian stations. She asks him if she's going to hell and he says yes."

"I didn't say you were going to hell. I never said you were going to hell."

"But you paused when I asked you. You *paused*. Let me ask you: If I'm going to hell, why are you with me?"

It took me two hours of strenuous argument to help him

clarify his position. He didn't know if I was brimstone bound, but he didn't know if he was, either. Which was good enough for me.

But soon after our engagement, John began reading his Bible before bed—pointedly, it seemed.

"It's the word of God, hon," he said. "It's also great literature. I would think that you, a writer, would know that."

"I can't get through one page. After a few paragraphs, I'm lost. I feel like I'm reading the tax code." I tipped my chin to the ceiling. "I'm sorry, God."

John looked at me and shook his head.

"I'm not going to hell," I said.

Still, my resistance to the Bible tugged at me like a puppy at the leg of your jeans. Why did I find Scripture so tedious? Was it, as Dana Carvey's Church Lady had asked, Satan? Worried, I asked God if I was a bad person for not reading the Good Book. He assured me that I was not. Although perhaps I could crack it open sometime. When I was ready. No hurry.

One night a few months later, as John showered, I eyed the Bible on his nightstand. Couldn't hurt to flip through it. My eyes fell on a passage in the book of Matthew.

When He had come down from the mountain, great multitudes followed Him. And behold, a leper came and worshiped Him, saying, "Lord, if You are willing, You can make me clean."

Then Jesus put out His hand and touched him, saying, "I am willing; be cleansed." Immediately his leprosy was cleansed.

John entered the bedroom, a towel around his waist. His eyes darkened with surprise. "You're reading the Bible."

"It would seem so. Read this and tell me what you think it means."

After a moment, John said, "It's about the nature of faith. The leper didn't say, 'Heal me.' He said, 'Heal me if you are *willing*.'"

"I got that," I said. "But do you think the leper knew that there was a reason for his suffering? That it had a purpose, even if he didn't know what it was?"

John just looked at me. Then he said, "I think you're overthinking things, hon."

"That's because you're an engineer." I put on my robe and went downstairs to Google leprosy, a disease older than Jesus.

Caused by the bacillus *Mycobacterium leprae,* leprosy is endemic in twenty-four countries, reported in almost a hundred. It is not a skin disease. Leprosy attacks nerve endings, which in turn destroys the body's ability to discern pain and protect itself from injury.

As I clicked through the photos of blind eyes and eaten-away fingers and noses, a memory flared like a match. A book I'd read at work while researching cancer—*The Gift of Pain*, by Paul Brand. A surgeon and missionary who had treated lepers in India, Brand contended that pain was vital to life—a necessity, like air or water. His book had focused on physical pain, but at that moment metaphor lit up my brain like the moon. I understood that, like physical pain, emotional pain warns you that something is amiss. That smoking had muted that warning in me, as alcohol had.

That in the weeks and months ahead, I could expect all the pain I'd never allowed myself to feel a rise, like that boil under my eight-year-old arm, and that I'd have to face it without the anesthesia of smoke.

Christianity—other religions, too—sometimes uses leprosy as a metaphor for the sin that isolates us from God. I have come to see it as a metaphor for the self-hatred that quarantined me inside my head with only cigarettes for company. Many smokers say they feel like lepers when they light up in public, but I felt like one before I ever tasted smoke.

Don't we all, at one time or another. It doesn't matter which end of the cigarette we're on. We are all contagious. Life is the contagion. *Contagion* derives from the same Latin root as *contiguous,* which means "touching." We are, as they say, all in this together. We touch each other, we infect and inspire.

Maybe God lifted my desire to drink to ensure my physical survival. If he hadn't, I might have perished in my midtwenties—maybe the night that, drunk and finding myself on the wrong subway platform, I jumped onto the tracks and over the electrified third rail to get to the other side. But God didn't take away my compulsion to smoke until I was willing to live. Touch and be touched. Accept the pain that was rightfully mine, a free gift for finally joining the human race.

Generations of Dutchy couples have cut their cakes at the VFW Picnic Grove in Adamstown; it's a perfect setting for a country wedding. Parentheses of maples curve around a pavilion of thirty picnic tables worn by age and weather, wounded by gouged declarations of love. In back, a full kitchen with plenty of outlets for the Crock-Pots and a counter for the endless platters: the thick pink coins of ring bologna nestled against cubes of sharp cheddar, the deviled eggs like rheumy eyes, the cold cuts and potato rolls and tubs of sickly-sweet potato and macaroni salad. Open the screen door, trot thirty feet past the kegs of beer, and there's your outhouse. At the front of the pavilion is the concrete slab where the bride and groom lead the first dance. The other couples follow after a moment, one leading the other. Their linked hands form the shape of a human heart, each wrist the fine fragile tube of an artery. Knotted tight as pearls, they sway, eyes closed, refusing age and loss and death.

Today John and I will lead the dance, on this rainy mid-September afternoon that steams like a lathered horse. I bounce up the grove's rutted dirt road in my maid of honor Susan's new Grand Am, my bridesmaids in back, the sound of the rain on the roof as soft and indistinct as an argument on the other side of a wall. Susan parks twenty feet from the canvas tent in which one hundred friends and relatives wait, umbrellas stashed under their metal chairs. Waiting for me.

"We had to have an outdoor wedding." I pull at a bead on my white bag, which holds the essentials: lipstick, compact, cigarettes. The murmur of rain hardens; then the roar and crackle of cloudburst.

"It's not that bad." Ignoring the monsoon, Tiffany fiddles with my crown of baby's breath.

"It's horrendous. I don't care for me—I've done this before. But I feel bad for your dad. This is his first wedding."

"You say it like there'll be a second," says Susan. Even after her breakup with Kathy six months before, we've managed to stay close. When I asked her to be my maid of honor, I expected her to turn me down; Kathy is in the tent with her new girlfriend. But Susan has guts. And a new girlfriend, Lisa. Both are solid Berks County girls, bosomy, thighs like mortadella sausages, hips like Vermeer's milkmaid. In their dark blue gowns scattered with tiny silver spangles, they look like an expanse of night sky, Lisa's hair a red Orion.

"Give him time," I say.

"Oh, stop. I've never seen him so happy."

"It's good luck when it rains on your wedding day," says Tiffany. "Wait, keep your head still. Good."

"Let me look." I peer into the tiny mirror on the visor. "I'm sweating like a pig." Reaching into my bag for my compact, I dab powder on my nose.

"You're dewy," says Lisa.

"Oh, God, my *hair*."

Heat and flood. A little Vietnam, a little Johnstown. Infernal weather has marked both my weddings. I married Matt in July on a riverboat in Philly. Two hundred people, one hundred and three degrees, one air conditioner, zero wind. I danced in a heavy silk wedding dress with long sleeves and a bustle; I bought it in March, how hot could it get? I chose wrong. Bloated with heat, her face puffed with tears, my mother wandered the top deck like a refugee, afraid for me—could I live happily ever after? Something in her said no. She was right. Why should this marriage, this man, be different?

I've made an enormous mistake. Doom settles like plaster dust on my frizzy hair, my bare shoulders.

I need a cigarette, but the rain, my dress. I turn to Susan—whose Grand Am still smells like showroom—hold up my pack of cigarettes, and laugh, one syllable of desperation and apology that lets people know that you know you're nuts.

"Three drags," I say. "Please. I'll blow them right out the window." Fouling a friend's new car. These are the depths to which a desperate smoker will descend.

Susan sighs. "Fine, but you're walking up that aisle in two minutes."

"Bless you." I crack the window an inch and light up. Vivaldi's *Four Seasons* wafts from the tent, rich round notes scented with rain. Fat drops pelt my right cheek, my upper arm; one splotches my cigarette. The paper turns translucent, the smoke cools. I suck harder. A cloud fills the car.

"I'm going to walk up the aisle smelling like smoke," I say. "So are you. Damn it. I'm sorry."

"You're stopping soon. Right?" says Tiffany, who regularly lectures John Senior about his smoking.

"Right."

I'm lying, shivering with the cold certainty that I am about to ruin a man's life. I have fooled him into believing that I am worth having but I am nothing, just a smoky bride in a white gown of indeterminate function, purchased at a consignment shop—I may be wearing a prom dress. It looked pretty when I bought it, but I chose wrong. Again.

I suck on my rain-splotched cigarette. The smoke catches in the filter. Fucker. Betrayer. Every one of them has let me down since I started smoking again last September. Skinny and mean, cold as a turned back in bed.

God whispers: *You're getting married. Be happy, damn you.*

Happiness. A piece of bright cloth snagged on a branch. *Idiot. Breathe. I'm offering you joy. Take it.*

"It's time." Susan swings her legs out of the car, pops open a giant green-striped golf umbrella, and runs around to the passenger's side. She raps on my window. "Let's go let's go let's go!" Clambering from the backseat, Lisa and Tiffany run, heads tucked, for Susan's umbrella. There's just enough room underneath it for me. I open the door and just sit there, looking up at Susan. The flat broad planes of her face shine like a just-scrubbed pan.

"You look beautiful," she says. "Gorgeous."

Take it.

She yanks me out of the car—I'm still clutching my cigarette—and bustles me into the center of female flesh away from the rain. My silver-spangled Cinderella slippers sink into the sodden earth. The hem of my dress drags in the mud.

"Shit!" I hiss.

"Wait, wait," says Tiffany, and stoops to pick it up.

"It doesn't matter. It only cost thirty bucks."

The four of us stand for a moment under Susan's giant umbrella, in the mud. Our faces are almost touching; their breath brushes my face. *Take it.* The moment trembles.

DAY 7

Take it. We are soap bubbles seconds from nothing. *Take it.*

I look at each of them, here because of me, for me. The rain drips from the umbrella. My cigarette hisses and dies. I step on it and it splits like a pod. I split too. My rib cage spreads, my heart opens, and my friends flow in, all the world flows in.

"Thank you," I say. "For this." *I don't deserve you or John, but I love you all the same. I don't deserve my life, but I can't let it go.*

"You're welcome," says Lisa. "Now please get married. I'm standing in a very large puddle."

I can't let it go.

We turn, my friends and I, edge toward the tent as one. Outside the flaps, my father waits to deliver me to my future.

⁓

We blast up Route 476 on this fine October night, John aiming the bullet-nosed Sebring toward home from the Tower Theater in Philly. John drives, his father rides shotgun, Roxy and I shift gently in the back like bags of groceries. It's after eleven, but heavy traffic braids the Blue Route's three lanes into a single streaking blur. I shut my eyes when John passes, but my closed lids still play the brake lights in front of us, flaring and fading like sparks.

John and his father critique the night's entertainment, Comedy Central's Insomniac Tour. "He was definitely stoned," John says, referring to a loopy comedian who would die fifteen months later, on my forty-second birthday.

"When you lie down on the stage and read your jokes off a page in a notebook, you're stoned."

"He was terrible. Just terrible," says John Senior. "And that Dave character—what a filthy mouth. He's not funny, he's sick." He cracks the window and lights a cigarette. Smoke seeps into the backseat. I imagine smoke curling under the doors in *The Towering Inferno,* Jews at Auschwitz awaiting their Zyklon-B showers. *You're making me sick. You're killing me.* Sipping thimblefuls of air, I fight the urge to kick the back of his seat.

"Lewis Black was good," says John. I stare at the back of his head. *Tell your father to open his window. I'm dying.* "I love his End of the Universe monologue—'There's a Starbucks across the street from a Starbucks.'" *I can't fucking breathe!* In the passing headlights, smoke hangs like a thunderhead between the front and back seats.

I inspect John Senior's profile. The chiaroscuro lighting of the night highway pleats and bleaches his face. His eye sinks into a hollow. A crescent of cheek teeters atop a deep fold that tugs at his voracious mouth. When I met him two years ago he was so alive he seemed to strain at his skin, uncontainable. Now he eats and smokes, naps and smokes. I've often wondered if he smokes to burn up the remainder of his life, to turn over his odometer so that it displays a row of mean dumb zeros. Tinkering with his death gene. Or maybe he's like me, who smokes for the same reason a woman in childbirth clenches a rag between her teeth: to bear the pain.

I could smoke too, if I wanted to, fill this car with the smell of life on fire. I don't want to. Jesus Christ, I don't. *I*

*don't want to die. Don't let my son see me die in an oxygen
tent. Please God. Lift this obsession.*

I wait. I am not me now, I am not sitting silent next to
the smiling Roxy wreathed in smoke. I am the nucleus of a
U-235 atom hit by a neutron, oscillating in the microsecond
before it splits to light up the world. I am one atom among
millions, one tiny link in a chain reaction formed by the
hand of God, the sound of it like wind, the wailing wind,
the tundra wind that whistles inside my head.

I pray harder. *I love you I believe in you I would get
down on my knees if I could but I'm in the car. You have
given me everything a beautiful son a good man good health
loving parents good looks okay I am getting old but I
looked pretty good even two years ago you have given me
so many gifts and I crush them like butts in an ashtray. I
hate cigarettes I fucking hate them please make me stop.*

I wait.

Then, like the scratching of a dying bird in a shoebox,
the rustling allure of smoke. Fuck shit piss hell cocksucking
cigarettes. I don't want to smoke, I want to smoke, I
shouldn't, I must; smoke is the finger of steam that wafts
from a cartoon pie cooling on a sill, beckons me toward
death. It's God's will that I die with a cigarette between my
fingers.

Please, God, no.

Please—whoomp! Floosh!

A white-hot point of light rockets up from the core of
me, screams into my dark empty head, and explodes like a
flare. White light floods my skull, and in its illumination a
steel-wrapped fist glints in a roaring ring of fire.

"Yes," I say.

"What," John says, his eyes on the road.

"I'm going to chain myself in the house for a week to quit smoking."

"Ha ha ha," peals John Senior, each "ha" perfectly enunciated. "You're too much."

"John, we need to go to Home Depot tomorrow."

"You're demented." My husband keeps his eyes on the road.

2:12 p.m.

I'm unloading the dishwasher when the front door screaks open. The next moment, a slam I feel in my feet. Only one person in this house slams a door like that. "Daniel," I cry. I hurry from the kitchen and there he is, pretzel-legged on the floor by the door, rooting in a plastic bag from Wal-Mart. More booty, courtesy of his father—comic books, gaming magazines, action figures from his private stash. Matt stands behind Daniel, his hands in his pockets.

"Hello," he says, the accent, as always, on the first syllable. He shifts his weight from foot to foot, a boxer's shuffle without the bounce. It's a kind of tic, the kinetic equivalent of throat-clearing. Daniel has it too.

"Hey." I kneel and bury my nose in Daniel's hair. "Yikes. When was his last shower?" Gamey as a buck, my son trails dirty drawers and sweaty hair and a hint of

chicken fingers, his signature scent. I could find my son in the dark, like a wild dog.

"Mom. Mom. You know what?" says Daniel. "Dad gave me Lord of the Rings: Return of the King. And I got to the third level of Dragonball Z Budokai 2 on my Game-Cube."

"The third level? Awesome. You are a video-game wizard."

"And look." Daniel rummages in the bag and extracts a blue monster made of plastic, with thick eyebrows and a melancholy half-smile. "It's Sulley from Monsters Inc."

"Really? It looks like Abe Vigoda on Fish."

"Who's Abe Vigoda?"

"Never mind." I nuzzle him again. He bats me away, but I am in love all over again. He looks older than he did a week ago, his eyes less shiny and graver, adult. I have this crazy impulse to eat him to keep him inside me forever. Mom probably felt the same. We love and loathe our children, cast them away and gather them up again like dice. If he wants to play hide-and-seek with the cushions tonight, I will seek until I drop.

John comes downstairs, greets Matt with a smile. "She smoking yet?" my ex-husband asks, his tone a conspiratorial elbow in the ribs. I give him a playful shove.

"No, she's doing good," says John.

"I told you, I'm officially an ex-smoker," I say. "I'm working on the snotty attitude. How did things go with Daniel?"

"Oh, you know. He had his moments. A little backtalk

*here and there—I sent him to his room a few times. But
basically, he was good."*

"*I was very good.*" Daniel snaps together a Bionicle.

"*Let's not go overboard, kid.*"

"*You want coffee?*" I ask.

"*Can't. I have to finish a model. It was due two weeks
ago but I couldn't get much done last week because—you
know.*" He looks down meaningfully at Daniel, then prods
him gently with his foot. "*Commere, you. Daddy has to
go.*"

Daniel stands up and wraps his arms around his father.
"*Bye, Dad.*"

"*You be good for Mommy. I'll see you Tuesday after
school.*"

"*See you Tuesday. Miss you. Love you.*" Turning back
to his bag, Daniel digs out two more Bionicles and bashes
them together. "*Mom. Mom. This one has a flamethrower
built into his arm. See? But this one has invisible powers, so
he's going to win this battle.*"

"*I can see that. Hold on, okay? I'm saying good-bye to
your dad.*"

At the door, Matt turns to me. "*I wanted to tell you
something Daniel told me.*" He speaks softly, so our son
doesn't hear. "*I know he can be a handful. So I'm not crit-
icizing, okay? But Daniel says you yell at him a lot.*"

I sigh. "*I do.*" My guilt clings like wet clothing.

"*I do too. Too much. Sometimes it seems like all I do is
yell at him. I yelled at him a lot this week, made him cry. I
felt so bad. So I wanted to say that we, both of us, have to
remember that he's our baby. The same little baby who*

popped up from his crib after his nap all smiley saying, 'Hi, Mommy' or 'Hi, Daddy.'" His face softens, glows; he has entered the cathedral of memory, a holy place.

I step in and take my place beside him. My son is nine months old again, standing at the bars of his crib in a yellow-and-orange-striped onesie, his Huggie bearing gifts. The buds of two teeth glimmer in milky gums.

"Remember?" Matt asks. "He was always happy. Remember?"

"Yes. I remember." Our marriage, the three of us in our bed, shining links in a chain with no end. Smoking could rip my child from my arms. It could kill me. Me.

A current of fury crackles through me. I don't deserve to die that way. I have a right to occupy my small piece of the planet. I deserve to live.

For so long, I didn't believe that. I believed that no one could possibly love me. I smoked to endure that knowledge. I believed that to love is to be weak and that you allow love into your life at your peril. I smoked to make it true. I believed that pain is to be avoided at all costs and that I didn't deserve happiness. I smoked to mute pain and deny pleasure. I believed that it was life that was chaotic and empty, and not me. I smoked to prove it. I don't believe those things anymore.

I'm leaving cigarettes behind, as I left alcohol behind, as I'm trying to leave my shame and self-hatred behind. They brought me to my knees and can again if I let them. I have to choose not to let them, again and again. To choose to live is my life's work.

"See you Tuesday." Matt walks to his Stratus parked

across the street, trailing loneliness like toilet paper on the heel of a shoe. I shut the door gently, then turn to John and Daniel. "Let's walk to the Rose Garden."

Daniel, halfway up the stairs, groans. He wants to play his PlayStation 2, which he hasn't touched for a week.

"Oh, come on, Dan," I say, irritated in spite of myself. "It's only three blocks, and you probably haven't played outside all week. And there will be dogs to pet. No, keep your coat on. I said keep it on!"

"Come on, Daniel. Let's go," says John, reaching for his sweatshirt on the coffee table.

Daniel stomps down the stairs again. As he rounds the coffee table, he sees the chain. "What's that?" He stops to investigate.

Oh, hell. The chain. I'd decided to leave it in the living room but hadn't yet worked out what to say. My mind examines and discards explanations. Daniel lifts a loop, then lets it drop with a clatter. "Cool." He does it again.

The sound of my chain, singing my story. I was a smoker, and then I died; I rose from the dead a nonsmoker. I'll give Daniel the CliffsNotes version.

"The chain helps Mommy not smoke," I tell him.

"Why don't you just wear the patch?" Seven years old. I can't help but be proud of him.

"The patch doesn't work. This is a new thing. Every time I want a cigarette, I pick it up and let it drop, just like you did. The noise is so horrible that it reminds me that smoking is horrible, too. Let's go."

"Oh. Can I play my PlayStation when we get back?"

Day 7

"Sure. Let's go."

But he's not quite done. He drops the chain once more, picks it up, drops it again.

"Enough!" I shout. John watches from the door, laughing.

Daniel looks at me. "Do you want to smoke?"

"Nope. See? It works."

EPILOGUE

I started to write about Lockdown a few days after John unshackled me. That's why when I started smoking again six weeks later—on New Year's Eve, a holiday universally dreaded by smokers—I knew that I was in deep shit.

John and I had been invited to Kathy's for a typical Berks County blowout—Crock-Pots of greasy meats and macaroni and cheese bubbling on the kitchen counter, eight different desserts for twenty people, coolers of lager nestled in beds of ice. And smoke. Cigarette smoke always smells different at a party—not stale and dead, but convivial, exuberantly alive. The smokers, who vastly outnumbered the nonsmokers, commandeered the sunroom. A sliding-glass door separated them from the main house and the few smoke-free revelers—me, John, Roxy, the kids playing darts and bumper pool in the family room (Daniel was celebrating with Matt), and a quiet older couple who kept to themselves. I pouted on the other side of the door, relegated to the kiddie table at Thanksgiving: It wasn't fair, I had nothing, *nothing*. Through the glass, I watched them spout smoke, heard the rippling chorus of their laughter, the faint *crack!* of pull tabs. They existed firmly in the moment, a place I'd heard of but never visited. Their smoke formed a cozy igloo around them. I was locked out in the cold to die.

A few smokers emerged from the sunroom to play darts in the family room. As they passed by, swaddled in a thick blanket of smoke, I sniffed enviously. They clattered downstairs. When John followed, I saw my opportunity and sidled up to Kathy's girlfriend Patty, a menthol gal like me.

"Give me a cigarette." I didn't say please; I didn't have to. She must have heard the plea in my voice.

"Are you sure?" Her brow furrowed with pity. She knew about Lockdown. Everyone in John's family knew, agreed that I was nuts.

"Yes. I need one. I just need it."

Silently she handed me her pack and mini-Bic. Smokers are like cops or firemen: We have a code. We support each other. We do not turn each other in.

I stole out the front door and lit up alone, expecting my need to snap back up inside me like a window shade. But that cigarette tasted of treachery—against John, who trusted me; against Daniel, who depended on me. Against myself, too. A moment of madness had seized me by the hair and dragged me out that door. I truly did not want to smoke. All I wanted was for the loneliness in my heart to flutter away like a butterfly across a field. It remained, trapped, beating its wings against its cage of blood and muscle.

Yet an hour later, hating myself, I bummed another. John was back upstairs in the sunroom, too happily drunk to notice. By one thirty I was filching from Patty every time she left the sunroom to use the bathroom or replenish the beer coolers.

On New Year's Day, I drove to CVS, bought a pack of Basic Menthol Lights, and began a double life. By day, at work, I smoked in the Bunker. By night, and on weekends, I lit up in the basement at any opportune moment, usually when John and Daniel were away or asleep. My sneaking lent each cigarette the feel of a tryst: pain, yearning, bittersweet rapture. I closed my eyes and inhaled hard, my lungs holding that smoke like the hand of someone dangling off a cliff. Before I ventured upstairs, I sprayed the laundry room—along with my clothing and hair—with Lysol.

After a few weeks, I got sloppy, like a killer who wants to get caught. One Saturday afternoon, I trudged up the cellar stairs into the kitchen and came face-to-face with John, who was pouring a soda—into a glass, over ice, as usual. He sniffed. His eyes narrowed.

"Were you smoking down there?"

"No." Terror gripped me, as if I were hiding a lover. In a way, I suppose I was.

John clattered downstairs and smelled the smoke—traitorous, good-for-nothing Lysol!—and yelled at me. I cried in humiliation. And relief: Caught, I could smoke in the open again.

I continued to write about Lockdown, however, astounded by the new level of absurdity I had achieved: smoking while writing a book about quitting smoking. Night after night, after Daniel and John had gone to bed, I dug up my past, writing for hours about the loneliness and anger that marked my life like a scar and how smoking both relieved and perpetuated it. Every thirty minutes, I took a cigarette break. That's how I spent most of 2004: smoking and writing, smoking and berating myself, smoking and rattling my chain—still lying like a dead serpent in the living room—in frustration.

In September 2004, disgusted, I booked myself into an inpatient nicotine-cessation program, where I would spend another five days not smoking. This Lockdown, however, cost seventeen hundred dollars. I arrived Sunday night. One by one, the seven other women and one man with whom I would quit drifted in with their suitcases and duffel bags. Their rides kissed them, whispered a few encouraging words, and left. We huddled in the living room, pale and silent and stunned, waiting for our room assignments.

During the day, we met as a group with a therapist, cried, enacted psychodramas, cried, attended lectures about stress reduction and deep breathing, cried, ate starchy snacks, cried. I was astounded by their stories, so similar to my own, yet unique. The youngest was a single mother in her twenties. The oldest, a woman in her fifties, had early-stage emphysema; she'd worked this program three times. One sweet middle-aged woman, whose daughter was about to deliver her first grandchild, mothered us all, soothing, clucking. The lone man, polite but reserved, revealed himself cautiously, in stages, unfolding like reverse origami.

At night, on our own, we recalled our first tastes of tobacco at eleven and fourteen and twenty, the allure and deceit of smoking. The *power* of it, the way it just takes over the small sweet acre of your life, smoke twisting and tangling through like kudzu, choking it. How we'd never experienced an adult thought or emotion unpolluted by smoke. We were eleven and fourteen and twenty again. What would we do, how would we act, who would we *be?*

Then it was over. We exchanged phone numbers and email addresses and went home to embark on our new and joyful smoke-free lives.

Three weeks later I was smoking again. The craving had built over a few days' time, driving me mad like a mosquito's whine in the dark, and I said fuck it, rolled that *fffff* with malicious pleasure. I went to CVS, bought a pack, smoked one cigarette, threw the pack out the window on the way home, returned to CVS a few hours later and bought another pack. Shit. Seventeen hundred dollars up in smoke. I emailed my comrades and confessed. They implored me not to give up. More cigarettes, more despairing tears, more writing.

Then, one morning a few months later, I sat down at the computer and lit a cigarette—my third or fourth of the day. An hour later, interrupted by need, I reached for my pack. A quiet, gentle voice inside me—God's? My own?—said *No. Wait awhile.* So I did. Twenty minutes later, the impulse to light up nudged me again. Again, that gentle voice: *Wait.* Hours passed. Then a day. Then a week.

My Last Cigarette was as sudden, and simple, as that— a momentous event wrapped in an ordinary moment, like an expensive gift in newspaper.

Did Lockdown help me quit? I think so. All that I experienced, thought, and felt during that week raised the stakes.

Although I started again, it became harder to rationalize my habit. Every cigarette amplified, rather than muted, the feeling that I lit up to avoid. I could not escape my story—the tale of how and why I began to smoke and why I continued. What I loved and hated about cigarettes, what they gave me and what they took away, what the world felt like with and without them.

Every addict's story goes beyond physical addiction and unfolds much like that of anyone who has abused his or her body and lived to tell about it. So many of us disconnect from our flesh even as we use it to act out our most profound struggles. The drunk, the cokehead, the bulimic, the cutter—all fight it out on a battlefield of blood and bone.

But while alcoholics and junkies tend to elicit the public's pity, smokers receive only its contempt. Perhaps that's because smoking lacks inherent drama. No one loses a relationship, beats their child, or jumps off a bridge because they smoke too much. No one cavorts in a fountain under the influence of nicotine or credits their smoking for inspiring great art. Smoking is the addiction in plain sight. We read memoirs about addictions to alcohol and drugs and food with a cigarette between our fingers. There are so many books on smoking—the how-to-quit programs, the elegant analyses of tobacco's impact on world history and culture, the trenchant exposés of the tobacco industry, the textbooks only researchers and clinicians understand. Are they relevant? Edifying? Of course. But they miss the point. It frustrates me that smoking is viewed solely as a cultural, political, or public-health issue when, at its core, it is a personal one.

I wrote this book to make smoking personal. In the end,

though, my story comes down to this: I smoked to survive my life. And then, to save it, I quit.

Between 1950 and 2000, death rates from lung cancer among white women in the United States increased by 600 percent, and lung cancer now accounts for 25 percent of all female cancer deaths.

In 1999, lung cancer research received about $900 per death, compared to $9,000 per breast cancer death.

Lung cancer kills 68,000 women a year, 27,000 more than breast cancer, but you see far more women wearing pink ribbons than black ones.

I pull up to my nineteen-year-old self, that brittle girl in the VW Bug. Her elbow is out the window. A Newport burns between her fingers. Our eyes meet and hold. She lifts her hand, the one holding the cigarette, and tosses me a crooked smile. I return it, then pull ahead. I watch her in the rearview mirror until I can't see her anymore. But I know that she's still on the road.

I found the chain in my garage a few months back and dragged it up to my office, where I could see it as I wrote. As my story continued to reveal itself, the chain underwent a transformation. When Lockdown began, it was only my addiction that slithered behind me. Now, I see the chain as a kind of umbilical cord that connects me to the people and events that shaped my life and, for better or worse, made me who I am.

Who I am is a smoker. I choose not to smoke.

ACKNOWLEDGMENTS

For their support of this book, I am indebted to my agent, the incomparable Lisa Bankoff of ICM, and my editor, the inimitable Liz Stein. Thanks, too, to Martha Levin and Dominick Anfuso of the Free Press and to Amy Scheibe, my almost-editor, who was the first to champion it.

Special thanks to Ginny Faber for her critiques, suggestions, and inspiration. Her excellence imbues every page.

Finally, I want to acknowledge Bill Roorbach, who read early drafts and believed that I had a story worth telling.

ABOUT THE AUTHOR

JULIA HANSEN was born in 1963 in Vineland, New Jersey. She lives in Reading, Pennsylvania, with her husband and son.